Assessing
General Education
Programs

Assessing General Education Programs

Mary J. Allen

Professor Emeritus of Psychology,
California State University–Bakersfield and
former Director of the California State University
Institute for Teaching and Learning

ANKER PUBLISHING COMPANY, INC.
Bolton, Massachusetts

Assessing General Education Programs

ISBN 1-882982-95-9

Composition by Lyn Rodger, Deerfoot Studios
Cover design by Dutton & Sherman Design

Anker Publishing Company, Inc.
563 Main Street
P.O. Box 249
Bolton, MA 01740-0249 USA

www.ankerpub.com

Library of Congress Cataloging-in-Publication Data

Allen, Mary J.
    Assessing general education programs / Mary J. Allen.
        p. cm.
    Includes bibliographical references and index.
    ISBN 1-882982-95-9
    1. General education--United States--Evaluation. 2. Education,
Higher—Aims and objectives--United States.   I. Title.
LC985.A55 2006
378.01—dc22
                                                        2005031622

Table of Contents

List of Figures

About the Author

Mary J. Allen is professor emeritus of psychology, California State University–Bakersfield, and former director of the California State University Institute for Teaching and Learning. She served as department chair and founded the faculty development center and assessment center at California State University–Bakersfield, and supported faculty development and assessment efforts for the California State University System. She holds a master's degree in statistics and a Ph.D. in psychology from the University of California–Berkeley. In the last decade she has offered assessment workshops and support to more than 60 colleges, universities, and college districts, and has led invited workshops at a variety of conferences, including presentations for the American Association for Higher Education, the Association of American Colleges and Universities, and the Western Association of Schools and Colleges.

Preface

I wrote this book as a compact, practical guide for busy professionals who want to assess their general education program in meaningful, manageable, and sustainable ways. I also discuss first-year experience programs because they are linked to student retention and success, providing additional support for student achievement in general education coursework. My goal is not to present one approach, but to help readers understand what other campuses are doing and to help them develop a repertoire of methods so they can make informed decisions about their own programs.

Most campuses work independently as faculty develop and assesses their general education programs, so it is not surprising that many models exist. Sections of this book provide descriptions and examples of approaches from a variety of campuses, including two-year and four-year institutions. Even the basic vocabulary varies across campuses. Colleges and universities may offer a *general education* program, a *core* program, a *general studies* program, a *university* program, a *liberal arts* program, or a *critical foundations* program; but all these programs provide a broad foundation for students' future academic, civil, cultural, economic, and social lives. Campuses also vary substantially in the number of stated learning outcomes for their programs, ranging from around ten to nearly 200 outcomes; their assessment programs may focus on the course, program, or institutional level.

Chapter 1 establishes a broad context for general education programs, first-year experience programs, and assessment, and summarizes relevant ideas from a variety of professional organizations. Chapter 2 provides general advice about developing mission, goal, and outcome statements and analyzes examples from dozens of campuses. Chapter 3 focuses on the alignment of curricula, pedagogy, and institutions with general education learning outcomes; develops an array of alignment questions that might lead to assessment projects; and describes how campuses can use course certification to promote alignment. Chapter 4 describes approaches for assessment planning, criteria for selecting assessment strategies, and ethical issues that should be considered. Chapters 5 and 6 provide examples of an array of direct and indirect assessment strategies, including the use of rubrics and content analysis. Chapter 7 brings it all together, including a discussion of the infrastructure for general education assessment and some friendly suggestions for effective collaboration.

I began studying assessment in 1997, and I had no idea that I eventually would work full-time in this field. Over the last eight years I have had the privilege of working with more than 60 colleges, universities, and college systems and with thousands of professionals at various retreats and conferences, and I continue to be impressed with how a few simple steps can change perspectives about professional roles, curricula, and courses.

Although the process seems overwhelming and sometimes unnecessary to the uninitiated, most who have earnestly examined their programs have seen their relationships with colleagues and students changing. Done well, faculty and other campus professionals develop a shared vision of their desired impact on students, and they work together to provide a more cohesive, effective learning environment. This requires a willingness to honestly examine their impact on students, to listen to student voices, and to be flexible when change is needed.

Over the years I have worked with many colleagues to promote quality assessment, and I wish to thank them for their many contributions to my own understanding. In particular, I have learned a great deal from Richard Noel, Amy Driscoll, Peggy Maki, and Beth Rienzi. I appreciate their friendship, and I respect their professionalism. I hope the readers of this book find congenial colleagues who share a dedication to student development so the assessment of their general education program is a collegial and rewarding experience.

CHAPTER 1

General Education Programs

G eneral education is the core of the undergraduate curriculum for all
students, regardless of major. It contributes to the distinctiveness of
college-educated adults and guarantees that all college graduates have a
broad, balanced education. Students may take their only science or humanities courses as part of their general education program; faculty who design
and staff such courses have a responsibility and opportunity to share their
enthusiasm for their disciplines and leave a lasting foundation for lifelong
learning, understanding, application, and appreciation of various approaches to understanding individuals, cultures, and the world we live in.

Assessing General Education

The assessment of academic programs is a best practice in higher education, and all colleges and universities are expected to assess the impact of
their general education program. *Assessment* is an ongoing process designed
to monitor and improve student learning. Faculty explicitly define what
they want students to learn, verify that the curriculum is designed to foster
that learning, collect empirical data that indicate the extent of the learning,
and use these data to improve the program. Assessment provides the context for ongoing consideration of general education programs and their
impact on students.

Assessment has become commonplace for two major reasons. First,
higher education has been moving from being teaching-focused to being
learning-focused, changing the emphasis from what faculty do to what students learn (Kuh, Kinzie, Schuh, Whitt, & Associates, 2005; Weimer,
2002). This change naturally leads to the question: Did students learn

what we wanted them to learn? Assessment helps us identify what is working well and what needs attention, and we make adjustments when we are disappointed with results.

Second, virtually every accrediting body requires the ongoing assessment of academic programs. They expect a climate of institutional reflection and continuing improvement based on empirical evidence. This contrasts with earlier models based on periodic reviews of programs and institutions every three to ten years, traditionally focusing on inputs to the system (e.g., library holdings, faculty degrees, course schedules) rather than outputs from the system (student learning). This focus on accountability for the impact of our efforts affects entire institutions, and student affairs professionals who coordinate and staff units such as counseling centers, tutoring centers, and advising centers also are expected to assess how their efforts affect those whom they serve. Agencies that accredit campuses expect to see evidence of a quality assurance process and ongoing improvement as evidence for institutional effectiveness. The assessment of general education programs is one part of such efforts.

Challenges in Assessing General Education

The assessment of general education presents special challenges for a number of reasons. Most faculty owe primary allegiance to their disciplines, rather than to general education. They may be willing to assess their own majors, but they may have less interest in assessing a program to which they contribute only a course or two. Most of their energy is tied to staying current in their discipline, mentoring majors, conducting research, and providing service to their department and community.

General education assessment often requires the coordination of many faculty and departments, making the process more complicated to schedule and coordinate than single-department reviews. An administrator or committee generally has responsibility for coordinating the general education program and its assessment, but often this is one of many assignments and the assessment task may seem like an overwhelming burden or an activity that has lower priority than other responsibilities.

Another challenge involves the faculty who teach general education courses. Adjunct faculty staff a high portion of general education courses on some campuses, and adjunct faculty generally are not expected to contribute work beyond teaching the courses they were assigned. The reliance on adjunct and part-time faculty continues to grow throughout the nation, and, overall, about half of all college faculty now serve in part-time positions (Faculty Hiring in Recent Years, 2005). Those who coordinate general education programs must find ways to engage all general education faculty in the assessment process if they are to effect meaningful improvements to the program.

In spite of these challenges, institutions are making progress in assessing general education programs, and we can learn from their experiences. This book reviews assessment models and activities at a wide range of campuses, and I hope you find ideas useful for your campus. Every college or university has its own mission and culture; strategies that work on one campus may fail on another. As you read this book, think about how you might adapt what others have done to help you and your colleagues develop or refine your general education assessment program.

Focusing on Learning

What does it mean to be learning focused, rather than teaching focused? The last couple of decades have seen enormous changes in institutional culture as campuses move toward focusing on student learning, and this affects how we conceptualize and review general education programs.

Professionals on many campuses used to think about general education programs in terms of courses, as if each course were a "silo" of learning that sits alone and operates independently. Students completed general education programs by accumulating a list on their transcripts that allowed a clerk to certify that all requirements were met. Debates about general education generally focused on which courses would be approved for which requirement, and, once approved, courses could be taught by any faculty member assigned by the relevant department. Faculty recognized that sections of the same course might significantly differ, but this was inconsequential.

As campuses move toward being learning centered, the focus changes. The emphasis is on determining what students should learn in the general education program and how the curriculum should be designed to foster that learning. Many campuses develop an array of general education learning goals that are neither course nor discipline specific, such as communication, critical thinking, information literacy, problem solving, leadership, and collaboration skills. Faculty who teach specific general education courses are expected to help students attain all or most of these outcomes.

Faculty in learning-centered institutions develop a cohesive general education curriculum designed to promote agreed-upon student learning outcomes. Each general education course is structured around an array of program and course-specific learning outcomes that are invariant, regardless of instructor. This does not mean that faculty give up control of the general education courses they teach. They may augment the common list of outcomes with some of their own, and they determine the pedagogy they will use to support student development. Each instructor has the responsibility to foster student mastery of the course outcomes, but there are many ways to teach well.

We have learned much about adult learning in the last few decades. Students construct meaning by integrating new learning into what was already known, and learning occurs through discussion, practice, feedback, and reflection. Comeaux (2005) describes this paradigm:

> Constructivist learning paradigms are learner centered and posit that learning occurs when students are actively engaged in making sense of phenomena as well as constructing and negotiating meaning with others. They emphasize the interdependence of the learners and the communal nature of the process as knowledge . . . is negotiated and constructed through dialogue, problem solving, and authentic experiences. (p. xx)

These ideas are not new in higher education, and the classic publication in this area is Chickering and Gamson's (1987) "Seven Principles for Good Practice in Undergraduate Education." Good practice:

1) Encourages contacts between students and faculty.

2) Develops reciprocity and cooperation among students.

3) Uses active learning techniques.

4) Gives prompt feedback.

5) Emphasizes time on task.

6) Communicates high expectations.

7) Respects diverse talents and ways of knowing. (p. 3)

Teaching in this environment requires considerable skill, and faculty generally develop a repertoire of teaching techniques to meet the needs of all students and to promote different types of learning outcomes. For example, faculty might design courses with:

- Active learning

- Collaborative and cooperative learning

- Community service learning and internships

- Homework and laboratory assignments

- Lectures and discussion

- Online learning

- Problem-based learning

- Student reflections on their learning

General education courses may require an array of pedagogical approaches beyond those used when teaching courses to majors who have more interests and skills in common. As faculty experiment with new pedagogical approaches and new types of learning outcomes, they often find the need to collaborate with colleagues from other disciplines, and they can benefit from the growing literature on effective practice. This often is facilitated within a formal faculty development program—an important component of a learning-centered institution. New faculty, as well as senior faculty, can benefit from well-run faculty development programs. Representatives of the Association of American Colleges and Universities (2002) make a strong case for faculty development, concluding, "The dark secret of higher education is that most college professors are never trained to be teachers. As doctoral students, their dissertations demand research; teaching skills are assumed to be easy for intelligent people to acquire" (p. 16). However, teaching is a complex, interpersonal process that few have perfected.

The term that is most often used to describe effective pedagogy is *engagement*. We want students to be engaged in their education. Members of the Association of American Colleges and Universities (2002) speak about *intentional learners* who are actively engaged in their educations:

In a turbulent and complex world, every college student will need to be purposeful and self-directed in multiple ways. Purpose implies clear goals, an understanding of process, and appropriate action. Further, purpose implies intention in one's action. Becoming an intentional learner means developing self-awareness about the reason for study, the learning process itself, and how education is used. Intentional learners are integrative thinkers who can see connections in seemingly disparate information and draw on a wide range of knowledge to make decisions. They adapt the skills learned in one situation to problems encountered in another: in a classroom, the workplace, their communities, or their personal lives. (pp. 21–22)

They recommend that faculty focus efforts on helping students develop this intentionality.

Faculty instructional roles are broad in learning-centered institutions. Faculty:

- Design learning environments to meet student and program needs

- Share interests and enthusiasm with students

- Help students become intentional learners

- Grade student work and provide students with formative feedback on their progress

- Mentor student development in and out of the classroom

- Collaborate with colleagues who support students outside of the classroom

- Assess class sessions, courses, and programs to improve their effectiveness

Given this range of activities, it is small wonder that faculty development assistance is needed.

Faculty who are learning centered focus on learning and routinely assess student progress to grade students, to provide students with formative feedback, and to improve courses and programs. Experienced faculty always have paid attention to their students' learning, and we are accustomed to recognizing that quizzical look that suggests confusion and that glazed-over look that suggests exhaustion or disengagement. We also have an array of *classroom assessment* techniques to more formally monitor learning in our day-to-day courses (Angelo & Cross, 1993), and many faculty could not imagine teaching without using these tools. Faculty who offer online courses face extra challenges because they are physically removed from their students. Moallem (2005) describes a project-based assessment system for monitoring and improving these courses.

Professionals at learning-centered institutions recognize the complexity of the teaching and learning process and are purposeful in planning, delivering, and assessing their courses and other contributions to student development. Assessment allows them to determine the impact of innovations and to compare alternative delivery systems, such as online and face-to-face courses, and they should share what they learn with colleagues. The scholarship of teaching and learning has received considerable attention over the last few decades (e.g., Boyer, 1990; Hutchings & Shulman, 1999); and faculty who engage in assessment can make important contributions to this growing literature (Banta & Associates, 2002). The Carnegie Center for the Advancement of Teaching web site is a valuable source of information on the scholarship of teaching and learning (http://www.carnegiefoundation .org). Faculty and staff who conceptualize assessment as meaningful research are likely to make important contributions to their students, campus, and professional colleagues. For example, the University of Portland situates assessment within a model of "scholarly teaching" (Maki, 2004), and they used this model as a framework for the development of a new core program and its assessment structure.

Professionals at learning-centered institutions work together to support student learning. Student affairs staff who organize the cocurricular environment coordinate with faculty to complement what happens in courses. For example, if global awareness is among general education learning goals, campus-wide events might include foreign films, international visiting artists and lecturers, and opportunities for students to learn from each other. Tutors and advisors are aware of general education expectations and align efforts to promote them. Tutors' services complement faculty efforts in courses, helping to improve institutional effectiveness, and advisors carefully monitor student progress and verify that students take courses in appropriate sequences. Librarians throughout the nation have taken the lead in the promotion of information competence, and their efforts can have greater impact when they collaborate with faculty so that assignments and activities are effectively designed to help students develop these skills.

Campus procedures at learning-centered institutions also support student learning. Recognition and reward systems value contributions to learning, and faculty and staff development programs encourage flexibility to uncover new ways to foster student development. Program reviews and campus decision-making rely on empirical findings and encourage the ongoing use of assessment to improve learning. Professionals who work in learning-centered institutions are accustomed to routine campus conversations about learning among administrators, faculty, and staff; they know that promoting student learning has high priority in the institutional culture.

General Education Models

Although all undergraduate institutions have general education programs, they may label them in different ways. Mauldin (as cited in Bowen, 2004) surveyed the titles of general education programs at 200 institutions and found that "general" was the adjective most often used (67%), but another 20% had a "core," 8% used the adjective "university," and 7% used the word "liberal." Sometimes these terms indicate important or subtle distinctions, and sometimes different terms are used for very similar programs. Your campus may have a "general education" program, a "general studies" program, a "core" program, a "university" program, a "liberal arts" program, or a "critical foundations" program, but all are designed to provide the foundations that mark a college-educated adult.

American general education programs tend to be variations of three models developed in the 19th and 20th centuries (Katz, 2005):

- A distribution model that guarantees breadth in the undergraduate curriculum

- A specially created set of core courses that integrate the liberal arts

- A specially created set of courses that emphasize processes and individual student growth

The Distribution Model

The first general education program model, developed at Princeton in the 1880s (Katz, 2005) and common in public colleges and universities, uses discipline-based courses and a menu from which students can select classes to meet each of a set of requirements. For example, students may be required to take two courses in the social sciences, and they may select among designated courses in Anthropology, Economics, Political Science, Psychology, and Sociology. These are often introductory survey courses required of majors, and they tend to focus on the concepts, theories, classic research findings, and approaches of single disciplines, with little attention to connections between disciplines. Faculty often require texts with titles like "Introduction to Sociology" or "Principles of Economics," and they generally are comfortable teaching these courses because they know their disciplines well and do not have to do extensive background work to develop course content.

Schwartz (2004) criticizes the distribution model, comparing it to a shopping mall eager to please student customers. Students on some campuses are encouraged to "window shop" by sitting in on classes before enrolling in them, although on other campuses students blindly take any section that is open before it is filled to capacity. Although Schwartz recognizes some benefits associated with providing options, he argues that "tyranny of choice" can lead to scattered, unfocused development; poor choices by learners who are not yet aware of what they need; and "a generation of students who use university counseling services and antidepressants in record numbers, and who provide places like Starbucks with the most highly educated minimum-wage work force in the world, as they bide their time hoping that the answer to the 'what should I be when I grow up' questions will eventually emerge" (p. B6). He argues that college and university faculty have the responsibility to structure a cohesive general education program that helps all students develop in agreed-upon ways. Students may be given a few choices, but the overall curriculum should carefully foster the development of our vision of a college-educated adult.

Not everyone agrees with Schwartz, and some campuses are proud of the wide variety and quality of options they provide students. For example Stanford University's general education web site (2005) stresses "Requirements as Opportunities":

> The Stanford curriculum will not force you into specific courses that do not interest you. Instead, it will remind you at every turn why you wanted a strong liberal arts education in the first place. . . . Remember that our General Education Requirements give you the flexibility to

take the courses you want when you want them. Take a range of courses in the various disciplines that excite you and you will complete your General Education Requirements without worry. View them not as obstacles but as opportunities, not as growing pains but as growth spurts. By approaching the curriculum from that perspective, you will learn more, enjoy what you are learning, and satisfy your requirements by satisfying your curiosity. (¶ 1, ¶ 3)

Distribution models can be effective, but they do require coordination, planning, and careful academic advising.

The Core Liberal Arts Model

Columbia University is the most well-known developer of the second approach to general education, which places more emphasis on interdisciplinary thinking. As America prepared to enter World War I, Columbia faculty became concerned that students were too often emphasizing science and were not learning enough about the liberal arts. They developed new interdisciplinary courses that stressed citizenship and "Contemporary Civilization." This approach became popular among elite universities. For example, University of Chicago faculty developed a Great Books curriculum in the 1930s and a core curriculum that required students to go beyond disciplinary boundaries, and Harvard faculty revised requirements in 1945 to emphasize a synthetic approach to learning about classic ideas (Katz, 2005).

Many faculty are attracted to elements of the Great Books approach, epitomized by Charles Eliot's "Five-Foot Shelf" of Harvard Classics (1909, cited in Satterfield, 2002). The Great Books model is not just a reading list; faculty engage students in discussion of the readings to promote learning outcomes, such as critical thinking and deep understanding of the complexity of human behavior. If you want to learn more about this approach, the Great Books Foundation (www.greatbooks.org) provides much support, including implementation advice, links to colleagues, a magazine (*The Common Review*), suggested discussion topics for Penguin Books classics, and an anthology, *Great Conversations 1* (Born & Whitfield, 2004), for semester-long humanities and first-year experience courses. Some campuses have adapted the idea and require a single book that all incoming freshmen read before their first semester so that campus-wide conversations and discussions in general education courses can be informed by a common text.

The Individual Student Development Model

The third approach to general education programs, emphasizing individual development, was promoted by John Dewey at Columbia and Arthur O. Lovejoy at Johns Hopkins University. Based on emerging understanding of cognitive development, students at these universities engage in reflective thinking in a curriculum focused more on process than on content (Katz, 2005). Reflection encourages students to think about their own learning and to integrate what they are learning, creating deep, long-lasting learning.

Many campuses combine elements of these models, with a required interdisciplinary core of coursework supplemented with a set of distribution requirements. In addition, most campuses update their general education curriculum periodically. For example, Harvard developed a core curriculum in the 1970s organized around general concepts like "social analysis," and they reorganized their program in 2004, adding freshman seminars and emphases on international studies and scientific literacy (Katz, 2005).

The Growth of General Education

The whole concept of general education evolved toward the end of the nineteenth century as campuses began requiring students to complete majors (Bowen, 2004). Most of us have only experienced universities in which students complete general education, major, and sometimes minor requirements, accumulating the necessary 120 or so semester units needed for graduation. Notions of what constitutes the college degree continue to evolve. For example, who in the 1950s could have imagined the importance of information literacy, technology, and globalization in today's curriculum and the growth of for-profit universities and online degree programs present today?

First-Year Experience Programs

Receiving considerable attention are first-year experience programs. "Over the past two decades nearly every campus in America has launched initiatives specifically designed to improve the success of new students" (Swing, 2004b, p. ix), and these first-year experience programs require assessment. The National Resource Center for the First-Year Experience and Students in Transition at the University of South Carolina, with support from the

Pew Charitable Trusts, has taken the lead in providing support for the implementation and assessment of first-year programs, including a web site (http://www.sc.edu/fye/), several listservs, conferences, a monograph series, and other publications.

First-year experience programs generally focus on improving the freshman retention rate. Nationally, about two-thirds of freshmen return for their sophomore year at the same campus, and this varies by type of college, ranging from 51% at two-year public colleges to 83% at doctoral-granting private colleges. Two-year private colleges fare better than their public counterparts, with a 62% retention rate. Bachelor's-level institutions, both public and private, and master's-level public institutions have about a 70% retention rate, private master's-level institutions have about a 75% retention rate, and public doctoral institutions have about a 78% retention rate (ACT, 2005). Of course, not every student who leaves an institution is making a bad personal decision, nor does every freshman intend to stay at his or her first campus. For example, a student may take a few courses at a local community college while saving money to attend a more-distant campus, or a student may decide to major in a program that is only available elsewhere.

One problem with student retention data is that campuses may not know if students have stopped/dropped out of school or have merely switched to another campus. The National Student Clearinghouse offers Enrollment Search services to campuses, and, for an annual fee, they track student enrollments, even across state lines. For example, Prince George's Community College used this service and determined that it has a high proportion of "successful dropouts" (students who succeeded elsewhere), mitigating some of their concern about students who leave the institution without completing a program (Ward, 2004).

Enrollment Growth and Student Diversity

Colleges were elite institutions earlier in American history, serving a small fraction of the population. In my parents' generation, a high school diploma was beyond reach for many who, like my parents, grew up on farms and could not relocate to communities with opportunities beyond the eighth grade. Times have changed, and a college degree has replaced the high school diploma for entry into many careers. Currently 75% of high school graduates enroll in college within two years of completing high school, and many older adults attend college for personal and professional growth. Between 1960 and 2001 American college enrollments more than tripled, from 4.1 million to 14.8 million, and many new campuses were created, including 743 new community colleges (Association of American Colleges and Universities, 2002).

Campuses not only are enrolling more students, they are serving an increasingly diverse student body, including many for whom English is not their primary language and whose childhoods were not spent in the U.S. In addition, the majority (57%) of traditional-aged students (ages 18 to 26) attend more than one undergraduate institution, including multiple community colleges before and during their enrollment at four-year institutions (Ramaley, 2004). How can we develop reasonable general education programs and expectations for our graduates when so many of our students do not have their entire college experience in our institution? Communication across campuses seems essential—not to standardize general education programs, but to reach an understanding about some basics. For example, the states of Illinois (Illinois Articulation Initiative, 2005b) and South Dakota (South Dakota Board of Regents, 2004) have established a common core of general education curriculum outcomes. We have the responsibility to serve the students we admit, even if they may transfer to another institution or receive our degree with courses taken elsewhere.

Assessment Vocabulary

Every emerging field, including assessment, develops a vocabulary that is used as a shorthand for important concepts. Some of these terms are borrowed from other areas, and some are adapted to have special meaning. Because so many people are working in assessment and many campuses work autonomously, differences in how words are interpreted exist, but the terms presented here are used quite consistently.

Alignment refers to how well two systems converge for a common purpose, and we use the term in many ways. For example, we ask if the curriculum aligns with learning outcomes, i.e., do we have a *cohesive curriculum* that systematically fosters student development of the outcomes we desire? If students are given options within the program, does each option ensure that the appropriate outcomes are addressed? We also ask if pedagogy aligns with course outcomes. For example, lecturing students about critical thinking probably is less effective than engaging students in thought-provoking exercises that provide opportunities for practice, feedback, and reflection. We ask if grading procedures align with course outcomes. Although our syllabi might specify our intentions to foster deep learning, students will study for the exams we give them. If we are interested in developing higher-order thinking skills, but only grade students using objective exams that focus on details, students probably will spend more time learning these details and less time developing the broad concepts, skills, and values we desire.

We also ask about institutional alignment. Do campus units align efforts to support learning? For example, if leadership, collaboration, and global awareness are among general education learning outcomes, do all campus professionals, including faculty, student affairs professionals, coaches, advisors, tutors, and residence hall managers, find ways to promote these outcomes when they interact with students and design courses and cocurricular activities? In addition, does the campus promote dialogue among these groups so they are aware of each other's efforts and can work together on the institutional level to promote student learning?

Authentic assessment occurs when students participate in exercises that simulate or are embedded in real-world activities. For example, we might assess critical thinking skills by asking students to analyze news articles or letters to the editor, and we may test their ability to integrate what they're learning by giving them a real-world problem and asking them to propose solutions that take into account cultural, social, physical, and economic conditions. Few professionals take multiple-choice tests for a living, and most deal with complex questions that must be answered with uncertain and incomplete knowledge. Authentic assessment helps us examine how well we are preparing students for life after graduation.

Assessment findings can be based on *direct* or *indirect* evidence. Direct assessment involves examining student demonstrations of the extent of their learning. If we want to know if students can write well, we ask them to write something and we look at the quality of the writing. If we want to know if students understand the scientific method, we give them a task that requires them to show the extent of their understanding, and we assess their work. Indirect evidence is based on opinions. For example, we could ask students to rate how well they write and how well they understand the scientific method, or we might conduct a focus group and invite students to discuss how well they have mastered these learning outcomes. Direct assessment provides the primary evidence concerning how well students have learned what we want them to learn. Indirect assessment provides supplementary information.

Opinions can be important, even if they are inaccurate or self-serving, because they can be the basis for student decision-making. For years educators relied on indirect assessment, generally periodic student and alumni surveys, but indirect assessment is no longer considered sufficient. Chapter 5 describes a variety of techniques for collecting direct assessment data, and Chapter 6 describes indirect assessment strategies.

Embedded assessment is frequently used to analyze the impact of general education programs. Students routinely take exams and do projects, and their products can be used as assessment data. Usually, the students' work is graded by course instructors, and the assessment of learning outcomes can be integrated into the grading process or can occur later. The alternative is to have *add-on assessment*. For example, students could be invited to take an exam or participate in a focus group outside of their regular coursework, perhaps on a designated Assessment Day.

Assessment data may be *quantitative* or *qualitative*. Quantitative data are numerical scores, such as a score of 82 on an exam. Qualitative data are verbal summaries of findings, such as a summary of what was learned in a focus group. *Scoring rubrics* (see Chapter 5) combine aspects of quantitative and qualitative assessment. They describe the criteria we use to classify student work into categories with verbal labels, such as unacceptable, marginal, competent, and exemplary, but these categories vary along a quantitative continuum. Some argue that only quantitative measures with an array of precise scores have validity, but a well-done qualitative study or the application of a rubric can provide outstanding assessment data.

When we do assessment, we are asking a simple question: Are we satisfied with the student attainment of our learning outcomes? We are less interested in knowing that the average is exactly 79.14 than in learning how many of our students meet or exceed our expectations. Assessment does not require the measurement precision required by grading, and not all data must be quantitative. When grading, the difference between a score of 79 and a score of 80 might mean the difference between a C+ and a B-grade, so precision of measurement is important. The use of rubrics is sufficient for assessment work, and using this approach may allow us to save much time and effort compared to generating a precise array of scores.

Assessment is a formative process. When we evaluate something, we can have summative or formative goals. A *summative* evaluation results in an overall assessment of the quality of what we're assessing. For example, a student might receive a B+ on a paper, and this B+ is a summative evaluation of the overall quality of that paper. A *formative* evaluation, though, focuses on improving what is being evaluated. For example, the teacher might provide helpful comments and suggestions on that B+ paper, and these are provided for formative purposes—to help the student improve. The distinction is important. Assessment policies and procedures should promote its formative purpose. For example, if faculty fear that disappointing assessment results might put their careers or their departments at risk, they will find ways to undermine or trivialize the process to always find positive results. Assessment should be conducted as an open inquiry, focused on learning that is important, and we have to recognize that some learning outcomes will be hard to achieve.

Some people use the words *formative* and *summative* in another way to indicate points in students' development (e.g., Suskie, 2004). *Formative assessments* evaluate students' abilities while they are still learning, and *summative assessments* evaluate their abilities as they're about to complete the program. For example, assessing the quality of students' writing at the beginning of the sophomore year is formative assessment; assessing their writing as they are about to graduate is summative assessment. We would expect summative results to indicate more complete mastery of our learning outcomes than formative results.

Assessment Steps

Six steps are involved in the assessment of academic programs (Allen, 2004):

1) Develop learning outcomes.

2) Check for alignment between the curriculum and the outcomes.

3) Develop an assessment plan.

4) Collect assessment data.

5) Use results to improve the program.

6) Routinely examine the assessment process.

Campuses have tried to skip some of the steps, but usually this results in a waste of energy, time, and money. For example, campus leaders might decide to spare faculty the time and effort to develop explicit learning outcomes, and opt, instead, for a *standardized test* that appears to target some important aspects of general education. They spend a few thousand dollars on the test and entice some students to take it, then are left with a set of results that no one really cares about. Would you consider changing your course or the curriculum based on a set of scores that bear no direct relationship to what you or your students are doing?

Step 1: Develop Learning Outcomes

Step 1 involves specifying what students should learn in the general education program, and this list forms the basis for curriculum development, review, and assessment. Creating the list engages the campus community in important discussions about what they are trying to accomplish. Chapter 2 provides examples of learning goals and outcomes from many campuses.

Step 2: Check for Alignment Between the Curriculum and the Outcomes

Once the list of outcomes is determined, the next question concerns the relationship between practice and these outcomes. We cannot hold students accountable for learning unless we have given them relevant learning opportunities. For example, does the curriculum introduce students to desired information literacy skills and does it provide sufficient practice and feedback to develop these skills? If it is possible for students to select course or instructor options that do not provide this instruction, how can we expect students to develop these skills? Chapter 3 describes a variety of ways to consider alignment.

Step 3: Develop an Assessment Plan

An assessment plan is essential because of the complicated nature of general education programs. Assessment requires ongoing contributions by faculty from an array of departments, and department chairs and faculty should be able to anticipate requests for assessment data, volunteers to review student work, participants in the discussion of findings, and efforts to modify courses to improve student learning. Campuses do not have to assess every general education outcome in every student every year, and attempting to do so may lead to the trivialization or abandonment of efforts.

A well-designed plan describes a series of assessment studies that systematically address all outcomes in a multi-year cycle. For example, if the campus has ten major goals, the plan might specify examining two or three of them each year, repeating the cycle every four years.

The plan specifies how a relevant, representative sample of students will be selected for each study, how data will be collected and analyzed, and how the campus will *close the loop* by identifying and integrating implications for change into campus operations. For example, an outcome may be assessed by collecting specific types of assignments from identified courses every three years, analyzing them using a rubric that focuses reviewers on the outcome being examined, discussing results at an annual assessment retreat, and providing needed follow-up services to support change.

The assessment plan should result in meaningful, manageable, and sustainable assessment. Faculty are too busy to waste time doing trivial tasks. When the general education assessment team invites faculty to participate, these faculty should see value in their efforts. They should learn how well students are mastering outcomes that faculty care about, and they should engage in fruitful discussion of changes if results are disappointing.

The assessment process should be manageable under reasonable constraints. No campus has unlimited financial resources, and time is the most important commodity for faculty. Although we are creative enough to design complicated assessment processes requiring hundreds of hours of professional time and thousands of dollars, most campuses seek a manageable process that efficiently generates valid answers to important questions. Creating a process that is overly complicated or expensive is likely to lead to dissatisfaction and abandonment, or to the perception that the purpose is to check off boxes on a list to satisfy some external agent, rather than do meaningful assessment for the purpose of improving student learning.

Assessment is ongoing, and those who design the assessment plan have to consider its sustainability. Maybe the general education assessment committee can beg, borrow, or steal enough resources to implement a complex plan, but can they do this year after year? Chapter 4 discusses suggestions for developing meaningful, manageable, sustainable general education assessment programs.

Step 4: Collect Assessment Data

Once the assessment plan is developed and approved, the campus is ready to implement the first year of planned studies. A designated budget should support efforts requiring financial assistance, and sometimes release time is necessary so leaders have time to do their work. If the campus has an assessment center, staff may provide the organizational structure for the assessment, such as collecting and copying student work samples, facilitating the development and application of a relevant rubric, and summarizing the data for subsequent discussion. Most faculty also will be engaged in assessing their own major programs. Assessment coordinators should organize everything to make efficient and effective use of faculty time when they contribute to general education assessment, and extraordinary efforts should be recognized in the faculty reward and recognition system.

Campuses can avoid costly errors by routinely pilot-testing procedures before implementing full scale studies. Invite a few students to think out loud as they respond to the study's instructions. Are students interpreting them as you intended? If not, revise them before beginning actual data collection. If the assessment process will involve subjective judgments, develop the rubric or scoring criteria that will guide these judgments and pilot-test the assessment using actual student work. Do your pilot judges understand the criteria, or do they need more explanation? Do the criteria lead to consistent judgments, i.e., do you have high *inter-rater reliability?* If not, revise the scoring criteria before you invite faculty to invest time assessing student work. Pilot-testing procedures reduces confusion and increases the likelihood that the assessment will result in useful information.

Step 5: Use Results To Improve the Program

Closing the loop can lead to a variety of decisions. If the assessment demonstrates that students are mastering the outcome at appropriate levels, you and your colleagues can celebrate. If some aspects of the results are disappointing, change is called for. Four major types of changes might be made, relating to curriculum, pedagogy, faculty support, and student support. For example, what if an assessment of student writing has disappointing results?

Faculty may decide to add another course to address writing in more depth, or they may decide to require more emphasis on writing within already-existing courses. For example, some campuses require each general education instructor to assign writing and give students feedback to improve their writing. Other campuses designate writing-intensive classes within the general education program, and campus policies restrict the enrollment in these courses so faculty have time to provide the necessary feedback. Some campuses develop linked courses, such as linking writing courses with content courses such as introductory psychology. Students enroll in both courses simultaneously, and they write papers that are reviewed by the psychology instructor for content and by the writing instructor for writing skills. The non-writing course provides a meaningful context for paper assignments, and both sets of faculty do what they do best.

Sometimes a disappointing result will lead faculty to the conclusion that they need special training or assistance to support an outcome, such as a faculty development program on helping students improve writing skills or the provision of specially trained teaching assistants who provide individual support and feedback on writing. Composition faculty might train and supervise these teaching assistants. The assistants might be paid, or their work might be part of a practicum integrated into a course on teaching college writing. Other campuses might respond to an identified writing problem by developing or enhancing a campus writing center to provide one-on-one guidance to students as they draft papers. Writing center staff and/or library staff may work closely with general education faculty to help them create effective writing assignments and to provide student training in writing and information literacy skills.

Closing the loop may involve the collaboration of many campus groups—faculty, campus governance leaders, administrators, student affairs professionals, and faculty development staff. General education is the core of the undergraduate program, and it sits at the intersection of much campus effort. General education assessment can provide the framework for important, institution-wide conversations about how to improve student learning.

Step 6: Routinely Examine the Assessment Process

We all are learning how to do assessment well, and we are likely to make mistakes. This is not a catastrophe; it is a learning opportunity. Consider ending each assessment study with some questions:

- How can we do this study better next time?

- What have we learned about doing assessment well?

- How can we share what we have learned about assessment with our colleagues, so they can benefit from our experience?

Your first general education assessment study may not be perfect, but subsequent studies should be more effective and more efficient. Perhaps your campus could host an annual event, such as an assessment forum, in which colleagues share what they are learning about doing meaningful, manageable, sustainable assessment.

Accreditation

Many countries have a federal agency that oversees colleges and universities, but in the United States we have multiple, independent accreditation commissions that base their judgments on peer evaluations using agreed-upon criteria. Someone on your campus probably has served on an accreditation team.

Although American accrediting bodies are not government agencies, they are reviewed and officially recognized by the Secretary of Education (U.S. Department of Education, 2005), as well as two national private organizations, the Council for Higher Education Accreditation (1998) and the Association of Specialized and Professional Accreditors (2005). Faculty sometimes are surprised to learn that accrediting agencies go through an accreditation-like process themselves, to verify that they meet national standards.

Accreditors assess campuses' capacity to offer their programs (e.g., qualified faculty, sufficient library resources, fiscal stability) and the effectiveness of their operations. American accreditors share a set of core academic values: "institutional autonomy, academic freedom, collegial governance, independent intellectual inquiry, general education, and education in the liberal arts" (Eaton, 2003, p. B15), and their evaluations certify that these are in place. Assessment is one of the major ways that campuses demonstrate effectiveness, and institutions are expected to have quality assurance processes in place to monitor and improve their impact on students.

Value of Accreditation

Most colleges and universities agree that accreditation is essential for many reasons:

- Accreditation is a certification that the campus is meeting its mission based on professional judgments by peers who apply a carefully defined, agreed-upon set of criteria.

- Students and their families are more confident that an accredited institution is viable, effective, and honest in its dealings with students.

- Students who transfer from colleges that are not accredited risk not receiving credit for their academic work and may be ineligible for entry into graduate programs on other campuses.

- Many agencies that provide grants to colleges and universities restrict support to accredited institutions.

- Students at colleges that are not accredited by a federally recognized accrediting body are not eligible for federal financial aid.

- Accreditation is earned through an extensive self-study process that engages the institution in periodic reflection, strategic planning, and data analysis. Accreditation encourages campuses to be thoughtful and purposeful in their operations.

- Accrediting agencies oversee campuses on a continuing basis, and each institution must be periodically reaccredited, verifying that the campus continues to meet professional standards.

Accreditation Agencies

Six regional accrediting bodies accredit American colleges and universities:

- Middle States Association of Colleges and Schools (Delaware, the District of Columbia, Maryland, New Jersey, New York, Pennsylvania, Puerto Rico, the U.S. Virgin Islands, the Republic of Panama; http://www.msche.org/)

- New England Association of Schools and Colleges (Connecticut, Maine, Massachusetts, New Hampshire, Rhode Island, Vermont; http://www.neasc.org/)

- North Central Association of Schools and Colleges (Arizona, Arkansas, Colorado, Illinois, Indiana, Iowa, Kansas, Michigan, Minnesota, Missouri, Nebraska, New Mexico, North Dakota, Ohio, Oklahoma, South Dakota, West Virginia, Wisconsin, Wyoming, including schools of the Navajo Nation; http://www.ncahigherlearningcommission.org/)

- Northwest Commission on Colleges and Universities (Alaska, Idaho, Montana, Nevada, Oregon, Utah, Washington; http://www.nwccu.org/)

- Southern Association of Schools and Colleges (Alabama, Florida, Georgia, Kentucky, Louisiana, Mississippi, North Carolina, South Carolina, Tennessee, Texas, Virginia; http://www.sacs.org/)

- Western Association of Schools and Colleges (California, Hawaii, the U.S. territories of Guam and American Samoa, the Republic of Palau, the Federated States of Micronesia, the Commonwealth of the Northern Marianas Islands, the Republic of the Marshall Islands; http://www.wascweb.org/).

In addition to the six regional accrediting agencies, the United States has dozens of specialized bodies that accredit specific programs or types of institutions, such as teacher education programs or dental schools. This is an enormous undertaking. For example, 80 different organizations accredited about 6,300 institutions and 17,500 programs in 2001 (Eaton, 2003). For more information on the various accreditation organizations, see the Council for Higher Education Accreditation (http://www.chea.org) and the Association of Specialized and Professional Accreditors (http://www.aspa-usa.org) web sites.

Accreditation and General Education

The six regional bodies accredit entire institutions, and general education receives special attention because it is an essential component of every institution that offers undergraduate degrees. For example, the *Handbook of Accreditation* for the Western Association of Schools and Colleges (WASC) Accrediting Commission for Senior Colleges and Universities (2001) specifies that:

> Baccalaureate programs engage students in an integrated course of study of sufficient breadth and depth to prepare them for work, citizenship, and a fulfilling life. These programs also ensure the development of core learning abilities and competencies including, but not limited to, college-level written and oral communication; college-level quantitative skills; information literacy; and the habit of critical analysis of data and argument. In addition, baccalaureate programs actively foster an understanding of diversity; civic responsibility; the ability to work

with others; and the capability to engage in lifelong learning. Baccalaureate programs also ensure breadth for all students in the areas of cultural and aesthetic, social and political, as well as scientific and technical knowledge expected of educated persons in this society. (p. 20)

The community college arm of WASC, the Accrediting Commission for Community and Junior Colleges (2004), also specifies general education expectations:

General education has comprehensive learning outcomes for the students who complete it, including the following:

a. An understanding of the basic content and methodology of the major areas of knowledge: areas include the humanities and fine arts, the natural sciences, and the social sciences.

b. A capability to be a productive individual and life long learner: skills include oral and written communication, information competency, computer literacy, scientific and quantitative reasoning, critical analysis/logical thinking, and the ability to acquire knowledge through a variety of means.

c. A recognition of what it means to be an ethical human being and effective citizen: qualities include an appreciation of ethical principles; civility and interpersonal skills; respect for cultural diversity; historical and aesthetic sensitivity; and the willingness to assume civic, political, and social responsibilities locally, nationally, and globally. (pp. 19–20)

The Middle States Commission on Higher Education (2002) has similar expectations:

The institution's curricula are designed so that students acquire and demonstrate college-level proficiency in general education and essential skills, including oral and written communication, scientific and quantitative reasoning, critical analysis and reasoning, technological competency, and information literacy. . . . General education incorporates essential knowledge, cognitive abilities, and an understanding of values and ethics, and it enhances students' intellectual growth. General education programs draw students into new areas of intellectual experience, expanding their cultural and global awareness and sensitivity, and

> preparing them to make enlightened judgments outside as well as within their academic specialty. Information literacy—the understanding and set of skills necessary to carry out the functions of effective information access, evaluation, and application—is an essential component of any general education program and is promoted by the participation of professional library staff. (pp. 37–38).

All the regional accreditors require campuses to explicitly state the outcomes associated with their general education program, assess these outcomes, and use results to improve the program. Assessment is not a temporary fad. It is a best practice in higher education that is required to acquire and maintain accreditation.

What Do We Want Students to Learn?

Greater Expectations

Because of its importance in higher education, many individuals and organizations offer advice about the nature of general education. Among the most seminal is a publication by the Association of American Colleges and Universities (2002): *Greater Expectations: A New Vision for Learning as a Nation Goes to College.* This initiative calls for:

- Articulation of and focus on forms of learning that are widely needed in the modern world;

- A new intentionality about addressing expectations for student achievement across successive levels of learning, from school through college;

- Involvement of students in "authentic assignments," i.e., the kinds of tasks that actually develop complex abilities while showing students how those abilities can be used with power in real contexts;

- Transparent assessments, linked to authentic assignments, that emphasize what students can do with their knowledge rather than their ability to pass standardized tests;

- Connection of desired capabilities to learning in each student's major, so that study in the major becomes an essential vehicle not only for developing those capabilities but also for learning how to put them to use. (Schneider, 2004b, p. 26)

Greater Expectations was developed over several years by a national panel of professionals representing public schools, community colleges, four-year colleges and universities, and the public sector; it is available in paper form and online (http://www.greaterexpectations.org). The report challenges us to promote deep and lasting learning and prepare students for citizenship, work, and participation in an interconnected world. The panel concludes that students should be empowered, informed, and responsible. Empowered learners should be able to:

- effectively communicate orally, visually, in writing, and in a second language

- understand and employ quantitative and qualitative analysis to solve problems

- interpret and evaluate information from a variety of sources

- understand and work within complex systems and with diverse groups

- demonstrate intellectual agility and the ability to manage change

- transform information into knowledge and knowledge into judgment and action. (p. xi)

Informed learners should know about:

- the human imagination, expression and the products of many cultures

- the interrelations within and among global and cross-cultural communities

- the means of modeling the natural, social, and technical worlds

- the values and histories underlying U.S. democracy. (p. xii)

Responsible learners should develop:

- intellectual honesty

- responsibility for society's moral health and for social justice

- active participation as a citizen of a diverse democracy

- discernment of the ethical consequences of decisions and actions

- deep understanding of one's self and respect for the complex identities of others, their histories, and their cultures. (p. xii)

As you and your colleagues examine your own general education program, you might like to ask how well your students will develop into the empowered, informed, and responsible citizens described in *Greater Expectations*.

Other Recommendations

The Association of American Colleges and Universities Board of Directors (2004) recommends that all campuses assess five key outcomes that prepare students for "work, citizenship, and a satisfying life" (p. 6):

1. strong analytical, communication, quantitative, and information skills—achieved and demonstrated through learning in a range of fields, settings, and media, and through advanced studies in one or more areas of concentration;

2. deep understanding of and hands-on experiences with the inquiry practices of disciplines that explore the natural, social, and cultural realms—achieved and demonstrated through studies that build conceptual knowledge by engaging learners in concepts and modes of inquiry that are basic to the natural sciences, social sciences, humanities, and arts;

3. intercultural knowledge and collaborative problem-solving skills—achieved and demonstrated in a variety of collaborative contexts (classroom, community-based, international, and online) that prepare students both for democratic citizenship and for work;

4. a proactive sense of responsibility for individual, civic, and social choices—achieved and demonstrated through forms of learning that connect knowledge, skills, values, and public action, and through reflection on students' own roles and responsibilities in social and civic contexts;

5. habits of mind that foster integrative thinking and the ability to transfer skills and knowledge from one setting to another—achieved and demonstrated through advanced research and/or creative projects in which students take the primary responsibility for framing questions, carrying out an analysis, and producing work of substantial complexity and quality. (pp. 5–6)

The board concludes that these are universal college outcomes for all students, regardless of major. Graduating seniors should demonstrate the most sophisticated understanding and capability, and this demonstration will vary across departments. For example, chemistry, history, and sociology majors will develop communication skills, but they will exhibit them in discipline-specific contexts and styles.

The League for Innovation in the Community College, supported by a grant from the Pew Charitable Trusts, invited representatives of fifteen community colleges to reach consensus on a list of learning outcomes for the 21st century. Eight categories of core skills were identified:

1. Communication skills (reading, writing, speaking, listening)

2. Computation skills (understanding and applying mathematical concepts and reasoning, analyzing and using numerical data)

3. Community Skills (citizenship; diversity/pluralism; local, community, global, environmental awareness)

4. Critical thinking and problem solving skills (analysis, synthesis, evaluation, decision making, creative thinking)

5. Information management skills (collecting, analyzing, and organizing information from a variety of sources)

6. Interpersonal skills (teamwork, relationship management, conflict resolution, workplace skills)

7. Personal skills (ability to understand and manage self, management of change, learning to learn, personal responsibility, aesthetic responsiveness, wellness)

8. Technology skills (computer literacy, Internet skills, retrieving and managing information via technology) (Wilson, Miles, Baker, & Schoenberger, 2000, p. 15)

Participants agreed that these skills are important for all adults and that community colleges are well equipped to foster them.

Researchers conducted a follow-up survey in 1999, inviting the chief academic officers of the 677 member institutions of the League for Innovation in the Community College to describe how their campuses are addressing these skills. The 259 responses indicated that most community colleges (92%) were discussing needed skills, and at least two-thirds of campuses that had developed lists of skills included collaboration/teamwork, communication, cultural/global studies/diversity, information management, mathematics, and technology literacy on their lists (Wilson, et al., 2000). When asked about barriers to integrating the 21st-century goals into their institution, the most commonly identified barriers were "inadequate time for needed activities" (88%) and "lack of agreement on how to assess 21st century skills" (87%; p. 25). Campus professionals never have enough time to do everything they want to do, but most campuses are finding ways to address the identification and assessment of their general education learning outcomes, in part because it is the right thing to do and in part because these activities are necessary to obtain and retain accreditation.

Other professional organizations also have suggestions. For example, the Council of Writing Program Administrators (2000) developed detailed learning outcomes for the first-year college composition course, and they describe how faculty can help students further develop writing skills as they complete their majors. Their outcomes are organized under four categories:

- *Rhetorical knowledge*—such as focusing on a purpose, taking the reader into account, and using multiple genres

- *Critical thinking, reading, and writing*—such as developing papers in a systematic way and using writing and reading for multiple functions (e.g., learning, communicating)

- *Processes*—such as iterating drafts, editing, self-critiquing, and using technology

- *Knowledge of conventions*—such as knowing about alternative formats, genre conventions, citations, syntax, and grammar

Ewell (2004) notes four major purposes served by general education, and most of his list deals with academic, personal, and practical outcomes, rather than course content:

1. Development of prerequisite skills needed for later work (e.g., in communication or in math)

2. Development of abilities that cut across disciplines, like critical thinking or problem solving

3. Development of general knowledge about particular disciplines and experiences with different modes of inquiry

4. Collegiate socialization—learning how to "do college" by learning how to use a library (or the Web), or how to plan and carry out an independent intellectual project. (p. 10)

Considerable disagreement among faculty exists about the relative focus on course-specific and broad learning outcomes. For example, I've heard faculty bemoan the fact that students don't know some specific facts that all educated people should know, such as the author of the *Iliad* or the date of the Emancipation Proclamation. In response, others defend the importance of process—it's not what facts students know; it's what they can do, such as critical thinking and problem solving. As with many dichotomies, the answer is somewhere between the two extremes. Students learn new knowledge *and* develop skills, strategies, and values in general education programs. Faculty often disagree on the proportional mix of knowledge, skills, and values. This discussion is common when general education learning outcomes are discussed, and you and your colleagues either have resolved this question or will do so in the future.

When we discuss general education, we are faced with a daunting task because we want to help our students develop satisfying and productive lives in the future. In the past America had an agrarian economy, then an industrial economy; but now it is a knowledge-based economy embedded in a global economy. Technology provides almost unlimited access to information and tools for manipulating data. General education should provide a foundation for students to manage and contribute to a knowledge-based economy and function in local, national, and international environments (Gaff, 2004).

Preparation for the Workplace

Greater Expectations promotes developing students' ability to apply what they're learning to practical, real-world problems, including problems in the workplace.

> A liberal education *is* a practical education because it develops just those capacities needed by every thinking adult: analytical skills, effective communication, practical intelligence, ethical judgment, and social responsibility. By expecting students to collaborate productively with people who are unlike them, a liberal education strengthens interpersonal skills useful in the workplace and community life. (Association of American Colleges and Universities, 2002, p. 26)

Most adults have multiple jobs and even multiple careers, and general education helps prepare them for lifelong learning and adaptation to different job demands and environments. Ramaley and Haggett (2005) suggest that among the basic skills required in the workplace are cognitive flexibility, creativity, knowledge transfer, and adaptability. The Business–Higher Education Forum (2003) defined nine necessary characteristics for the workplace: leadership, teamwork, problem solving, time management, self-management, adaptability, analytical thinking, global consciousness, and communication skills. Some campuses take career building seriously. For example, faculty at Kwantlen University College in British Columbia are encouraged to integrate twelve "employability skills" into their courses (Macpherson, 2001): creative thinking and problem-solving skills, oral communication skills, interpersonal skills, personal management and entrepreneurial skills, writing skills, reading and information skills, visual literacy, mathematical skills, intercultural skills, technological skills, and citizenship and global perspectives.

How well are we preparing students for the workplace? Newman, Couturier, and Scurry (2004), based on a five-year study (*The Futures Project*), found that 90% of college graduates reported that their college degree did not prepare them to succeed in the workplace. In addition, employers reported concerns about the graduates, including their critical thinking and writing skills. Ewell (2004) points out faculty and employers often use the term "critical thinking" differently:

> Academics tend to anchor the ability in a student's capacity to recognize flaws in reasoning, examine evidence, and compare two lines of

argument. Business people, by contrast, tend to emphasize performance in ill-structured situations—finding the "problem to solve," for
example, and knowing how to work around missing information or
when to stop after a "good enough" solution. (p. 6)

If we want our students to develop skills for the workplace, we should identify them among our learning goals and outcomes, integrate appropriate
learning experiences into the curriculum, and use assessment to identify
how well our students are meeting our expectations. Alumni and employers
can help with this task.

Local Discussion

Gaff (2004) warns that discussion of general education requirements often
involves turf battles and issues related to workload, resources, and curriculum details. He suggests that we set aside these concerns and begin our
conversation by focusing on what we want students to learn—the general
education learning outcomes—and the characteristics of a high-quality
curriculum. These conversations should not be restricted to a committee,
but should involve the faculty, as a whole, in "open, inclusive, and constructive dialogue" (p. 6) concerning issues like:

• Problems with the current general education program

• Student feedback on the current program and student retention data

• National general education curriculum trends and the current state of
general education on other campuses

• Relevant issues in the literature on higher education

• Feedback and suggestions from the local community and from those
who employ campus graduates

Retention data may seem out of place on this list, but 29% of African-
American freshmen and 31% of Hispanic freshmen do not complete their
first year of college (Newman, Couturier, & Scurry, 2004). Campuses
should disaggregate retention data to explore the success rates of various
groups to verify that students who are given access also succeed.

Gaff (2004), who has facilitated general education discussions on multiple campuses, suggests an exercise called "The Fives." He asks faculty to
list five (p. 6):

- "ideas and skills they want students to learn"
- "persons (living or dead) they would want their students to know"
- "places they would like their students to visit"
- "musical or artistic performances their students should see"
- "books students should read"

The ensuing discussion helps faculty identify differences, clarify priorities, reach consensus, and take collective responsibility for the general education program. Faculty refine their general education learning outcomes, and these outcomes become the framework for the assessment of curriculum alignment, student achievement, and enhancing student learning.

CHAPTER 2

General Education Mission, Goals, and Outcomes

All American general education programs share a common core of broad expectations. For example, expectations for written and oral communication, critical thinking, and information literacy are virtually universal. Some colleges and universities, though, have a mission that distinguishes them from other institutions, and this should be reflected in their general education program. For example, they may include expectations for spiritual development, global citizenship, or civic engagement; or they may place greater emphasis on the arts or the sciences. The diversity of our campuses and their missions is a strength of American education, allowing students many different opportunities for learning.

> Unlike the single, unified system found in many other countries, we have a vibrant enterprise of private and state-supported colleges and universities. Institutions with diverse missions have flourished, from community colleges to research universities; small, rural residential colleges to large, urban comprehensive universities; church-affiliated campuses to minority-serving institutions, and everything in between. Our network of higher education spans the nation, forming a rich resource of multiple approaches for the multiple audiences as the United States, more than any other country, moves toward universal participation. (Association of American Colleges and Universities, 2002, p. iii)

Our institutions and accreditation system share the important task of certifying that generally agreed upon standards are met at all institutions.

Mission, Goals, and Outcomes

Learning outcomes often are organized into a hierarchical system. The highest level is the *mission* statement, a description of the overall vision or purpose of general education within the institution. Associated with the general education mission are a set of *goals*, broad statements about the types of learning that are fostered within the program, such as communication and problem-solving skills. *Learning outcomes* (sometimes called *objectives*) are associated with each of these goals; and they describe, in behavioral terms, how students can demonstrate that each goal has been met. For example, a goal might be information competence, and the outcomes would be the array of things that student could do to demonstrate the extent of their information competence skills.

Knowledge, Skills, and Values

Learning goals and outcomes describe the knowledge, skills, and values that students should display when they complete the general education program. They answer these questions:

- What should students know when they complete the general education program?

- What should students be able to do when they complete the general education program?

- What kinds of attitudes, values, or predispositions should students have when they complete the general education program?

Some campuses are careful to integrate general education expectations into the majors, and these campuses would rephrase the three questions, asking about all students, regardless of major:

- What should students know when they graduate?

- What should students be able to do when they graduate?

- What kinds of attitudes, values, or predispositions should students have when they graduate?

We use goals and outcomes when we align curricula with expectations and when we assess general education programs, so it is important that we carefully articulate them. They should not be so narrow as to trivialize the process, nor so broad that they lose meaning.

Properties of Goals and Outcomes

How many goals and outcomes should a campus have? As you will see later in this chapter, there is no best answer to this question. Some campuses have a few broad goals, while others may have as many as 50 but each is more narrowly defined. You and your colleagues will have to decide which approach is better for you.

Learning goals and outcomes should focus on the learner, not the instructor. For example, "We teach students to be critical thinkers" focuses on what faculty do. When we focus on the learner, this changes, that is, "Students become critical thinkers," "Students become better critical thinkers," or "Graduates are able to think critically." Notice the differences among these examples. "Students become critical thinkers" and "Graduates are able to think critically" set *absolute* standards, but "Students become better critical thinkers" sets *value-added* standards. Sometimes campuses with absolute standards discuss the *mark* of their graduates. For example, the mark of a graduate from Yale University is the set of characteristics that all Yale graduates display. As you think about the general education learning outcomes for your campus, ask about the mark of your graduates. What characteristics should all your students develop because of your general education program?

Value-added standards specify improvement. Students may start at levels 1 or 2 on a 10-point scale, but the general education program is expected to help them move to higher levels. Some students may improve to levels 3 or 4; some may begin at level 7 and improve to level 10. When value-added standards are in use, there is no absolute standard; for example, you cannot claim that all graduates reach at least level 6. When it's time to assess how well learning outcomes have been achieved, we can examine students who are about to graduate to see if they meet absolute standards, but we generally use a pre-post design to assess value-added standards because we want to demonstrate individual growth. We could assess each student's skills at entry and at exit to demonstrate value-added learning.

Developing Goals and Outcomes

As faculty determine the learning outcomes for general education courses, they might ask this question: If this is the only course students ever take in this area, what do we want them to retain? For example, imagine you are teaching a freshman-level general education course in your discipline, and you know many students in this course have low intrinsic interest in your discipline and are unlikely to take another course in this area. What lasting impact do you want to have on them—learning that persists past the final exam? You could offer them a traditional freshman introductory course for majors designed to help them learn the key terms and concepts that would be further developed within the major, but this might result in memorization to get through exams, rather than deep and lasting learning. You might decide to put greater emphasis on how your discipline can be applied to their lives and the decisions they're likely to face in the future, how professionals in your discipline develop and test ideas, and general skills, such as critical thinking and problem solving. You might be able to capture their imagination, engage them in activities that illustrate the usefulness of your discipline and its methodology, help them develop desired critical thinking and problem-solving skills, and leave lasting interest in an area they used to think was irrelevant to their lives.

Faculty on campuses with distributed general education programs might find the word *or* particularly useful when defining goals and outcomes. Typically, students can meet a requirement by selecting from a list of courses in a variety of disciplines. Faculty sometimes worry that they will not be able to find a common denominator among a set of disciplines, but the learning goal could be that students can demonstrate an understanding of X, Y, *or* Z. For example, faculty at the University of South Carolina (2003a) developed this humanities goal: "Students will demonstrate an understanding of the contributions of the literary, visual or performing arts and their cultural context and express informed personal responses to artistic creations" (Goal 5).

Depth of Learning

As faculty consider learning outcomes, questions emerge about the depth of learning. Should the outcomes be at the *surface* level or at a *deep* level? We gain surface-level learning through memorization and practice, and it can be long-term if sufficient practice occurs. For example, most of us first memorized the letters in the alphabet when we were children. We rehearsed the letters in grade school, and we continue to use them every time we read, write, or use a dictionary or file system arranged in alphabetical order. We retain this learning throughout our lives because of ongoing practice. The knowledge is memorized, making it difficult to manipulate what we have learned. For example, it is difficult to list every other letter in the alphabet without thinking of the intermediate letters, and it is even more difficult to break the pattern more fully, such as trying to say the alphabet in reverse. If memorized materials are not rehearsed or practiced, they fade away.

Deep learning involves conceptual understanding. The knowledge is personal and usable in a variety of situations. For example, if you understand how computer programs function, you "own" this knowledge and can use it in many situations. This deep understanding allows you to generalize and transfer what you've learned to new programs—not just the software covered in your coursework. Differences in deep learning separate experts from novices. For example, an expert logician, historian, political scientist, or sociologist is aware of issues and processes during a political debate that others might not even notice; and their analysis is habitual because it is how they process information.

Bloom's Taxonomy

Probably the best-known discussion of the depth of learning is Bloom's taxonomy (Bloom, 1956; Krumme, 2002). Bloom's six levels are:

- *Knowledge.* To know specific facts, terms, concepts, principles, or theories

- *Comprehension.* To understand, interpret, compare and contrast, explain

- *Application.* To apply knowledge to new situations, to solve problems

- *Analysis.* To identify the organizational structure of something; to identify parts, relationships, and organizing principles

- *Synthesis.* To create something, to integrate ideas into a solution, to propose an action plan, to formulate a new classification scheme

- *Evaluation.* To judge the quality of something based on its adequacy, value, logic, or use

Knowledge is surface-level learning, and, according to Bloom, the depth of learning increases as you go down the list, with evaluation viewed as the deepest level. Although not everyone agrees with this strict order, the taxonomy can be useful as you define and refine your outcome statements.

If, for example, your campus has a learning goal concerning the scientific method, you might consider a variety of outcomes:

- Students can define the scientific method. (Knowledge)

- Students can explain the scientific method. (Comprehension)

- Students can use the scientific method to design experiments. (Application)

- Students can identify independent and dependent variables, hypotheses, and results in scientific studies. (Analysis)

- Students can review a set of research studies on a given topic and reach a general conclusion about what they demonstrate. (Synthesis)

- Students can judge the scientific merit of a research study and its conclusions. (Evaluation)

Considering Bloom's taxonomy helps ensure that you and your colleagues have identified the *depth of processing* you expect students to develop. You may decide to have outcomes at varying levels of Bloom's taxonomy.

Examples of General Education Mission and Vision Statements

Let's review some examples of general education mission or vision statements. Brigham Young University (BYU; 2005) describes the mission of its University Core program:

> Within The Aims of a BYU Education, the objective of BYU's General Education Program is to prepare students with a broad, integrated foundation of knowledge, skills and cultural understanding which supports and enhances major education and facilitates the ability and desire for lifelong learning and service. In an environment which blends the spiritual and the secular, general education courses should improve the student's ability to think clearly, communicate effectively, and act wisely. (Mission Statement section)

Coastline Community College (2004) has the following general education philosophy statement:

The term "general education" refers to a broad-based and comprehensive program that introduces students to the major areas of higher education: the humanities, fine arts, social sciences, and natural sciences. The general education program at Coastline Community College is designed to help students develop the knowledge and skills that will contribute to their intellectual, personal, and professional growth. Specifically, the general education program will help students:

- improve the essential communication skills of speaking, writing, reading and listening.

- understand and apply the principles of the scientific method.

- develop competence in mathematics and analytical thinking.

- develop skills that will enable them to access information and resources independently for continued research and learning.

- understand and apply principles of critical thinking to a variety of situations, areas of study of fields of endeavor.

- understand and appreciate the heritage of their own culture and that of others.

- develop insight and knowledge in understanding self and others.

- understand the rights, responsibilities and privileges necessary to be an informed participating citizen in a democratic society.

- develop an understanding and appreciation of the visual and performing arts.

- gain information and experiences that will assist them in making effective career decisions.

- understand the effects of changing technology on society today and in the future.

Grand Valley State University's (2005) mission for its general education program is:

The Grand Valley State University General Education Program provides a broad-based liberal education experience that fosters lifelong learning and informed citizenship. The program prepares students for intelligent participation in public dialogues that consider the issues of humane living and responsible action in local, national, and global communities. (Mission section)

Olivet College (n.d.) describes The Olivet Plan:

The Olivet Plan's purpose is to implement the college's vision of Education for Individual and Social Responsibility.

The Olivet Plan is based on the college's historical mission of offering education to all, regardless of race or ethnicity, sex, or economic status. It seeks to help students integrate learning from the full range of their experiences, engage in active learning both inside and outside the classroom, and take genuine responsibility for their own learning. At Olivet College, we seek to place equal emphasis on engaging, challenging, and supporting our students. (¶ 1–2)

Sinclair Community College's (2004) vision statement for its general education program states:

We believe in unlimited human potential. General Education is a process whereby lifelong learners grow and fulfill that potential. General Education supports individuals in the quest to become whole, complete persons by encouraging development in areas such [as] thought, communication, values, creativity, feeling, adaptability and awareness. General Education provides foundation skills necessary for successful living in the ever-changing present and future global environment. In addition to encouraging uniqueness and personal development, General Education provides the commonalities which enable us to collaborate and achieve community. Indeed, as we face the challenges inherent in human existence, General Education is a key to solving the problems of survival for individuals, communities, nations and the species. (¶ 1)

Common Elements

Each campus, including your own, is unique, but a review of general education mission and vision statements allows us to identify some elements that commonly occur:

• Explicit ties to the campus mission

- Breadth of coverage of the liberal arts, including the cultural, social, and natural world, as well as mathematics and technology

- Development of communication skills

- Development of lifelong learning skills

- Development of citizenship skills and social responsibility

- Development of analytical, critical-thinking, and problem-solving skills

- Development of interpersonal and collaboration skills

- Development of a foundation for subsequent academic studies, work, and life in a complex environment

- Development of a foundation for participation in local, national, and global affairs

- Development of ethics and values, including those related to interpersonal relationships and the environment

- Development of research skills, including information competence and an understanding of the scientific method

- Personal development of the individual student, including self-understanding and health

- Some description of pedagogy and student roles, such as active engagement of students in their education and in making choices about general education coursework

- Exploration of contemporary problems

Not surprisingly, this list overlaps considerably with accreditation and *Greater Expectations* (Association of American Colleges and Universities, 2002) recommendations described in Chapter 1.

Examples of General Education Goals and Outcomes

Campuses vary in how they describe their learning targets. Some use the term goal (or competency) and have associated outcomes (or objectives or behaviors). Others just provide goals, outcomes, objectives, competencies, or behaviors without using the hierarchical format. Some develop a separate set of learning expectations for each segment of the general education curriculum (e.g., for the natural science requirement), and others use a more holistic approach, developing learning targets for the program, as a whole.

Regardless of format, campus statements explicitly communicate what students are expected to learn in the general education program. Faculty who decide to use brief statements concerning general education goals will eventually face the task of articulating how students can demonstrate that goals have been achieved. They may decide to expand their statement of learning goals/outcomes, or they may decide to integrate these details into the rubric or scoring guide they will use to assess student work. If you are unfamiliar with rubrics and are curious to learn about them now, glance at Chapter 5.

Goal and outcome statements should be clear to program administrators, faculty who staff general education courses, students, and others. Program administrators use these statements to approve general education courses and plan general education assessment efforts, faculty use them to design courses, students use them to guide studying, and others use them to plan support services and the cocurricular environment.

Examples from more than 45 institutions are provided in the following sections, and my intent is to offer a range of ideas that you might consider. Rarely can another campus's outcomes be cut and pasted into your own draft, but often you can save considerable effort by adapting the work of others to your own campus. The following examples are given in the language each campus uses, so the terminology often switches among *goals, outcomes, objectives, competencies,* and *behaviors.* In addition, because these are quotations from campus documents, language styles, bullets, numbers, and formats vary. If you are like me and always edit for consistent style, be prepared for the variations.

Written Communication

Goals concerning written communication skills are universal, although campuses describe them in different ways. Some campuses combine written and oral communication into a single goal, some include reading and/or listening, and some include writing in a broad basic skills goal. Some campuses simply list goals using generic titles, such as "Written Communication" or "Writing"; some campuses describe goals in more detail:

- "Students should develop competence in writing for personal and interpersonal communication as well as artistic expression. Through the practice of writing, students should develop the ability to:

  - reason critically;

  - assimilate knowledge; and

  - articulate what they have learned" (California State University–Northridge, 2005, Written Communication section A.1).

- "Students will plan and write well-structured compositions demonstrating the writing capabilities to express, inform, analyze, evaluate, persuade, argue, conduct research, and use primary and secondary sources" (Community College of Denver, 2005, ¶ 1).

- Students will "write effectively and responsibly and understand and interpret the written expression of others" (Dakota State University Assessment Office, 2000, ¶ 1).

- Students can "communicate conclusions, interpretations and implications clearly, concisely and effectively, both orally and in writing" (Washington State University, 2002; Outcomes section D).

Campuses have developed a variety of learning outcomes associated with written communication goals. For example, Cascadia Community College (Baker, 2000) defines communication outcomes in four areas:

- *Content Analysis and Evaluation.* Learners will listen to, locate, choose, evaluate context, comprehend, paraphrase, summarize, analyze, synthesize, and evaluate texts—oral, written, and electronic.

- *Development of Evidence.* Learners will use supporting evidence to create, develop, and present arguments and reasoning.

- *Creative Expression.* Learners will create communications that reflect audience, cultural awareness of self and others, disciplinary awareness, and historical and political settings.

- *Representation.* Learners will use standardized symbol systems (language, visuals and graphics, numbers, etc.) to interpret, evaluate, create, and express knowledge. (pp. 34–35)

The State of South Dakota (South Dakota Board of Regents, 2004) lists four writing outcomes. Their students are expected to:

1. Write using <u>standard</u> American English, including correct punctuation, grammar, and sentence structure;

2. Write logically;

3. Write persuasively, with a variety of rhetorical strategies (e.g., expository, argumentative, descriptive);

4. Incorporate formal research and documentation into their writing, including research obtained through modern, technology-based research tools. (p. 3)

The University of Arizona (2005) lists four outcomes for English Composition:

Read and summarize critical arguments.

Organize information coherently.

Choose language and format appropriate for different audiences.

Revise their writing effectively. (Outcomes section)

The University of Montana (2002) specifies that "a graduate's writing will demonstrate":

1. voice that is consistent and appropriate to the audience and purpose;

2. correct diction and sentence structure;

3. sound judgments unified by a clear message;

4. evidence of reasons supporting all judgments;

5. logical linkage of judgments and evidence;

6. transitions that connect a series of ideas and evidence;

7. correct spelling and punctuation. (Student Learning Outcomes for English Writing Skills Competency section)

California State University–San Bernardino (2005) has three written communication goals (dealing with effective writing, effective reading, and effective research using primary and secondary sources), and each has from four to nine objectives. For example, their reading goal and objectives are:

Read and comprehend a variety of written materials, including material at the entry level of professional work in their major discipline; extract ideas from written material; and value the printed word as a source of information and/or enjoyment.

Objectives:

1. Comprehend a writer's message literally, inferentially, and analytically

2. Identify both stated and implied main ideas

3. Differentiate between main ideas and supporting ideas

4. Evaluate the persuasiveness/effectiveness of the supporting details

5. Distinguish between fact and opinion

6. Recognize the organizational structure of written material

7. Discern the style and tone of a writer

8. Abstract thoughts and ideas from reading material

9. Appreciate the value of reading as a source of lifelong learning, recreation, and intellectual enjoyment (Written Communication section)

As can be seen in objective 9, outcomes do not always have to be about knowledge and skills. Some campuses want general education to affect attitudes. How might the inclusion of this outcome affect the teaching of related courses?

Oral Communication

Oral communication is also a very common goal, and, as noted above, it is sometimes combined into broad communication or basic skills goals. The National Communication Association (1996) argues that oral communication is an essential component of general education.

> Preparation for life in the modern world requires communication with a cross section of diverse people who often have conflicting needs and interests. Perhaps more than ever, educated persons need to communicate with sensitivity and skill with those of widely different backgrounds, cultural experiences, and values. Effective communication helps maintain a sense of community and an ability to craft consensus in an increasingly diverse and complex world. . . . Members of SCA agree that rather than focusing on narrow applications, a required oral communication course emphasizes the most basic and universal concepts and skills that cut across many fields such as listening respectfully and critically, explaining points clearly, asking questions to gain understanding, adapting messages to different contexts, and solving problems in groups. (¶ 5–¶ 6)

Here are some examples of goal statements that campuses have developed:

- "Oral Communication: . . . Students should acquire a clear understanding of the basic concepts and practices associated with public speaking and should appreciate the role of public speaking in a democratic society. Students should be able to deliver speeches in accordance with the principles of effective oral presentation" (California State University–Northridge, 2005, Oral Communication section A.4).

- Students will "communicate effectively and responsibly through speaking and listening" (Dakota State University Assessment Office, 2000, ¶ 1).

- Students will be able to "engage in articulate expression through effective writing and speaking. A generally educated person has mastered the various forms of written and oral communication that permit full participation in a society and world dependent on the free interchange of ideas and information" (Grand Valley State University, 2005, Goals section).

- "Students will communicate orally in a manner that unites theory, criticism, and practice to produce an effective communication" (University of South Carolina, 2003c, ¶ 1).

A variety of outcomes have been developed. For example, Eastern New Mexico University (2005b) combines written and oral communication into a single competency, and they include interpersonal skills among their outcomes:

The student is able to use written and spoken English effectively, including the ability to read and to listen with understanding and critical discernment.

- The student is able to write essays that are well-structured, well-developed, and well-edited.

- The student is able to comprehend basic readings and read critically.

- The student understands basic conventions of academic writing with respect to format, structure, paragraph development, style, and sentencing.

- The student is able to use multiple sources to develop, plan and organize written and oral presentations that analyze and evaluate the ideas and language choices of the sources.

- The student is able to practice effective small group and interpersonal communication. (The Competencies section 1)

The Illinois Articulation Initiative (2005a) specifies theory and practice competencies for oral communication:

Communication Theory—The student is expected to:

- have a theoretical understanding of communication;

- understand the relationships among self, message, and others; and understand the process of effective listening.

Communication Practice—The student is expected to:

- phrase clear, responsible and appropriate purpose statements;

- develop specific, well-focused thesis statements;

- analyze an audience and situation, and then adapt a message to those needs;

- generate ideas and gather supporting material;

- incorporate material from various appropriate sources, using proper verbal citations;

- use evidence, reasoning and motive appeals in persuasive speaking;

- prepare and use visual aids that promote clarity and interest;

- organize and outline an effective message;

- use language that is appropriate to enhance understanding and effect the desired result;

- establish credibility by demonstrating knowledge and analysis of topic;

- use extemporaneous delivery with reasonable fluency, expressiveness and comfort;

- cope effectively with the tensions involved in public speaking;

- demonstrate acceptable ethical standards in research and presentation of materials; and

- listen to, analyze and critique oral communication. (Oral Communication section)

Kellogg Community College (2001) has three communication competencies. Their students should be able to:

A. Communicate ideas and opinions clearly and correctly for a variety of readers and purposes through writing and speaking.

B. Examine a written or spoken work and recognize purpose, meaning, main ideas; locate additional information sources and apply that information in research or problem solving.

C. Use listening and speaking skills in interpersonal communication, one-to-one and in a group, with accuracy, insight, and effectiveness in a variety of settings. (Communication section)

San Francisco State University (1999) has ten oral communication learning objectives. They expect students to be capable of:

1. Demonstrating awareness of the complexity of communication in terms of its psychological, social, political, cultural, and ethical dimensions.

2. Demonstrating knowledge about verbal and nonverbal communication in various contexts (e.g., interpersonal, small group, public speaking, intercultural).

3. Reducing their own speech anxiety and projecting greater confidence as a speaker.

4. Listening actively and providing constructive feedback.

5. Considering an audience's knowledge, background and attitudes when constructing a message.

6. Recognizing and articulating issues from one's own perspective, while acknowledging the perspectives of others.

7. Locating, evaluating and reporting information in support of a view.

8. Assessing claims or arguments as a speaker and listener.

9. Organizing, constructing, and delivering prepared and spontaneous presentations.

10. Demonstrating effective verbal and nonverbal delivery skills. (Oral Communication section)

In addition to a set of more typical communication skills, Waukesha County Technical College expects students to develop group effectiveness skills:

• *Conflict Resolution.* Apply effective techniques to resolve interpersonal conflict.

- *Social Responsibility and Effective Citizenship.* Demonstrate awareness of the social and global environment by making informed decisions for effective participation in the community.

- *Teamwork.* Work effectively and cooperatively in a group setting.

- *Valuing Diversity.* Value differences among people.

- *Effective Relationships.* Develop positive relationships with family members, co-workers, friends, and others. (Schoenberger, 2000, p. 43)

Mathematics

Goals related to mathematics are labeled in different ways, such as quantitative literacy, quantitative reasoning, mathematical thinking, and numeracy. Some campuses combine mathematics with other areas, such as formal logic or computer science. Some campuses offer "math for poets" courses specifically designed for general education, and some faculty advocate the inclusion of fairly sophisticated calculations, such as conic sections, in the general education math course. Some want to include skills related to creating and interpreting maps and charts, and others are interested in "real world" math, such as making personal decisions about loans, investments, and retirement planning. Faculty also debate the role of technology in mathematics education. Which calculations should students be able to do on their own, and when can calculators or computers be used?

Many campuses have moved toward a focus on *quantitative literacy,* emphasizing the process of mathematics (mathematical and logical reasoning), rather than traditional mathematics curricula, such as algebra, geometry, and statistics (Steen, 2001). These campuses often encourage connecting mathematics with other disciplines by giving general education credit for courses, such as "Practical Physics," "Quantifying Judgments of Human Behavior," and "Introduction to Energy Sources" (Steen, 2004).

Writing-across-the-curriculum initiatives have been popular for decades, based on the recognition that all faculty share a responsibility for teaching effective writing. Perhaps the time has come for a math-across-the-curriculum movement in higher education, with increased emphasis on integrating quantitative literacy into the majors (Schneider, 2004b). Schneider concludes:

It is time to give up on the stand-alone general education mathematics requirement. . . . very little is actually accomplished through this traditional approach to quantitative reasoning, and we must fundamentally rethink it. One promising strategy is to make field-related quantitative competence the standard, holding students accountable for evidence of developed ability to actually use quantitative reasoning in ways keyed to their major field(s) of study. . . . Whatever strategy we choose, we must recognize that it really is malpractice to allow students to slip through college without developing the ability to use quantitative strategies to examine significant questions. We are only shortchanging our graduates with respect to the actual demands of a numbers-infused world. (p. 27)

Although not everyone agrees with all that Schneider suggests, most students probably would better develop mathematical competence and confidence if quantitative reasoning were fostered in the major after lower-division, general education mathematics coursework is completed.

In light of these controversies, how have campuses defined their mathematics goals and outcomes? Examples of campus goals are:

Students will analyze and use numerical data and qualitative reasoning skills, including applying proper formulas to mathematical data and calculating results, illustrating quantitative data graphically, rearranging general formulas to solve for any term, and interpreting graphic data and assessing importance of portrayed trends. (Community College of Denver, 2005, ¶ 4)

Quantitative Reasoning and Representation: [Students learn] To deepen understanding of the value and need for this type of reasoning, the ability to understand the graphical representation of data and to transform information into quantitative and graphical representations. (Portland State University, 2005, ¶ 4)

Mathematical Sciences. . . . The courses . . . are designed to develop the powers of formal reasoning through use of precise artificial languages as found in mathematics, computer science, statistics, or formal logic. These courses present broadly applicable techniques for formulating, analyzing, and solving problems, and for evaluating proposed solutions. (University of Chicago, 2000, Natural and Mathematical Sciences section D, ¶ 2)

Quantitative or Formal Reasoning: Courses in this area help develop analytical skills through the practice of quantitative or formal symbolic reasoning. Courses focus on the presentation and evaluation of evidence and argument, the understanding of the use and misuse of data, and the organization of information in quantitative or other formal symbolic systems including those used in the disciplines of computer sciences, linguistics, mathematics, philosophy, and statistics. (University of Iowa, 2005, Quantitative or Formal Reasoning section)

A variety of mathematical learning outcomes have been developed. For example, Arizona Western College (2003) has four outcomes for its quantitative goal:

1. Identify and extract relevant data from given mathematical or contextual situations.

2. Select known models or develop appropriate models that organize data into:

    a. tables or spreadsheets (with or without technology); or

    b. graphical representations (with or without technology); or

    c. symbolic/equation format.

3. Obtain correct mathematical results and state those results with qualifiers.

4. Use the results to:

    a. determine whether they are realistic in terms of the original situation; or

    b. determine whether the mathematical model/representation of data was appropriate; or

    c. describe a trend in a table, graph, or formula and make predictions based on trends; or

    d. draw qualitative conclusions in written form. (Quantitative Analysis section)

Eastern New Mexico University (2005b) has five outcomes related to mathematical competency:

- The student is able to perform the five basic mathematical operations: addition, subtraction, multiplication, division and exponentiation on whole numbers and fractions without assistance.

- The student understands mathematical relationships from verbal and written descriptions and can translate them into mathematical expressions.

- The student is able to solve basic equations and inequalities.

- The student understands the fundamentals of measurement and geometry.

- The student is able to use information from data represented in charts, graphs, tables and spreadsheets. (The Competencies section 2)

Mesa Community College (2002–2003) has four outcomes for its Numeracy goal:

1. Identify and extract relevant data from given mathematical situations.

2. Select known models or develop appropriate models that organize the data into tables or spreadsheets, graphical representations, symbolic/equation format.

3. Obtain correct mathematical results and state those results with qualifiers.

4. Use the results. (Numeracy section)

San Francisco State University (1999) has nine quantitative reasoning objectives. Their students should be capable of:

1. Translating between verbal statements and mathematical expressions.

2. Understanding mathematics both as a descriptive language and a set of techniques.

3. Applying quantitative information and procedures to contexts both inside and outside the classroom.

4. Presenting and summarizing information in quantitative form.

5. Interpreting, making judgments about and drawing conclusions from quantitative material.

6. Performing mathematical calculations.

7. Using appropriate technology for mathematical operations.

8. Evaluating critically the uses of quantitative procedures and descriptions, including identifying appropriate applications and deceptive or erroneous reasoning.

9. Constructing mathematical models. (Quantitative Reasoning section)

The University of South Carolina (2003b) has four math objectives:

Objective A. Students will demonstrate their understanding of the role of quantitative reasoning and its application.

Objective B. Students will demonstrate an understanding of the language of mathematics and basic mathematical concepts and operations.

Objective C. Students will demonstrate the ability to apply basic mathematical operations to problem solving in one's personal and working life. This criterion demonstrates ability to apply basic mathematical concepts and operations to situations which will be encountered beyond the university and in the "real world".

Objective D. Students will accurately comprehend and draw appropriate inferences from numeric data assembled in a variety of forms (e.g., graphs, charts, summary statistics, etc.) and in other disciplines. (¶ 1–4)

Critical Thinking and Problem Solving

Most campuses include some statements about critical thinking and problem solving among their general education outcomes, sometimes within separate goals and sometimes as outcomes associated with other goals.

Some campuses offer specific courses in critical thinking, and others help students develop critical thinking skills within a context, such as within social science courses. Illustrative campus goals are:

- "Students will actively reflect on, reason about, and form independent judgments on a variety of ideas and information, and use these skills to guide their beliefs and actions" (Bergen Community College, n.d., Critical Thinking section).

- "Students will demonstrate orally and in writing the critical-thinking skills of analysis, synthesis, and evaluation" (Community College of Denver, 2005, ¶3).

- Longwood University (2004–2005) promotes "the development of citizen leaders for the common good by promoting critical thinking and analysis in all aspects of the students' lives and by developing the knowledge and skills that lead to college success" (Goal 1).

Campuses have developed a variety of outcomes associated with critical thinking and problem-solving goals. For example, Arizona Western College (2003) has two critical thinking outcomes:

1. Learners will demonstrate the ability to take charge of their own thinking.

2. Learners will demonstrate an intellectually disciplined process of actively and skillfully conceptualizing, applying, analyzing, synthesizing, and/or evaluating information gathered from, or generated by, observation, experience, reflection, reasoning, or communication, as a guide to belief and action. (Critical Thinking section)

California State University–Bakersfield (2000b) developed six goals, each having two or three objectives, under Critical Thinking and Logical Reasoning. The goals are:

1. Construct a good argument.

2. Distinguish argumentative discourse from other kinds of discourse.

3. Distinguish different kinds of arguments.

4. Identify hidden aspects of arguments.

5. Evaluate the quality of reasoning.

6. Judge the credibility of different kinds of sources. (Critical Thinking and Logical Reasoning section)

Mesa Community College (2002–2003) has seven Problem Solving/ Critical Thinking outcomes:

1. Identify a problem or argument.

2. Isolate facts related to the problem.

3. Differentiate facts from opinions or emotional responses.

4. Ascertain the author's conclusion.

5. Generate multiple solutions to the problem.

6. Predict consequences.

7. Use evidence or sound reasoning to justify a position. (Problem Solving/Critical Thinking section)

Washington State University (2002) lists five outcomes for "Reason Critically":

1. Define and solve problems

2. Integrate and synthesize knowledge

3. Assess the accuracy and validity of findings and conclusions

4. Understand how one thinks, reasons, and makes value judgments

5. Understand diverse viewpoints, ambiguity and uncertainty

6. Understand differing philosophies and cultures (Reason Critically section)

American and World Cultures, Multicultural Understanding, and Citizenship

Another common general education learning goal or set of goals deals with American and/or world cultures and the development of multicultural understanding and/or citizenship. Goals related to this concept are given a variety of titles, such as American or World History, Western or

Non-Western Civilization, Citizenship or World Citizenship, World Perspectives, Cultural Diversity, Cultural Studies, Cultural Legacies, Multiculturalism, Global Consciousness, and Global Perspectives. Some campuses have an array of designated *multicultural* courses that meet other general education requirements, and students must take at least one of these courses within the program. For example, a course on African-American literature that satisfies a literature requirement or a course on the sociology of urban life that satisfies a social science requirement might also satisfy the multicultural requirement.

From 1989 to 1993 the Association of American Colleges and Universities, supported by a grant from the National Endowment of the Humanities, sponsored an initiative called *Engaging Cultural Legacies: Shaping Core Curricula in the Humanities.* Campus participants developed new curricula focusing on American and world cultural pluralism, and some campuses included among their goals the development of world citizenship (Schneider, 2004a). Information on this organization's initiatives and publications is available on their web site (http://www.aacu.org).

Smith (2004) argues that *cultural studies* is developing into a separate discipline that should be specifically integrated into general education programs. According to Smith, cultural studies, among other things, promotes critical thinking and informed citizenship, and it provides an important forum for the discussion of the impact of nature vs. nurture—a controversy that continues to generate heated debate with important personal and interpersonal implications (Stearns, 2004).

What kinds of goals have campuses developed? Here are some examples:

- "Students will demonstrate an awareness of the responsibilities of intelligent citizenship in a diverse and pluralistic society, and will demonstrate cultural, global, and environmental awareness" (Bergen Community College, n.d., Civic Responsibility section).

- "The Global and Cultural Awareness requirement seeks to help BYU students come not only to see the relativity of many of their own, culturally-derived notions but also to 'go forth and serve,' having had meaningful discussion about or hands-on experience in dealing with real world global issues and problems, approached with empathy and charity gained from learning to see the world through others' eyes" (Brigham Young University, 2004, p. 3).

- Students will "develop an understanding of diversity/pluralism in the world community and an awareness of civic and social participation and ethical and informed decision-making" (Santa Fe Community College, 2002, Community Skills section).

- Students will "develop an international perspective in order to live and work effectively in an increasingly global society" (Association of American Colleges and Universities Greater Expectations National Panel, 2000, University of Delaware, Newark section).

- "WSU students must be able to . . . understand the historical development of human knowledge and cultures, including both Western and non-Western civilizations" (Washington State University, 2002, section F).

Campuses have developed a variety of outcomes for these goals. Some emphasize understanding other cultures, and some include the development of self-understanding. For example, Indiana University–Purdue University Indianapolis (2003–2004) has three outcomes for its Understanding Society and Culture goal:

- compare and contrast the range of diversity and universality in human history, societies, and ways of life

- analyze and understand the interconnectedness of global and local concerns

- operate with civility in a complex social world (¶ 5)

Johnson County Community College (2005) lists five ways for students to demonstrate mastery of its Culture and Ethics outcome. Students should be able to:

1. Demonstrate a fundamental knowledge of world geography.

2. Demonstrate knowledge of the major cultural issues of a person's own culture as well as other cultures.

3. Demonstrate knowledge of major historical events affecting one's culture and other cultures.

4. Demonstrate familiarity with contemporary social issues.

5. Demonstrate an understanding of major ethical concerns. (¶ 1)

St. Cloud State University (2005) has four goals related to diversity:

- Students will recognize that contributions to a culture by individuals and groups within that culture significantly influence the culture of the larger global society.

- Students will examine beliefs, belief systems, and ideologies that may be different from their own.

- Students will recognize that the choices and behaviors of individuals establish and/or define the culture.

- Students will identify unjust, de-humanizing, and oppressive policies and practices of individuals, authorities, and social institutions within the dominant culture and their impact on the treatment of various disenfranchised groups. (Diversity Learning Outcomes section)

Citizenship may be given attention as a separate goal. For example, California State University–Los Angeles (n.d.) includes this as one of its eight general education goals:

Students have the knowledge, abilities, and values necessary for participation in American society and government.

Objective 1.   Students demonstrate an understanding of the historical development of American political and social institutions and ideals.

Objective 2.   Students demonstrate the knowledge, abilities, and values relevant to the democratic political systems established under the U.S. and California constitutions.

Objective 3.   Students demonstrate recognition of the contributions made by major national, ethnic, and social groups to the historical development of American ideals and the contexts in which these contributions were made. (Goal 4)

Some campuses require the study of a second language, and this requirement may be tied to multicultural understanding. For example, Longwood University (2004–2005) has this goal and outcomes:

The ability to communicate and function in a globally interdependent world as developed through foreign language study . . .

Outcomes: Students will

Demonstrate the ability to understand, interpret, and produce both oral and written communication in a foreign language.

Demonstrate an understanding of relationships among the products, perspectives, and practices of the culture(s) studied.

Develop insight into the nature of language and culture. (Goal 10)

Ethics

Many campuses include goals or outcomes related to ethics, sometimes combining ethics with other areas, such as multicultural understanding. For example, here are some goal statements:

- Students can "recognize the role of values and ethics in making personal, social, and professional decisions" (Bismarck State College, 2004, p. 2).

- Students will "engage questions of ethics and recognize responsibilities to self, community, and society at large" (Association of American Colleges and Universities Greater Expectations National Panel, 2000, University of Delaware–Newark section).

- "Values and Ethics: The ability of students to make judgments with respect to individual conduct, citizenship, and aesthetic. A sense of values and ethics is demonstrated by the ability of students to:

  - make informed and principled choices regarding conflicting situations in their personal and public lives and to foresee the consequences of these choices

  - use knowledge and understanding in order to generate and explore new questions" (Indiana University–Purdue University Indianapolis, 2003–2004, Values and Ethics section).

A variety of outcomes have been developed. For example, California State University–Monterey Bay (2005) lists five outcomes associated with Ethics:

Students identify and analyze real world ethical problems or dilemmas, and identify those affected by the dilemma.

Students describe and analyze complexity and importance of choices that are available to the decision-makers concerned with the dilemma.

Students articulate and acknowledge one's own deeply held beliefs and assumptions as part of a conscious value system.

Students describe and analyze one's own and others' perceptions and ethical frameworks for decision-making.

Students consider and use multiple choices, beliefs, and diverse ethical frameworks when making decisions to respond to ethical dilemmas or problems. (Ethics ULR [University Learening Requirements] - Learning Outcomes section)

Santa Clara University (2004b) lists its Ethics outcomes in a narrative:

Students will be able to think and write critically about classic and contemporary moral problems; moral concepts such as right/wrong conduct and good/bad character; and ideals such as justice, happiness, dignity, rights, and equality. They will be prepared with the conceptual resources for making moral decisions in their personal and professional lives. (Section 12, Ethics)

Santa Clara University (2004b) also requires a three-course Religious Studies Core sequence. Outcomes for the last of these courses are described in a narrative:

As the last course in the sequence, students will be able to use their analytic skills on real-life questions and current challenges. By confronting the complexity of questioning while taking a moral or religious position, this course enables students to integrate what they have learned about religion with other areas of the Core, their majors, and their full involvement in the world. (Section 13, Religious Studies)

Information Literacy

Technology has transformed campus and community libraries, and millions of postings exist on the Internet. Students must develop search strategies to access resources effectively. A simple search may lead to thousands of hits, requiring us to define and narrow searches to be productive. In addition, so much can be found in print and nonprint media, including many sources of questionable quality, that students must learn to discriminate among them, select what is reasonable and relevant, and analyze and synthesize what they have learned. Some campuses include information literacy skills among the outcomes for other goals, such as written communication or critical thinking, and some have a specific goal in this area.

Breivik (2005) argues that information literacy is a critical thinking skill with five components: computer literacy, library literacy, media literacy, network literacy, and visual literacy. She concludes that "few campuses have systematically addressed this need. Indeed, some academic programs do a good job—albeit unintentionally of making sure their students remain information illiterate" (p. 24) by not creating assignments that require students to develop sophisticated skills. Reference librarians have taken the lead on information literacy on many campuses, and they collaborate with faculty to help students develop these skills.

Most campus information literacy goals and outcomes borrow heavily from the five standards developed by the American Library Association (2000). They provide from three to seven performance indicators for each standard and from two to seven outcomes for each performance indicator. Details are provided on their web site (Standards, Performance Indicators, and Outcomes section):

- Standard One: "The information literate student determines the nature and extent of the information needed."

- Standard Two: "The information literate student accesses needed information effectively and efficiently."

- Standard Three: "The information literate student evaluates information and its sources critically and incorporates selected information into his or her knowledge base and value system."

- Standard Four: "The information literate student individually or as a member of a group, uses information effectively to accomplish a specific performance."

- Standard Five: "The information literate student understands many of the economic, legal, and social issues surrounding the use of information and accesses and uses information ethically and legally."

Health, Wellness, and Personal Growth

Some campuses include goals or outcomes that focus on the development of the individual student's health, wellness, or personal growth. For example:

> The wellness requirement is designed to 1) provide instruction based on revealed truth, current scientific understanding and practical information about what constitutes a healthy lifestyle, and 2) offer practical experiences in fitness, wellness, skill acquisition and wholesome family recreation activities that motivate individuals to pursue healthy lifestyles for them and their family members through their lifetimes. (Brigham Young University, 2004, p. 1)

> The physical education program [requirement] is designed to cultivate physical fitness, basic athletic skills, and an appreciation of the value of recreational physical activity. (University of Chicago, 2000, Physical Education section)

> Personal Management Skills. Develop self-sufficiency and responsibility for effectiveness in personal and occupational life. (Waukesha County Technical College; Schoenberger, 2000, p. 43)

Learning outcomes vary considerably. For example, Inver Hills Community College (2001) has an essential skill stating that each student achieves "a perspective on oneself and the world" (Appreciation section). This skill can be seen in five contexts:

Other's Viewpoints
Concerns the ability to "step" out of one's own personal point of view in order to see the world as others perceive it, whether that "other" is a character in a story; a real person of another ethnic, racial, or religious background; or a potential or real customer for a business.

Breadth of Vision
Concerns the ability to "step" out of one's viewpoint in order to see "the big picture," perceiving and understanding the larger, systematic patterns within which we live.

Attention to Excellence
Concerns the ability to attend to detail and nuance in a given field of endeavor, yielding a remarkable result that others can characterize as "excellent."

Commitment to Principles
Concerns the ability to conform to outside influences.

Personal Accountability
Concerns the ability to commit to a task and to follow through with that commitment. (Appreciation section)

Kellogg Community College (2001) has a Wellness goal with two competencies. Their students should:

A. Demonstrate a knowledge of relationships between mental and physical health principles.

B. Identify and apply health-related fitness components through an exercise program and/or through the acquisition of a leisure skill. (Wellness section)

Rose-Hulman Institute of Technology (2002) includes a goal related to professionalism and lifelong learning, with teamwork among its outcomes.

When assigned to teams, students will:

1. Share responsibilities and duties, and take on different roles when applicable.

2. Analyze ideas objectively to discern feasible solutions by building consensus.

3. Develop a strategy for action. (p. 1)

The University of Iowa (2005) lists three outcomes for its Health and Physical Activity goal:

• Students will understand the theoretical groundings of good health practices, become cognizant of major health risks, and learn strategies for overcoming those risks.

• Students will develop critical skills for assessing various structural factors that constrain good health practices and for making informed choices about health behaviors.

- Students will learn and practice the physical and mental skills associated with a specific activity or activities. (Health and Physical Activity section)

Waukesha County Technical College expects students to develop seven personal management skills:

- *Career Development.* Make career choices appropriate to current personal needs and to the changing nature of the labor market.

- *Career Securing.* Demonstrate effective job search skills.

- *Study Skills.* Use effective study skills in order to master course content.

- *Stress Management.* Manage stress in appropriate ways.

- *Coping with Change.* Understand and manage change appropriately.

- *Time Management.* Organize activities to accomplish desired tasks in the time available.

- *Self-Concept.* Evaluate one's self-concept in regards to self esteem, values, attitudes, interests, goals, strengths, and weaknesses. (Schoenberger, 2000, pp. 43–44)

Some campuses require volunteer or service-learning experiences within the general education program, with personal growth among the learning outcomes. For example, California State University–Monterey Bay (2005) has a Community Participation goal:

Purpose: The purpose of the CP ULR [Community Participation University Learning Requirement] is to foster the development of self-reflective, culturally aware and responsive community participants through reciprocal service and learning.

Outcomes:

1. Demonstrate critical self-reflection of one's own assumptions and stereotypes.

2. Comprehend their own social and cultural group identities and the relative privilege or marginalization of each.

3. Demonstrate intercultural communication skills.

4. Demonstrate knowledge of the demographics, socio-cultural dynamics and assets of a specific local community.

5. Examine and analyze a community issue in the context of systemic inequities.

6. Enter, participate in, and exit a community in ways that do not reinforce systemic injustice.

7. Demonstrate reciprocity and responsiveness in service work with community. (Community Participation ULR - Learning Outcomes section)

Technology

Technology sometimes is integrated into other goals and outcomes, and sometimes it is a separate goal. Campuses may emphasize the use of technology (e.g., using word processors and spreadsheets) and/or an understanding of the impact of technology. Examples of technology goal statements are:

Students must demonstrate comfort with technology and information search and discovery methods. They must also demonstrate the ability to use tools effectively for the discovery, acquisition, and evaluation of information as well as core computer tools for the manipulation and presentation of information in a creative and ethical manner. (California State University–Monterey Bay, 2005, Technology Information ULR - Learning Outcomes section)

The purpose of this requirement is to help the student integrate an understanding of the goals and social impact of technology, an understanding of how technology works (as described in its characteristic methods), and proficiency in applicable computer skills. Contemporary society, with its dependence on technology and its emphasis on technological change, demands awareness of and proficiency in appropriate technology in each discipline, especially computers. Moreover, the University's commitment to values, community, and justice demands a critical attitude to technology. (Santa Clara University, 2004a, Section 8, Technology)

Campuses have developed a variety of outcomes for technology. For example, Arizona Western College (2003) has five outcomes stressing the use of technology:

1. Learners will demonstrate a working knowledge of computer basics by opening and closing a program; by creating, saving, printing, finding, renaming, copying, moving and deleting files.

2. Learners will perform basic word processing operations including document creation, editing, formatting, printing, saving and retrieving a document.

3. Learners will perform basic spreadsheet operations including creating, editing, formatting, printing, saving and retrieving a worksheet including the use of formulas, simple functions, and the copy command.

4. Learners will demonstrate the ability to use the Internet in order to access information resources, evaluate their credibility, and apply them.

5. Learners will demonstrate the ability to send and receive E-mail including attachments. (Technology Applications section)

Kellogg Community College (2001) has two technology competencies. Their students can:

A. Demonstrate the ability to effectively use computers to achieve a personal or professional goal.

B. Understand how technology relates to the individual, society, and the environment. (Technology section)

Santa Clara University's (2004a) narrative list of technology outcomes is:

Through a combination of lecture and laboratory courses, the student will demonstrate an understanding of the nature of technology, its social context, the ways computer networks are structured and how they can be used as sources of information in the particular field of interest to the student, and some discipline-specific applications. (Section 8, Technology)

Arts and Humanities

General education programs often have three breadth requirements speci-fying coursework in the arts and humanities, natural sciences, and social sciences. Although many campuses set the humanities, natural sciences, and social sciences as three separate goals, some campuses have a single, broad goal. For example, California State University–Los Angeles (n.d.) has this goal: "Students understand the distinct perspectives and major achievements of the natural sciences, the social sciences, and the arts and humanities" (Goal 5).

Within the arts and the humanities, students are often given choices among various disciplines, such as communication, history, literature, music, theater, philosophy, religious studies, and the visual arts. Some campuses also include the study of second languages, other than English. Not everyone agrees with this model. For example, Vendler (as cited in Field, 2004a) argues that language, literature, and the arts should be the core humanities required for all students rather than history or philosophy, because they help students understand human culture. Kagan, in response to Vendler, argues that history is the "Queen of the Humanities," because the study of history allows students to understand the nature of human experience (Byrne, 2005). Davidson and Goldberg (2004) suggest the need for integrated preparation in all the humanities as the foundation for an educated person:

> The humanities provide the social and cultural contexts of the creation and application of knowledge, the critical reflections upon how knowledge is created and what its effects and implications are. The humanities promote a broad range of social and cultural literacies. They offer critical civic competencies, ways of comprehending cultural and technological values, and the worlds such values conjure; in short, ways of world making. A world without the humanities would be one in which science and technology knew no point of social reference, had lost their cultural compass and moral scope. It would be a world narrowly limited and limitlessly narrow. (p. B7)

Campuses have developed a variety of outcome statements. As you read through these examples, think about how campus curricula might differ.

Brooklyn College (n.d.) describes its "Classic Origins of Western Culture" core course in a narrative:

Core Studies 1 aims to help students achieve the following goals: to read closely and critically Greek and Roman literary texts in English translation; to understand those texts in their social, historical, material, and performance contexts; to relate the cultures which produced these texts to our contemporary culture in its diversity; to speak and write clearly and coherently about the issues that emerge from critical reading and comparison of cultures. (¶ 1)

Brooklyn College also requires a core course called "Shaping of the Modern World." Gerardi (2003) describes its objectives:

Working through the materials of this course will not only give you important information for understanding the development of our world. You also will learn skills of analysis, writing and reading. You will learn to place issues into historical context, to consider evidence, and to develop arguments. (Objectives section)

Cascadia Community College (Baker, 2000) presents humanities outcomes in three clusters:

- *Content Analysis.* Learners will gain knowledge of the core content of at least two humanities disciplines and apply that knowledge through analysis, synthesis, and evaluation.

- *Personalization.* Learners will investigate the context and language of the human experience to examine and explore their everyday worlds and to expand their experience and understanding of other cultures and times.

- *Creative Expression.* Learners will discover and use a creative process for self-expression to communicate an understanding and/or interpretation of human experience through visual, musical, dramatic, oral, or written products. (p. 36)

Eastern New Mexico University (2005b) has four outcomes associated with its fine arts and humanities competency:

- The student is able to describe basic relationships between history, literature, culture, and the fine arts.

- The student is able to articulate her/his own response to the work of an artist.

- The student is able to appreciate the fine arts and humanities, including the artistic perspective of people of other cultures and historic periods.

- The student understands the vocabulary for discussing basic elements of artistic expression in at least one area of the arts. (The Competencies section 4)

Mesa Community College (2002–2003) lists four outcomes for the Arts and Humanities. They want students to:

1. Demonstrate knowledge of human creations.

2. Demonstrate an awareness that different contexts and/or world views produce different human creations.

3. Demonstrate an understanding and awareness of the impact that a piece (artifact) has on the relationship and perspective of the audience.

4. Demonstrate an ability to evaluate human creations. (Arts and Humanities section)

The University of Iowa's (2005) Fine Arts goal has four outcomes for the Fine Arts and three for Interpretation of Literature:

- Students should develop the ability to recognize the constituent parts of an artwork and of the processing of producing art.

- Students should have ample opportunity to observe the performance of an art, or when feasible, be actively engaged in the making of that art.

- Students should be able to recognize how aesthetic and critical meanings are attached to artworks and be introduced to some of the ways in which quality can be recognized and assessed.

- Students should be able to recognize aspects of the context (e.g., historical, social, ethnic, economic, geographic) in which artworks are made, particularly how an artwork is linked to the identify of both the artist and the artist's culture. (Fine Arts section)

- Students use and refine their skills of reading, speaking, and writing to respond critically and sensitively to literary texts.

- Students learn to see themselves as readers, recognizing the influence of individual differences (such as gender, ethnicity, geography) and past experiences on interpretation.

- Students consider the connections between individual texts and broader cultural contexts. (Interpretation of Literature section)

The University of Iowa (2005) has two outcomes for its Humanities goal:

- Students will learn about one or more specific cultural topics, problems, artistic forms, value systems, philosophical concepts, or religious ideas in relation to the larger human context in which they become meaningful.

- Students will become familiar with one or more methods of humanistic research, critical inquiry, and analysis and have an opportunity to practice these methods. (Humanities section)

Natural Sciences

Science requirements are virtually universal in general education programs. Campuses may require an integrated core course in science, or they may allow students to select among options from a variety of science departments, such as astronomy, biology, chemistry, earth science, geology, and physics. Sometimes the requirement is broader and includes other fields, such as mathematics and computer science. Related goals may have a variety of titles, such as The Physical World, Scientific Reasoning, or Scientific Inquiry.

Most agree that too few American students develop interest in science and mathematics, and we face stiff international competition from other countries, notably China and India (Tucker, 2005). Recent reports suggest that American students' interest in computer science is "in a freefall. The number of newly declared computer science majors declined 32 percent from the fall of 2000 to the fall of 2004 . . . and the number of incoming freshmen who expressed an interest in majoring in computer science has plummeted by 59 percent in the last four years" (Foster, 2005, p. A31). In addition, American doctoral programs in science enroll many international students. For example, non-U.S. citizens earned 43% of doctorates in the physical sciences and 31% of doctorates in the life sciences at American universities in 2003 (Gravois, 2005). While their participation adds international perspectives to these programs, there is concern that America may be losing its position in the world's scientific community.

In addition, there is ongoing concern about the participation rate of women and students of color in science and mathematics (Schmidt, 2005), as well as engineering, prompting some faculty to rethink teacher education programs to provide better preparation in K–12 education (California Teach, 2005; Field, 2004b). Faculty also are examining how they teach college-level science courses. Evidence suggests that linking science to social problems and providing opportunities for hands-on, cooperative learning attract more women and students of color to science majors (Ramaley & Haggett, 2005). General education courses provide an opportunity for science faculty to share their enthusiasm for science and recruit potential majors, as well as help all students develop analytical and problem-solving skills and gain an understanding of the physical world and the scientific method (Ramaley & Haggett, 2005).

Raymo (2005b) argues that general education science should not be a watered-down introductory course in a discipline (e.g., "Physics 1 for Non-Majors"), nor should it be a "friendly" course like "Physics of Art." He suggests, instead, "The Art of Physics," a course that stresses the essence of the discipline, rather than its content. Students would learn how physicists identify questions, pose solutions, and empirically test theories to understand and predict aspects of our physical world. This course would help students understand the intellectual challenge and satisfaction that scientists feel when they explore, explain, and predict natural phenomena. Raymo (2005a) argues that "at the heart of the scientific way of knowing is organized skepticism that transcends religion, politics, ethnicity, or nationality. Scientific knowledge is partial, tentative, and evolving, but it has become the irreversible basis for our health, wealth and secular freedoms, and therefore a proud achievement of humankind" (¶ 2). This is what he wants general education students to learn about science.

Campuses have developed a variety of outcomes for general education science goals. For example, faculty at California State University–Bakersfield (2000a) developed four goals for their Life and Physical Sciences requirement. Students should be able to:

1. Demonstrate an understanding of the basic principles and concepts of the life and physical sciences.

2. Demonstrate an understanding of the scientific method.

3. Apply the principles, concepts, and methods of the life and physical sciences to everyday life.

4. Demonstrate an understanding of the role science and technology play in society. (Life and Physical Sciences and Thematic Courses of Natural Sciences and Technology section)

Faculty at Humboldt State University (2000) proposed eight outcomes for their lower-division general education science requirement:

1) Students should be able to explain what sort of experiments or observations would be necessary for a particular scientific hypothesis to be rejected (or accepted).

2) Students should be able to distinguish questions that can be answered by scientific approaches from those that can't.

3) Students should be able to distinguish a scientific explanation of a particular phenomenon from a non-scientific explanation.

4) Students should be able to recognize sound arguments (direct, indirect, or statistical) as they are applied to scientific phenomena, and distinguish them from arguments that are unsound.

5) Students should be able to demonstrate their understanding of the basic language and concepts of the field under study.

6) Students should be able to develop conclusions from a particular set of observations or experiments.

7) Students should be able to critically assess conclusions drawn from a particular set of observations or experiments.

8) Students should be able to find (e.g., in the library, on the internet) information relevant to the scientific understanding of a particular contemporary issue. (Lower Division Science GE Outcomes section)

Faculty at Longwood University (2004–2005) have three science outcomes. Their students learn to:

- Understand the major methods of natural science inquiry

- Recognize and explain major contributions of science to our cultural heritage

- Understand how natural science has been used to address significant contemporary issues (Goal 6)

The University of Montana (2002) sets four outcomes for its natural sciences requirement. A student is expected to:

1. use both creative and critical scientific questioning, and validation of scientific findings.

2. use the methodology and activities scientists use to gather, validate and interpret data related to natural processes.

3. detect patterns, draw conclusions, develop conjectures and hypotheses, and test them by appropriate means and experiments.

4. identify laws and rules related to natural processes by quantitative measurement, scientific observations, and logical/critical reasoning. (Student Learning Outcomes for Perspective VI: Natural Sciences section)

The University of Arizona (2005) integrates mathematics and communication into its outcomes related to science. They expect students to

Understand the nature and application of physical and/or biological science.

Apply ideas and processes beyond the classroom.

Recognize the complexity of many scientific issues.

Design experiments, generate and analyze actual data, use abstract reasoning to interpret these, and formulate and test hypotheses with scientific rigor.

Speak and write about scientific knowledge.

Appreciate the relative scale of objects, rates of change, and linear and nonlinear growth.

Present data in tables, graphs, and charts and perform appropriate mathematical calculations and data analysis.

Read and understand scientific literature from popular sources such as magazines and newspapers. (Expected Student Outcomes for NATS Courses section)

Social Sciences

Campuses vary in their names for and definitions of the social sciences. Some use the term "behavioral science," some refer to "social/behavioral science," and some include history among the social sciences.

A variety of goals and outcomes are in use. For example, the University of Chicago (2000) describes its goals for this requirement: "The following sequences [of courses] are designed to cultivate an understanding of fundamental concepts, theories, and philosophies of the social sciences and to demonstrate how the social sciences formulate basic questions and inquire about the nature of social life through acts of imagination as well as through systematic analysis" (Social Sciences section). Stony Brook University (1999) faculty want to "develop in students knowledge of how the social and behavioral scientists discover, describe, and explain the behaviors and interactions among individuals, groups, institutions, events and ideas" (p. 5).

Brooklyn College (1998) requires a course on "People, Power, and Politics" and describes its outcomes in a narrative:

Introduction to the social sciences through the study of power, authority, and social organization in American society. Emphasis on gaining insight into American society in broad terms, as well as in terms of such specific issues as social class, race, gender, community, equality, and opportunity. The unifying theme of the course is an understanding of the nature of power (social and political). A major goal of the course is an understanding of contemporary issues and controversies involving power in America. (¶ 1)

Cascadia Community College (Baker, 2000) has four outcomes for the social sciences:

- *Individual and Societal Levels of Analysis.* Learners will analyze inter-relationships between individual and sociohistorical forces.

- *Diversity.* Learners will evaluate how social structures impact diversity, inequality, and social change.

- *Evaluation of Evidence.* Learners will identify and evaluate qualitative and quantitative evidence to draw conclusions about human behavior consistent with social science theory.

- *Theory and Method.* Learners will demonstrate facility to move between frameworks, to use varieties of evidence, and to arrive at multiple conclusions. (p. 36)

The Illinois Articulation Initiative (2005c) states that social and behavioral science general education requirements should help students to:

- gain insight into individual behavior;

- develop an understanding of their own society and the world as part of larger human experience in time and place;

- analyze social, political, cultural, historical, and economic institutions and relationships that both link and separate societies throughout the world;

- develop analytical, critical thinking, and communication skills necessary to understand and influence the world in which they live;

- comprehend methods of inquiry employed by social and behavioral scientists. (¶ 1)

The University of Missouri–Columbia (2005) lists three outcomes for its social and behavioral sciences requirement. Their students should be able to:

a. Take an experiment/investigation reported in the popular press and examine the extent to which it reflects the methods of social or behavioral science, the ethics of inquiry, etc.

b. Examine competing perspectives within disciplines. For example, in the social sciences students could be asked to examine both functionalists and conflict theorists, positivists and poststructuralists. In the behavioral sciences, students could look at the assumptions that support both quantitative and qualitative research or competing explanations of behavior.

c. Examine the nature of civic responsibility, issues of social justice, and the continued evolution of democratic processes. (Social and Behavioral Sciences section)

Integration

A college education is more than an accumulation of courses in a variety of disciplines. College-educated adults should be able to use the knowledge, skills, and values acquired in the general education program, as well as the expertise developed in the major. Huber and Hutchings (2004) argue:

> One of the great challenges in higher education is to foster students' abilities to integrate their learning across contexts and over time. Learning that helps develop integrative capacities is important because it builds habits of mind that prepare students to make informed judgments in the conduct of personal, professional, and civic life; such learning is, we believe, at the very heart of liberal education. (p. 1)

Complex, real-world problems often call for the integration of what was learned. For example, understanding and responding to global warming, preventing child and elder abuse, and competing in a world economy require critical thinking, communication skills, and an understanding of culture, history, and science. Students are more likely to develop these integrative skills if they are given opportunities for practice within the curriculum, and this is more likely to occur if integration is included among the goals and outcomes for the general education program. Here are a few examples of goals and outcomes that specifically address this issue:

- "Creative problem solving" can be shown in synthesizing knowledge within and across courses and programs, integrating theory and practice, linking academic and life experiences, and relating one's self and culture to diverse cultures within the U.S. and globally (Bowling Green State University, n.d., Creative Problem Solving section).

- Students learn to "integrate different areas of knowledge and view ideas from multiple perspectives" (Grand Valley State University, 2005, Goals of the General Education Program section).

- "Integration and Application of Knowledge: The ability of students to use information and concepts from studies in multiple disciplines in their intellectual, professional, and community lives. This skill is demonstrated by the ability of students to apply knowledge to:

  - enhance their personal lives

  - meet professional standards and competencies

  - further the goals of society"

(Indiana University–Purdue University Indianapolis, 2003–2004, Integration and Application of Knowledge section).

- "Students acquire knowledge of past and present achievements of our own and other cultures in the arts, letters, and sciences; of the impact of people, institutions and communities involved in the creation, preservation and transmission of culture; of the distinctions and interconnections among disciplines" (James Madison University, 2005, ¶ 1).

- "Students will explore and integrate knowledge in order to understand how various disciplines interrelate" (St. Cloud State University, 2005, ¶ 2).

First-Year Experience Course Outcomes

First-year experience courses are very common, and a variety of learning outcomes have been developed for them. For example, Bryant University's required first-year seminar, "Foundations for Learning," is designed to "help students take responsibility for their education" by:

- Understanding the importance of being actively involved in the educational process

- Developing cognitive and metacognitive abilities

- Developing a fuller understanding of a range of learning and study strategies

- Learning how planning and prioritizing impact academic success

- Developing self-concept including an awareness of health and wellness issues

- Developing communication skills including those related to collaboration and leadership

- Engaging in scholarly activities such as group discussion, conducting research, and synthesizing materials

- Understanding the importance of respecting diversity as a member
  of the Bryant community and a citizen of the world (Hazard, 2005,
  p. 24)

The first-year seminar at Mount Mary College, "Leadership for Social
Justice," is strongly recommended to all new, traditional-aged students,
and it has six primary objectives:

- To introduce students to Mount Mary's mission and the Mount
  Mary Women's Leadership Model

- To increase self-knowledge leading to an understanding of personal
  leadership styles

- To develop and increase skills and strategies for dealing with difficult issues and conflict

- To expand knowledge of local and global social justice issues

- To experience service-learning as a means of growing in leadership,
  self-understanding, and knowledge of social justice issues

- To develop reading, writing, and oral communication skills (End,
  2005, pp. 97–98)

Northern Illinois University's "University Experience," course is an
elective for first-semester freshmen, and it is designed to help students:

- Understand the challenges and expectations of college

- Develop strategies for academic success

- Adjust to the university community and become involved

- Communicate with faculty

- Learn to manage time and money

- Learn how to use technology and NIU's resources

- Live in a diverse community
- Prepare for a career (House, 2005, p. 104)

Olympic College offers "General Studies 100: Strategies for Academic Success," a requirement for students requiring developmental English courses and an elective for other students. Students in this course learn:

- To demonstrate knowledge of the purposes, values, and expectations of higher education
- To demonstrate basic self-awareness and self-management
- To demonstrate academic skills of learning how to learn
- To write an educational/career plan
- To demonstrate knowledge of physical, social, and emotional wellness (Huston, 2005, p. 123)

Faculty at Temple University teach a one-credit, elective course, "Learning for the New Century," with four major goals:

- Enhance students' intellectual development and improve their study behaviors and skills
- Enhance students' social development and engagement in the campus community
- Promote collaborative learning and group work
- Allow students to practice technology applications and retrieval of information (Laufgraben, 2005, p. 152)

Lessons Learned

Looking through these many examples can be useful, but a bit daunting if you have not yet developed your own general education goals and outcomes. Many campuses have established ambitious expectations for their students, and their curricula offer rich opportunities for learning. What can we learn from reviewing their ideas?

The Number of Goals and Outcomes

There is no consistency in the number of goals and outcomes that campuses have developed. Some campuses have only a few goals; others have dozens. For example, the University of Judaism (2004) lists four educational goals and objectives for its core program:

1. to ensure that all students attain a richer understanding of the self and the larger world through the comparative examination of Jewish and other civilizations

2. to enhance students' critical thinking, writing and technological skills

3. to foster ethical thinking, behavior and leadership by encouraging students to examine their own ethical beliefs and develop a sense of global citizenship

4. to enhance students' appreciation for the interrelatedness of knowledge (p. 2)

Other campuses have many more. For example, California State University–San Bernardino (2005) faculty developed 56 goals and 190 outcomes for its general education program.

Perhaps one of the reasons for this variability is that campuses approach the task differently. On some campuses, it makes good sense to have a set of committees develop goals for different segments of the general education program. This is most likely to occur with a distributed general education program. If there are a dozen required segments, then twelve committees might be appointed. Perhaps the social scientists develop three goals, the humanities faculty develop four goals, etc. Soon the campus has 40 or 50 goals, and they might easily generate more than 100 outcomes.

Other campuses, though, approach the task differently, asking about broad conceptual expectations for students in the general education program. This probably is more likely to occur on campuses with integrated, core programs, although it can be done for distributed programs, too. This approach might lead to four to ten goals (e.g., Communication, Breadth of Knowledge, Problem Solving, Cultural Understanding) and maybe 20–30 outcomes.

Some campuses elect to stay at the goal level and do not develop outcomes, although at some time they will be faced with having to answer the question: How can students demonstrate to us that our goals have been reached? These campuses are postponing rather than avoiding this task, and they are running the risk of having ambiguous goals that are not clearly understood by faculty and students.

Terminology

We have not yet agreed on a common language. Campuses use words like goals, outcomes, objectives, and competencies in different ways. This can be a problem when we compare campuses, but it is not a problem on an individual campus as long as everyone agrees on a consistent set of terms and their meanings.

Different Outcomes for the Same Goal

Campuses do not have identical learning outcomes, even when they have goals that sound interchangeable. Each campus has its own history and mission, and each of the examples we've examined shows unique characteristics that distinguish between expectations and, presumably, curricula. For example, all campuses want to help students become better communicators, but some are more explicit than others about the range of writing, reading, speaking, listening, and interpersonal skills they're fostering. Some campuses choose to include outcomes associated with health and wellness; others may place more emphasis on civic engagement, spirituality, or workplace skills. This means that graduates of these campuses, who have experienced different curricula, cannot be compared on a common metric. A test that might be reasonable for one campus might be unfair to students on another campus who have not been exposed to the same learning opportunities. This argues against the use of standardized national exams for the assessment of general education programs.

Commonalities

In spite of the many differences, campuses have much in common. They may organize the goals, outcomes, and curricula differently, but many expectations are similar. General education provides a broad foundation in the liberal arts and develops basic skills, such as communication, quantitative reasoning, critical thinking, and information literacy. Campuses vary in the level of detail articulated in their goals and outcomes and there are differences, but they share a common heritage concerning the nature of general education.

Learning from Each Other

We can learn from each other. If your campus already has developed its general education learning outcomes, consider the examples in this chapter and the cited campus web sites. Were you inspired to advocate for changes? Which goals and outcomes appealed to you and appear consistent with your campus mission? Any assessment-related task, including agreeing on the goals and outcomes, is subject to revision. Sticking with a list just because it exists makes no sense if new ideas could enrich your curriculum and students.

A problem that most of us have is that we are working backwards by starting with a pre-existing general education curriculum that was not outcomes-based. We try to figure out the implicit assumptions for student learning. Imagine, instead, starting with a blank slate—no curriculum—and beginning with the question of what your students *should* learn in the general education program. Once these decisions are made, you then could design a curriculum to support this learning. If you and your colleagues could start with a blank slate, would you create your present general education program, or would it evolve differently?

Reaching Consensus on General Education Goals and Outcomes

If your campus has not yet refined its goals and outcomes for the general education program, you might be wondering how to begin. One powerful way to develop the list is to host a broadly attended retreat or series of retreats that are coordinated by a skilled facilitator or leadership team. The goal of the retreat(s) is to generate working drafts that will go through routine campus review and approval processes. Here are some ideas that might be useful if you are considering hosting a general education retreat.

Invite to the retreat people who care about general education and who contribute to it—experienced and new general education faculty, librarians and student affairs professionals who work with general education students, department chairs, academic governance leaders, and administrators. Consider also inviting some students. They add a unique perspective and their presence might affect the nature of the discussion. Some campuses pre-assign participants to teams to ensure that the various stakeholders are well-mixed during breakout discussions, and others encourage participants to create their own teams with this characteristic. In addition, some campuses designate team leaders and/or note takers in advance, and they participate in a pre-retreat orientation to develop a shared understanding of the retreat and their role in it.

Because your goal is to reach *consensus*, begin the retreat with a clear statement of what you want to accomplish and set ground rules that encourage free, respectful exchange of ideas. Figure 2.1 provides some general suggestions for achieving consensus (Allen, 2004; Johnson & Johnson, 1997).

Figure 2.1
Suggestions for Achieving Consensus*

- Consider establishing ground rules before the discussion begins that promote an open discussion and that encourage participants to "respectfully disagree" over issues.
- Encourage all participants to present their views and to explain the rationale for their opinions.
- Role model support for the airing of different viewpoints and repeatedly seek out differences of opinion by inviting everyone to contribute.
- Avoid a win-lose atmosphere. Instead, remind participants that the purpose is not to see whose ideas are the best, but to develop the best solution for the campus as a whole.
- Avoid conflict-reducing techniques that prematurely terminate discussion, such as voting for each goal or outcome separately.
- Regularly summarize positions in a fair way and seek common ground among them. Continue to question participants about their reasons for supporting certain ideas and not others.
- Once decisions appear to be agreed upon, check with all members to see if everyone can support the final ideas. If everyone supports the choices, you have reached consensus.

---

*Adapted from Allen (2004), p. 32

Begin at the broadest level—the general education mission statement. If you already have one, distribute copies of it at the retreat, as well as copies of your campus mission statement, documents relevant to your general education program (such as catalog copy, general education course approval criteria, and course syllabi), and examples of general education mission statements from other institutions. Begin with a general discussion of the various handouts, then ask participants to work in small, interdisciplinary teams to review the documents, verify that the campus's overall mission and general education mission align, brainstorm ideas, and suggest revisions. Post all suggestions, with similar ideas grouped together, and reach consensus on which should be implemented. Someone on the leadership team with good wordsmith skills can then draft a clean revision, perhaps during a refreshment or overnight break, and distribute copies to everyone for agreement. If you don't already have a mission statement, use a similar process to develop it. Distribute the above documents, minus the general education mission statement, of course, and ask teams to brainstorm bulleted lists of the essential components of your general education mission statement. End by reaching consensus on the list and a written draft, acknowledging that everyone will have an opportunity to reflect on it and suggest changes before the final draft is submitted for formal campus review and approval.

The first big decision about goals and outcomes is the approach you and your colleagues will take. Do you want a short list of more general goals and related outcomes (e.g., the marks of a graduate from your campus), or a longer list of outcomes, generally tied to specific general education requirements? Both approaches have strengths and limitations, as discussed in the next section of this chapter.

There is little need to start from scratch when generating goals and outcomes. Share relevant lists of general education goal and outcome statements from campuses that are similar to your own or that are respected by your faculty, as well as documents related to your own general education program (e.g., its mission statement, course approval criteria, syllabi). After a general discussion of the documents, ask small teams to review the handouts and suggest goals and outcomes for your campus. If you are working toward a short list of the marks of a graduate from your campus, teams should be interdisciplinary, and you should reach consensus on the list of goals before developing outcomes. On the other hand, if you are developing separate goals and outcomes for each general education requirement, teams should be predominantly composed of those who directly contribute to each requirement.

These retreats can be very effective, and I have seen campuses that have been stalled for months make significant progress in a weekend. Temporarily away from the distractions of their offices and other obligations, participants have the opportunity to reach consensus on their shared vision of the mission and expectations for the general education program. Most documents created at retreats require thoughtful inspection to verify that important details were not forgotten, and they profit from some editing to create a cohesive document with segments written in a common format.

Too Many Outcomes?

Ewell (2004) argues that in our attempt to build a comprehensive list of outcomes, "we tend to name an awful lot of abilities" (p. 5). He suggests that colleges and universities focus on a shorter list of goals that are nurtured throughout the undergraduate experience, such as problem solving and civic participation. Students begin mastering these goals in general education, but continue developing them throughout their undergraduate experience. Strengths and limitations of developing fewer, more general goals and outcomes as opposed to more, requirement-specific goals and outcomes are summarized in Figure 2.2.

One major advantage of a shorter list is that people might remember the outcomes and use them as they plan curricula, courses, and general education policies. For example, Indiana University Purdue University Indianapolis has six major institution-wide goals, and they distributed thousands of laminated three-hole punched copies so faculty, students, and others can integrate them into binders and refer to them easily (Association of American Colleges and Universities, 2002). If these lists spanned multiple pages, few would want to carry them around or attempt to keep them in mind.

Another good reason to develop a shorter list is that assessment should be meaningful, manageable, and sustainable. Although some campuses have developed systems for assessing many outcomes, the assessment program may be easier to manage and more effective if the outcome list is shorter. If your campus is one of those with 60, 70, or 100+ outcomes, you might consider shortening the list to focus on the most important outcomes, or you may seek redundancies that could be consolidated. For example, campuses with long lists developed by many committees might discover repeated references to communication skills, critical thinking and problem solving, and information literacy.

One way to create consolidated lists is to invite key faculty and academic leaders to develop them together. Campus general education leaders and I generally refer to this as a *cluster party*. We invite to the party people who support the general education program and who represent all the

Figure 2.2

Strengths and Limitations of Two Models for General Education Goals and Outcomes

	Strengths	Limitations
More General Goals and Outcomes	• A short list can be remembered. • A short list can help to shape a campus culture. • A short list describes the mark of a campus graduate, clarifying learning priorities to everyone. • Assessment planning is less complicated and focuses on key indicators of student success that can be monitored and tracked across time. • A short list can form a strong basis for the design of a core curriculum. • A short list can lead to important, campus-wide discussion of teaching-and-learning topics, such as how all faculty can help students develop communication or quantitative reasoning skills.	• Assessment results may be too general to determine what needs to be changed. • Goals may be ambiguous to faculty and students. • Goals may be so broad that every course, even those ill-suited for the general education program, may be considered acceptable. • Assessment criteria may be difficult to determine because of honest differences in opinion that were not sufficiently addressed when the goals were developed. • Assessment will not be done without strong, on-going leadership and the coordination and cooperation of many departments and individuals.
Goals and Outcomes Related to Requirements	• These lists can be very useful in the course certification process. • Course-embedded assessment can be done with specific outcomes in mind. • Rubrics are easier to develop because relatively clear criteria have already been agreed upon. • Assessment can be decentralized because fewer departments and courses are involved in each assessment study. • Outcomes with similar themes can be assessed simultaneously, similar to the more general model.	• The overall assessment task might seem overwhelming and might be reduced to a "check off each box" mentality. • Assessment may take more time and resources because so many outcomes are examined. • Assessment might be too focused on details, rather than on major areas of concern; key indicators of student success may not be monitored or tracked. • Important campus-wide conversations about teaching and learning may not occur.

major segments of the program. The process is probably most effective (and more fun) if participants have good analytical skills and the respect of their peers, and are flexible and collegial. I've done this in about two or three hours with 10–20 people. More could participate, but the process might take longer. The outcomes have already been established, and the purpose of the cluster party is to look for meaningful groupings.

We began with the complete list of general education outcomes. In preparation for the party, we listed each outcome on a numbered card and created decks of cards. If there were 80 outcomes, each deck had 80 cards. We were concerned that the language on each card might be ambiguous out of context, so we provided background information, such as the general education requirement that was being considered.

When participants were ready to begin, we explained that our purpose was to reduce the number of general education assessment studies that will be planned by clustering together similar outcomes. We provided and briefly discussed some lists of goals from other campuses so participants could see how others had accomplished this task. We wanted to reach consensus on the number and nature of the clusters and, at the same time, ensure that everyone's voice was heard and respected. We asked participants to form small groups of two or three people and suggested that they work with a colleague or two outside of their area. For example, a historian and a chemist might work together. Each team was given a deck of cards and was told to sort the deck into piles with common themes, aiming for about six to ten piles; and we asked them to name each cluster. We gave each team a sheet for recording their clusters and cluster names so we would have a record of their deliberation.

After all the teams were done with their sorts, we invited them to share the cluster names they developed, and we looked for conceptual commonalities and consensus. After a few teams had given their cluster names, subsequent teams added to the growing list any unique clusters that had not yet been mentioned. We built a tentative list of clusters that seemed comprehensive and then, as a group, assigned each outcome to the cluster that seemed most appropriate. Occasionally a new cluster would emerge during this discussion, but at the end of the process we had accomplished our task. We had reduced the number of conceptual areas to assess, simplifying our assessment planning.

Results from the cluster party can be useful for multiple purposes. In addition to simplifying assessment planning, the party offers an opportunity for program leaders to closely examine the already-identified outcomes. The long list of outcomes usually was developed by a number of subcommittees, generally in consultation with relevant peers. Lists generated in this way tend to vary significantly in level of detail and attention to depth of processing. For example, party participants may wonder why something like understanding the scientific method is on the social science list, but not the natural science list, or why critical thinking shows up almost everywhere except in the technology goal. Leaders may decide that some revisions in the long list are required, which requires consultation with relevant subcommittees. The long lists should not be abandoned. They continue to be useful for course certification purposes and as guides for the assessment of the clusters, because they identify how broad goals like problem solving are interpreted by those who staff segments of the general education curriculum.

Cluster party results also provide opportunities to check for alignment of the newly generated general education clusters with the campus mission, general education mission, and accreditor's expectations. When the long lists were originally created by subcommittees, these overriding expectations may have been lost because participants focused on segments of the curriculum. For example, mission statements often emphasize the development of civic engagement, cultural sensitivity, and leadership skills, but one or more of these broad areas may not occur in the long lists of outcomes or the clusters. If the clusters do not align with mission statements or accreditation expectations, more work is required. Discrepancies suggest that campus leaders might have to revise a mission statement, augment the outcomes and perhaps the clusters list, or advocate for changes in their accrediting commission's expectations. The general theme of alignment is the concern of Chapter 3.

Alignment of General Education Programs

A lignment is a key concept in the design and assessment of general education curricula. We ask if the campus provides a cohesive learning environment that supports its general education mission, goals, and learning outcomes. Biggs (2002) reminds us that "teaching and learning take place in a whole *system*, embracing classroom, department and institutional levels" (p. 1), and he argues for "constructive alignment" to support student construction of higher-order learning. If everything runs as planned, "The learner is 'trapped', and cannot escape without learning what is needed" (p. 2). Although this may be optimistic, it is an ideal worth seeking.

Curriculum Alignment

"Well-designed curricula are more than collections of independent courses; they are pathways for learning" (Association of American Colleges and Universities, 2002, p. 30). General education programs may consist of a core curriculum that all students take, a distributed curriculum with many options, or some combination of optional and required coursework. Regardless of the model, faculty have the responsibility to offer a cohesive curriculum that systematically fosters the agreed-upon general education learning outcomes. Alignment asks if the pathways that individual students take systematically lead to these outcomes.

A Cohesive General Education Curriculum

A *cohesive curriculum* systematically provides students multiple opportunities to synthesize, practice, and develop increasingly complex ideas, skills, and values. Important learning outcomes are introduced early, and they are reinforced and further developed throughout the curriculum (Allen, 2004; Diamond, 1998). This is easier to do in a general education program if courses are taken in a set order, with some courses prerequisite to others. For example, students may be required to complete a basic skills sequence before enrolling in other general education courses, so they develop basic communication, critical thinking, information literacy, and quantitative skills before continuing. Subsequent general education courses then build on this foundation, giving students opportunities to practice and further develop these basic skills.

Four-year colleges and universities often require upper-division general education courses, and faculty who teach them can build on the lower-division foundation to further strengthen student mastery of general education outcomes and promote the integration of learning. Although most community colleges only offer lower-division courses, some require a capstone general education course that is taken after other general education requirements have been met. This course can promote the consolidation and integration of learning, and it provides opportunities for embedded assessment of the program.

A simple way to conceptualize a cohesive program is by summarizing it in an *alignment matrix* or *curriculum map* that shows where learning outcomes are fostered in the program. Figure 3.1 shows a simplified model of a cohesive curriculum for developing basic skills in a general education program. *I*, *D*, and *M* indicate that a learning outcome is introduced, developed to foster more sophistication, and demonstrated at a level of mastery acceptable for graduation, respectively. A *D* indicates that students are given opportunities to practice, learn more about, and receive feedback to develop more sophistication. Only four outcomes are listed in Figure 3.1 to simplify this discussion, but, as we saw in Chapter 2, campuses might have dozens of general education outcomes

This alignment matrix uses *I*, *D*, and *M*, but these notations may not work as well for you as some others. For example, you might prefer *I*, *E*, *M* for introduce, enable, and master; *I*, *P*, *D* for introduce, practice, and demonstrate learning; or *B*, *I*, *A* for basic, intermediate, and advanced expectations for learning. Campuses with a professional focus might separate

Figure 3.1
Cohesive Development of Basic Skills

Course	GE Outcome 1	GE Outcome 2	GE Outcome 3	GE Outcome 4
Freshman Basic Skills Course 1	I			
Freshman Basic Skills Course 2		I		
Freshman Basic Skills Course 3			I	
Freshman Basic Skills Course 4				I
Sophomore-Level Courses	D	D	D	D
Capstone/Upper-Division Course(s)	M	M	M	M

I = *Introduce*—outcomes are introduced at the basic level.
D – *Develop*—students are given opportunities to practice, learn more about, and receive feedback to develop more sophistication.
M = *Mastery*—students demonstrate mastery at a level appropriate for graduation.

didactic from experiential (e.g., internship) learning, so they may prefer something like *I, E, P, M*, where

I = Introduce at the basic level.

E = Enhance learning; increase sophistication beyond the basic level using didactic methods.

P = Practice with real or simulated clients and receive feedback to develop practical skills.

M = Demonstrate mastery at a level appropriate for graduation.

You and your colleagues should decide what distinctions help you map your learning outcomes onto your curriculum. You could just use check marks, but more details show how the curriculum builds on itself. This *scaffolding* systematically provides opportunities for consolidating learning and developing increasing sophistication.

The alignment matrix focuses on outcomes, rather than goals, because we want to verify that students receive appropriate support to master all outcomes. If we focused at the goal level, some outcomes might be lost. For example, if we aligned our curriculum with an oral communication goal, the program might look cohesive, but if we focus on a specific outcome associated with oral communication, such as interpersonal skills, we might discover that no course fosters the development of this specific outcome. This matrix also serves another important purpose. When we begin to develop our assessment plan, any alignment matrix entry of *D* or *M* alerts us to the existence of products or behaviors that could be evaluated in an embedded assessment study.

Many colleges allow students to take general education courses in almost any order, without a capstone requirement, and this makes scaffolding difficult. For example, see Figure 3.2. Here each course works relatively independently. Faculty cannot be confident about what students already know, so students may receive multiple introductions to something like information literacy, but they may never experience coursework beyond the introductory level. Students may be required to take only one course to meet each requirement, and this course often is expected to introduce, develop, and elicit the demonstration of mastery-level learning. Some basic skills, such as written communication, may overflow into other courses, as shown for Outcome 1 in Figure 3.2, and this should be recognized by including the relevant outcomes on course syllabi.

Perhaps making some minor changes that create a few prerequisites within the general education program would provide students opportunities to integrate and practice what they learned multiple times, as well as develop higher levels of learning. Freshman experience courses, for example, might introduce all new students to basic information literacy skills, so faculty who teach subsequent general education courses have opportunities to build on this foundation. Including capstone courses in the humanities, natural sciences, and social sciences and/or an overall general education capstone course would allow students to focus on integrating what they have learned.

Sometimes faculty are surprised by their general education alignment matrix. Look at the alignment matrix in Figure 3.3, pretending that this program has only five outcomes and four courses which students take in alphabetical order (A, B, C, and D). Does this campus offer a cohesive general education curriculum?

Figure 3.2

Less Cohesive Program

Course	GE Outcome 1	GE Outcome 2	GE Outcome 3	GE Outcome 4
English 100	I, D			
History 101	D, M	I, D, M		
Biology 100	D		I, D, M	
Sociology 100	D, M			I, D, M

I = Introduce; D = Develop; M = Mastery

Figure 3.3

General Education Alignment Matrix Example

Course	GE Outcome 1	GE Outcome 2	GE Outcome 3	GE Outcome 4	GE Outcome 5
A	I, D	I, D			
B	D			D	
C	D				I
D	D, M			D, M	M

The first outcome in Figure 3.3 is well-integrated into the general education program. Faculty introduce students to it in the first course, provide development and practice with feedback in every course, and expect students to demonstrate mastery at the end of the general education program.

Outcome 2 is introduced and developed in one course, but students do not systematically improve beyond this course nor demonstrate mastery within the program. This is fine if students' majors provide subsequent opportunities for development; otherwise it appears to be a problem. Campus faculty can determine this.

Outcome 3 was forgotten in the curriculum, and you might think this never happens, but I have seen it in practice. A campus might have a broad communication goal that includes writing, reading, speaking, and listening, but an examination of the curriculum might reveal that no instruction or feedback is provided for one or more of these skills. Other goals or outcomes might share this problem. For example, Emporia State University (2001) discovered that none of its general education courses addressed their goal related to developing "a commitment to scholarship, intellectual curiosity and life long learning" (Events During 1998–1999 section).

Outcome 4 is fairly well integrated into the curriculum, but it was never introduced. Perhaps faculty know that incoming students do not need an introduction, and this assumption could be verified by a simple assessment when students begin Course B. If students do well on this assessment, the present curriculum is reasonable. If not, the faculty should determine where the introduction will occur.

Outcome 5 is introduced and students demonstrate their mastery in Course D, but students are never given opportunities to learn more, practice, and receive corrective feedback. For example, faculty may lecture students on speaking or scientific reasoning, but they may not provide students formative feedback on their ability to give a speech or to analyze a phenomenon from a scientific perspective. Most students require more than just an introductory lecture to develop and retain such skills.

Pedagogy and Grading Alignment

Learning-centered teaching requires careful attention to the alignment of learning outcomes with pedagogy and grading. Traditional lectures, reading assignments, and objective exams might serve surface-level learning well, but may not support some aspects of deeper learning. In addition, teaching methods and curriculum structures that used to work may not be optimal for the wide variety of students in our classrooms today. We have the responsibility to help our students learn, and this might require changes in how we design courses.

Pedagogy

Decades of research in higher education and in cognitive science have allowed us to identify characteristics of the teaching and learning environment that support deep and lasting learning. Researchers at the Berger Institute (n.d.) at Claremont McKenna College review this literature and summarize nine learning principles:

- The single most important variable in promoting long-term retention and transfer is "practice at retrieval"—learners generate responses, with minimal retrieval cues, repeatedly, over time.

- Varying learning conditions makes learning more effortful but results in enhanced long-term retrieval.

- Learning is generally enhanced when learners are required to take information that is presented in one format and "re-represent" it in an alternative format.

- New information learned depends heavily upon prior knowledge and experience.

- Learning is influenced by our students' as well as our own epistemologies (theories about learning).

- Experience alone is a poor teacher.

- To promote in-depth understanding, avoid passive learning situations where a lone teacher mostly lectures while learners take notes.

- The process of remembering influences what learners will and will not remember in the future.

- Less is more, especially when considering long-term retention and transfer. (¶ 2).

These principles provide an empirical foundation for the cohesive curriculum that offers students repeated opportunities to remember, expand, and use their learning in a variety of contexts. Students should be expected to communicate well, think critically, and use what they have been learning throughout the curriculum—not just in the courses that satisfy specific general education requirements; and they should learn how to learn. Faculty should engage students in active learning opportunities that promote the establishment of links between previous and new learning and the development of deep, conceptual understanding.

Feedback is crucial. One does not improve just by doing something. Imagine you have been told to shoot basketballs through a hoop that is ten feet away. Someone requires you to use a blindfold and earplugs, then leads you to a basketball court. The person keeps passing you balls, and you throw them again and again. Without any feedback, your basketball skills will not improve. However, take away the blindfold and the earplugs, and your shooting accuracy can improve because you can see the target and you can see and hear the "swish" as the ball goes through the hoop. Sometimes the environment provides the feedback that the learner needs, as in the basketball example, but often the instructor must provide the feedback. As will be seen in Chapter 5, grading rubrics can be used to give effective feedback and save faculty grading time.

The concept that "less is more" is a lesson many experienced faculty have learned the hard way. They may begin their teaching careers as walking encyclopedias, and they want to somehow transmit that entire encyclopedia into the head of each of their students. Frustrated and disappointed, they recognize that their graduate-level understanding of what they're teaching is inappropriate and impossible for their general education students. The undergraduates do not have the necessary background or experience to make sense out of everything, and there is simply too much to memorize. Faculty learn that the "less is more" approach actually improves learning. They begin each class period with two or three learning outcomes for the day, and students hear about those things, practice them, discuss them, and leave the room understanding them.

Most faculty teach the way they were taught, and this may not optimize learning for the students in their courses today. According to Halpern and Hakel (2003), "ironically (and embarrassingly), it would be difficult to design an education model that is more at odds with the findings of current research about human cognition than the one being used today at most colleges and universities" (pp. 37–38). The active learning classroom is different from the typical lecture classroom, and doing it well requires some risk taking and proficiency in an array of techniques. An important active learning principle is that students don't just do something—they learn something. Occasionally, the class seems noisy or out of control, but the effective teacher has carefully thought through each activity and assignment so that students consolidate and extend their learning.

To use class time effectively, faculty motivate their students to complete homework, such as reading assignments, before coming to class so that class time can be spent working with the material, not learning about it for the first time. This often is a challenge in general education courses, and even some courses for majors, but we want our students to develop lifelong learning skills that will assist them during school and after graduation. Some faculty find that setting expectations early and using learning journals, short writing assignments on the readings, study groups, or quizzes helps to motivate students to get their first exposure to course materials before coming to class.

Each course has explicit learning outcomes, and the faculty member organizes the course to facilitate mastery of those outcomes by deciding what students should do, how they should receive formative feedback, and how they should be graded. Figure 3.4 illustrates the planning for two course outcomes.

Figure 3.4

Course Planning Grid for Two Course Outcomes

Course Outcome	Activity	Feedback and Grading
Students learn to give effective oral presentations.	Students hear a lecture on effective speaking and develop two oral presentations: one to summarize key concepts in a chapter section and one to describe how a theory from this course could be applied to an event in a recent newspaper article. Immediately prior to each speech, they provide an outline of their presentation to everyone in the class.	Students are given peer feedback and instructor feedback on each presentation using a rubric that describes the content and delivery style. Each presentation counts as 5% of the course grade.
Students learn to design experiments to test theories.	Students participate in a series of demonstrations designed to show how research hypotheses are generated and tested to evaluate psychological theories. Students develop hypotheses and aggregate data to reach conclusions. After each of these, the class, as a whole, discusses how the theory was translated into testable predictions about observable phenomena.	Students write short reports on two of the demonstrations and identify how the theory was tested and what was learned. In addition, the final exam requires students to develop and explain a simple experiment to empirically examine a theory learned in the course. The reports count as 5% of the course grade, and the exam question counts as 10% of the final exam.

Faculty Development

If you want to learn more about active learning and learning-focused instruction, much help is available. Perhaps your campus has a faculty development program that provides support. If not, you might consider inviting some colleagues to join you in a collaborative learning group to explore the teaching-and-learning literature. There likely is a journal dedicated to the scholarship of teaching in your discipline, and many of these are linked to a web site maintained at Indiana University Bloomington (Subject and Area Librarians Council, 2001–2005). In addition, dozens of excellent books have been written on teaching and learning. Faculty reviews of a variety of these books are published in *Exchanges: The Online Journal of Teaching and Learning in the CSU* (http://www.exchangesjournal.org).

Grading

Grading, whether by letter grade or narrative summary, can be a powerful tool for promoting student learning. Grading serves a number of purposes:

- Exams and assignments communicate to students what we want them to learn.

- Exams and assignments can provide opportunities for learning. For example, preparing for comprehensive exams helps students consolidate learning, and writing critical analyses engages students in thinking about course concepts.

- Exams and assignments can be used to provide formative feedback to students.

- A series of exams and graded assignments motivates students to keep up with the coursework, reminds them that learning is important, and rewards them for learning.

- Faculty can use embedded assessment to improve courses and programs by reviewing student work on exams and assignments.

Grading procedures should align with course outcomes, and course grades should indicate the extent to which students have mastered them. Figure 3.5 summarizes the analysis of the grading components for one course with four learning outcomes. Each of the graded components contributes from 5%–30% and each of the four outcomes counts from 21%–31% of the course grade. An *S* indicates that the grading procedure is at the surface level. This is usually done using objective exams that require students to recognize or recall specific facts. A *D* indicates that the grading procedure requires students to demonstrate deeper levels of learning. For example, students may be required to explain, apply, analyze, synthesize, or evaluate something using what they have learned.

Figure 3.5

Grading Alignment Matrix I*

Grading Element	Grading Weight	Week	Course Outcome 1	Course Outcome 2	Course Outcome 3	Course Outcome 4
Quiz 1	5	2	S (3)	S (2)		
Homework 1	5	3	D (2)	D (3)		
Quiz 2	5	5	S (1)	S (3)	S (1)	
Homework 2	5	7	D (2)	D (3)		
Community Service Report I	5	7	D (2)	D (3)		
Midterm	15	8	S, D (7)	S, D (8)		
Lab Report	5	9	D (1)		D (2)	D (2)
Oral Report	5	9			D (5)	
Homework 3	5	11	D (2)			D (3)
Quiz 3	5	13		S (1)	S (2)	S (2)
Group Project	10	15		D (3)	D (3)	S (4)
Community Service Report II	5	15		D (2)	D (1)	D (2)
Final Exam	25	16	S, D (4)	S, D (4)	S, D (8)	S, D (9)
Total	100	-	24	32	21	22

S = Surface-level learning is assessed.
D = Deep learning is assessed.
*Numbers in parentheses are the percentage of the course grade for each outcome.

The faculty member who teaches the course described in Figure 3.5 has 13 graded activities that assess both surface and deep learning, and they appear to be aligned with the course learning outcomes. Brief quizzes at the surface level focus students on key concepts, and the homework assignments, community service reports, oral reports, and group projects provide opportunities to practice and receive feedback on deeper understanding of the material. The midterm and final, together worth 40% of the grade, measure both surface and deep learning; and each is preceded by relevant activities to help students prepare for the larger exams. The assignments are spread across the semester to encourage ongoing student engagement, and the most important learning outcome (judging by its weight in the course grade) is introduced early and practiced throughout the semester. In reviewing a grading alignment matrix, faculty might ask:

- Do the course grading procedures give appropriate weight to each of the learning outcomes? (For example, should the second outcome in Figure 3.5 generate the highest proportion of the course grade?)

- Are outcomes assessed at an appropriate level? (For example, is too much of the course grade determined by surface-level learning?)

- Are students provided with sufficient formative feedback to benefit from mistakes before the final exam? (For example, are the exams and assignments timed to give students time to reflect on and learn from the feedback? Does the feedback help students develop deep learning?)

- What is the intended function of each exam and assignment and does it serve this function? (For example, if the faculty member is using quizzes to motivate students to keep up with reading assignments, is this strategy working?)

Examine the grading alignment matrix summarized in Figure 3.6, and ask if the grading procedures align with course outcomes. Assume that all four outcomes require some deep learning.

Your first response to Figure 3.6 may be that too few grading elements are used. When I was an undergraduate, admittedly quite a few years ago, this was the typical grading scheme, and I am confident that some faculty use something like it today. Faculty teaching large sections without assistance cannot be expected to develop and provide feedback using dozens of

Figure 3.6

Grading Alignment Matrix II

Grading Element	Week	Grading Weight	Course Outcome 1	Course Outcome 2	Course Outcome 3	Course Outcome 4
Midterm	8	30	S (15)	S (15)		
Term Paper	15	20		D (15)		D (5)
Final	16	50	S (10)	S, D (10)	S (15)	S (15)
Total		100	25	40	15	20

procedures, and the real question is if the procedures align with course outcomes and promote student learning.

An examination of Figure 3.6 demonstrates that Outcome 2 receives the most weight for the course grade (twice the weight given to outcome 4), which may be reasonable if it has the highest priority for this course. In addition, Outcomes 1 and 3 are not graded at the expected, deep level. Course grades will not indicate deep learning for these outcomes, and students who focus on exams will be more likely to study for surface-level learning. In addition, much of the grading for Outcomes 2 and 4 is at the surface level, suggesting a similar problem. The grading procedures do not appear to provide early formative feedback, especially for deep learning, but ungraded exercises may be embedded in the course to serve this function. Courses must be considered as a whole. An array of active learning exercises can even be integrated into huge course sections, reducing the need for reliance on graded components to provide necessary feedback.

Institutional Alignment

Learning does not happen just in courses. Institutions, as a whole, should support the general education program. Advisors should provide timely, useful advice to students about options in the general education program, the order in which courses should be taken, and course sections that seem particularly suited to their needs or interests. Tutoring center staff should be familiar with general education learning outcomes, as well as individual course outcomes, and they should tailor their services to help students meet these expectations.

Faculty and staff should be particularly aware of *gateway* or *roadblock* courses that frequently challenge students and result in failing grades, and they should work together to facilitate student success. "Taking pride in 'flunking out' large numbers of students is a distant memory on most campuses," (Swing, 2004b, p. ix), and we want to solve this problem by finding ways to help more students meet our expectations. First-year experience courses generally focus on reducing student attrition, but a single course is unlikely to solve everything.

The cocurriculum can support a variety of general education learning outcomes. For example, student government, clubs, social organizations, and athletic, political, and cultural events provide opportunities to develop communication, leadership, collaboration, civic engagement, and ethical decision-making skills. They present a natural laboratory for applying what students learn in a variety of general education courses, and they can provide opportunities to develop multicultural awareness and an understanding of cultural, social, political, and economic issues.

Aligning the work of student affairs and academic affairs staff requires deliberate effort, especially when these units are functionally independent within the institution. Leaders should find ways to institutionalize collaboration. For example, on many campuses librarians are assigned to particular departments and programs, and part of their responsibility is to reach out and work with relevant faculty to support the development of information literacy skills. The campus should host events to foster collaboration between and among faculty, staff, and administrators concerning how they can work together to support learning in the general education program. An annual campus-wide assessment retreat may be instrumental in initiating collaboration.

Faculty and staff development programs should include a focus on support needs for general education, and program decisions should be affected by assessment findings. For example, if an assessment resulted in the conclusion that students were taking writing-intensive general education courses before completing basic college composition requirements or that students were not meeting faculty expectations for the development of ethical reasoning, faculty and staff development professionals could target these problems.

One indicator of campus commitment to general education is the types of faculty who contribute to it. On some campuses the full range of faculty, including senior faculty, teach in the general education program, but on others general education courses are assigned to adjunct faculty and new faculty. In my experience, some of the best teaching in general education is by dedicated, long-term lecturers; but if senior faculty denigrate their contributions and believe that general education teaching is inferior and to be avoided, the wrong message is sent. A well-taught general education course can change the course of students' lives. Most of us know students who changed majors or added a minor after taking an especially interesting general education course. Faculty of all ranks should take advantage of this opportunity to share their discipline with a new audience of potential enthusiasts.

We are in the age of learning-centered instruction, and many campuses claim to be learning-centered. Recognition and reward systems and campus policies should align with this vision. Are faculty and staff who make extraordinary contributions to student learning in the general education program publicly honored and respected by peers and institutional leaders? Do personnel decisions recognize such efforts? Are faculty expected to demonstrate effective teaching before they are eligible for tenure, promotion, or ongoing classroom assignments? Are staff expected to demonstrate positive impact on students when they are reviewed for retention, promotion, or salary increments? Are administrators evaluated, in part, on their active and vocal support for student learning? If yes, the campus is aligned to foster student success.

The DEEP Project

An interesting study of institutional effectiveness is the DEEP (Documenting Effective Educational Practice) project conducted by the Center for Postsecondary Research at Indiana University (Kuh, Kinzie, Schuh, Whitt, & Associates, 2005). Project staff identified 20 colleges and universities using two major criteria. Compared to similar institutions, DEEP campuses have higher than expected graduation rates and higher than expected scores on the National Survey of Student Engagement (NSSE). In effect, these campuses, compared to similar campuses, have students who report being more engaged in their learning and who are more likely to complete their degree. In addition, researchers wanted to examine a variety of campuses. Their sample included public and private, residential and commuter, research-intensive and undergraduate-intensive, and large and small institutions. Two are historically black campuses, two are Hispanic-serving, two are women's colleges, and one is a men's college.

What do these effective campuses have in common? Researchers spent time on each campus attending classes and meetings, interviewing campus representatives, reviewing documents, and evaluating the campus environment. Kuh and Associates (2005) are careful to point out that what works on one campus may not work on another and that each DEEP campus was unique, but they found "six features that appeared to foster student engagement and persistence" (p. 24):

- A "living" mission and "lived" educational philosophy

- An unshakeable focus on student learning

- Environments adapted for educational enrichment

- Clearly marked pathways to student success

- An improvement oriented ethos

- Shared responsibility for educational quality and student success (p. 24)

DEEP campuses have a clearly defined mission or philosophy, and everyone on campus "lives" it. They have a shared vision that guides decision-making and priorities. When asked about the campus, representatives of DEEP campuses tend to refer to their shared mission; it is salient in their day-to-day decision-making. For example, Alverno College's mission permeates the campus: "Alverno exists to promote the personal and professional development of women" (Kuh, et al., 2005, p. 29). Representatives of Fayetteville State University share the mantra of "meeting students where they are" (p. 35), and faculty at Longwood University designed their general education program for "preparing citizen leaders for the common good" (p. 39). The University of Michigan's mission is "to serve the people of Michigan and the world through preeminence in creating, communicating, preserving, and applying knowledge, art, and academic values and in developing leaders and citizens who will challenge the present and enrich the future" (p. 48). According to Kuh and his colleagues, taking their missions seriously helped these DEEP campuses promote student engagement and persistence.

DEEP institutions are learning-focused: "Student learning and personal development at DEEP schools is a priority. Though this might seem to be a simplistic and hardly revolutionary statement, DEEP schools are special precisely because their commitment to this priority is authentic and they pursue it with a high degree of effectiveness" (Kuh, et al., 2005, p. 88). Researchers concluded that these campuses share four characteristics related to student learning. They value undergraduate learning, engage students through active learning, share "a cool passion for talent development" (p. 65), and make time for students. Institutional commitment to undergraduate learning runs deep, and these campuses provide an array of enriching activities and support mechanisms, such as honors programs, tutoring centers, technology centers, and interdisciplinary courses. Faculty believe in their students' capacity to learn, they provide extensive feedback to help students develop, and they diligently provide support for multiple learning styles. They are available to students and encourage interaction inside and outside the classroom, in person and via email. In addition, DEEP campuses are careful to recruit faculty who are dedicated to student learning, and they support faculty in their teaching by providing services, such as faculty development programs and internal grants to support teaching innovations.

DEEP institutions adapt environments to support learning. For example, classrooms are well designed, and undergraduate services are easily accessible. Students are encouraged to stay on campus, even if they are commuters. Campuses provide places for students to study, to interact outside of class, to exchange and discuss ideas, to exercise, to eat, and to relax. Residence halls may be organized as living-learning communities, and groups of students may take classes as a cohort. These institutions develop mutually beneficial town-gown relationships, and students, as well as faculty, provide community service and use the community as a laboratory and internship site.

DEEP institutions help students understand campus expectations and opportunities. They acculturate new students into the institution and its mission, and they communicate high standards as well as welcoming support. Students feel as if they belong on campus, and they are empowered to take advantage of available services. For example, Wofford College invites newly admitted students to "join" Wofford and become part of its family. Gonzaga University hosts a Gonzaga Experience Live (GEL) program for prospective students—a weekend featuring campus and community tours, samples of academic experiences, an overnight dorm stay with a current student, and social activities. Participants learn about student clubs, the campus mission, and the nature of the Gonzaga experience. Most DEEP colleges have summer transition programs for at-risk students and first-year experience programs to ensure that all students feel welcome, understand what is expected of them, know how to take advantage of campus services, and become part of the campus community. Campus staff take the advising role seriously, and they monitor student progress and reach out proactively to help students who are experiencing academic difficulty.

"DEEP schools seem to be in a perpetual learning mode—monitoring where they are, what they are doing, where they want to go, and how to maintain momentum toward positive change" (Kuh, et al., 2005, p. 133). This is assessment at its best, and it requires administrative and academic leaders who are willing to make hard decisions to prioritize learning, even when budgets are tight. Professionals on DEEP campuses recognize that any complex system is imperfect. They're willing to investigate their impact, and they're flexible enough to experiment with new approaches when their criteria aren't met.

The last characteristic noted by the research team was that DEEP campus professionals share responsibility for student success. They respect the contributions of others, and they recognize the value of ongoing collaboration between academic and student affairs professionals. Faculty, administrators, and staff—both individually and collectively—support student development. "DEEP campuses benefit from large numbers of caring, supportive individuals who perform countless daily acts of kindness and thoughtfulness that make students feel wanted and important" (Kuh, et al., 2005, p. 172).

As you consider the alignment of your campus' courses, curriculum, cocurriculum, policies, and activities with general education outcomes, ask if your campus exhibits some of the learning-centered characteristics of DEEP campuses. If you conduct assessment studies and are disappointed with results, the DEEP project may provide some provocative ideas for responding to these findings.

Promoting Student Engagement in Community Colleges

The DEEP project examined four-year colleges and universities and used the NSSE to identify campuses that actively engage their students. The Community College Survey of Student Engagement (CCSSE) is the community college version of the NSSE, and its results are summarized in an annual report. Authors of the 2005 report, *Engagement by Design: 2004*

Findings (CCSSE, 2005), acknowledge that community colleges face serious challenges, including tight budgets and students who work and have families, attend college part-time, and vary considerably in their academic background and goals; but "these challenges do not make student engagement impossible. They simply indicate that student engagement is not likely to happen by accident. Engagement, therefore, must be intentional. It must happen by design" (CCSSE, 2005, p. 2). CCSSE staff take this responsibility seriously:

> And this work is essential. Community colleges tend to serve students who have the fewest options; if they do not succeed in their community college, students likely will not have access to productive jobs, further education, or any of the benefits these next steps bring. Community colleges, moreover, are not just preparing students for their own benefit. They are preparing students to contribute to their neighborhoods, the nation, and the world. Providing effective learning experiences is critical for both the students themselves and our society, which increasingly relies on every individual to participate productively in our economy, our democracy, and the global village. (p. 3)

The CCSSE can be a powerful tool for monitoring and strengthening student engagement in their educations, and this should lead to increased learning. The authors of *Engagement by Design* (CCSSE, 2005) describe four strategies to expand student engagement and provide campus examples for each strategy:

- *Strategy 1.* "Engage early; engage often" (p. 6). Community colleges can't wait for students to become engaged; they must be proactive. For example, Tallahassee Community College sets up information tents at the beginning of each term to help students locate classes and support services, office staff wear "Ask Me" buttons, and faculty and staff create stations in classroom building lobbies with refreshments, maps, and willing assistance.

- *Strategy 2.* "Stress academic advising" (p. 7). CCSSE results indicate that more than one-third of community college respondents rarely or never see an academic advisor, and nearly half fail to make use of career counseling services. Unfortunately, this puts these students at risk because goal setting and developing a concrete strategy for meeting long-term goals help students succeed. Campuses should be proactive. For example, Sinclair Community College provides counseling and support to encourage students to develop a "Student Success Plan," which has resulted in increased student persistence and success.

- *Strategy 3.* "Emphasize effective developmental education" (p. 7). Nationally, about half of all entering community college freshmen are not prepared for college-level work, and developmental education helps them develop the skills they need to succeed in school, at work, and in the future. For example, Prince Edward Community College requires developmental work for students who need to develop reading, writing, and computational skills.

- *Strategy 4.* "Redesign educational experiences" (p. 9). Faculty can engage students in and out of the classroom in many ways, such as using active learning techniques during class, assigning work that promotes reflection and deep learning, requiring group projects, and providing opportunities for students to join learning communities. For example, Northwest Vista College's weekend college combines two or three disciplines and offers team-taught, multidisciplinary courses that students take as a learning community. Students work together on final projects that integrate what they learn each semester.

Efforts to Increase Student Retention and Success

Because of concern about student retention, general education programs are often given the added responsibility of helping students learn to succeed in college. Habley and McClanahan (2004), representing ACT, analyzed survey data from more than 800 two- and four-year colleges and universities to identify factors related to student retention. When asked to identify three effective campus retention practices, at least 10% of campus representatives identified freshman seminars (13%), tutoring programs (13%), advising interventions for special student subgroups (13%), and required placement testing programs (10%). Based on a review of all their findings, Habley and McClanahan recommend that campuses:

- Designate a visible individual to coordinate a campus-wide planning team.

- Conduct a systematic analysis of the characteristics of your students.

- Focus on the nexus of student characteristics and institutional characteristics.

- Carefully review the high impact strategies identified in the survey.

- Do not make first-to-second-year retention strategies the sole focus of planning team efforts.

- Establish realistic short-term and long-term retention, progression, and completion goals.

- Orchestrate the change process.

- Implement, measure, improve! (Executive Summary section)

In short, they recommend that campuses systematically plan and coordinate their interventions, align programs with specific goals, and use assessment to improve their efforts—good advice for any initiative.

Many strategies have been used to promote student retention and success, and assessment is essential to verify that interventions have the desired impact. For example, a research team at the University of Mississippi empirically verified that course absences among first-year students are directly related to their grades, and they created a pilot Absence-Based Intervention Project. Faculty who taught freshman English reported students with at least two absences, and graduate students intervened by calling or visiting identified students and telling them about available support services. Compared to a control group of students who were not contacted, project freshmen earned significantly higher grades. Based on these findings the campus expanded the program and anticipates continuing success (Anderson, 2004).

The most common intervention is a first-year experience course, and these courses have emerged all over the country. They specifically target the development of the knowledge, skills, and values required for sustained academic success.

Types of First-Year Experience Courses

Barefoot (1992, cited in Tobolowsky, Cox, & Wagner, 2005) identified five types of first-year experience courses:

1. *Extended orientation seminar.* Sometimes called a freshman orientation, college survival, college transition, or student success course. Content likely will include introduction to campus resources, time management, academic and career planning, learning strategies, and an introduction to student development issues.

2. *Academic seminar with generally uniform content across sections.* May be an interdisciplinary or theme-oriented course, sometimes part of a general education requirement. Primary focus is on academic theme/discipline but will often include academic skills components such as critical thinking and expository writing.

3. *Academic seminars with variable content.* Similar to previously mentioned academic seminar except that specific topics vary from section to section.

4. *Pre-professional or discipline-linked seminar.* Designed to prepare students for the demands of the major/discipline and the profession. Generally taught within professional schools or specific disciplines.

5. *Basic study skills seminar.* The focus is on basic academic skills such as grammar, note taking, and reading texts. Often offered for academically underprepared students. (pp. 7–8)

Of course, no typology of academic programs can be complete, and campuses have created first-year experiences that are combinations of some of the above approaches. Experiences at nearly 40 campuses are described in the third volume of the First-Year Experience Monograph Series, *Exploring the Evidence: Reporting Research on First-Year Seminars* (Tobolowsky, Cox, & Wagner, 2005).

Alignment of First-Year Experience Courses

Faculty and staff who contribute to first-year experience programs may be working outside of their primary expertise, and assessment is essential to verify that their interventions have the desired impact. Regardless of course structure, alignment is also a concern. To test the alignment of first-year courses with campus intentions and to understand how these courses change over time, faculty on some campuses develop *course diaries:*

> A course diary documents the content of a course including assignments, texts used, subjects discussed, handouts distributed, and any other pertinent information and supplies a record of overall student performance and expectations. Historical archives of course records also help faculty members guard against "content creep"—the addition of more content with each new offering of the course—and "curriculum drain"—the elimination of content related to the course goals and objectives. . . . First-year programs that have used course diaries report greater control over student outcomes, increased student retention, and more involvement from courses typically relegated to low-priority status. (Scheffel & Revak, 2004, pp. 17–18)

In addition, Scheffel and Revak (2004) report that the use of course diaries encourages faculty to be reflective about their teaching and helps them maintain high standards that reduce grade inflation.

Alignment Questions

As you and your colleagues consider the alignment of various factors with your general education program, you might like to ask these broad questions:

Curriculum Cohesion

- Is the general education curriculum cohesive? Does it systematically provide students multiple opportunities to synthesize, practice, and develop increasingly complex ideas, skills, and values?

- Are students given opportunities to find connections between the disciplines and to consolidate their learning?

- Do all general education courses have explicit course learning outcomes that align with program-level outcomes?

- Are needed developmental courses, including a first-year experience course, available and required?

- Should some general education courses be prerequisite to others? For example, should students take mathematics before science courses or should they take English courses focusing on reading and writing before history courses? Does a check of transcripts demonstrate that students without these prerequisites are at a disadvantage?

- Are prerequisites strictly enforced?

Pedagogy and Grading

- Does the pedagogy in general education courses align with course learning outcomes?

- Do students receive formative feedback on program learning outcomes throughout the general education program?

- Are students actively engaged in the general education program?

- Do faculty use grading as a tool to promote student attainment of course outcomes?

- Do course grades reflect the extent to which students master course outcomes?

- Do course exams and assignments measure each outcome at the appropriate level (surface vs. deep learning)?

Support Services

- Do general education advisors take a personal interest in each student's development?

- Do students understand general education requirements and options?

- Do students develop personal plans to attain their academic and career goals?

- Are tutoring center staff, librarians, and others on campus aware of general education course and program outcomes? Do they collaborate with faculty to provide needed support?

- Does the cocurriculum provide enrichment activities that support general education outcomes?

- Do faculty and staff development programs support contributions to general education and address needs identified through the assessment of the general education program?

General Education Instructors

- Does the campus recruit faculty who are learning-centered and eager to contribute to the general education program?

- Are general education courses taught by an appropriate array of faculty, including senior faculty?

- Do campus recognition and reward systems encourage contributions to the general education program?

Learning-Centered Campuses

- Does your campus have a general education mission or philosophy that everyone shares?

- Does your campus have an "unshakeable" focus on student learning in the general education program?

- Does your general education program have adequate, easily accessible space for advising, teaching, studying, and interacting?

- Does your general education program include ties to the community?

- Do faculty and staff who work with general education students believe in students' capacity to learn and provide opportunities for students who learn in different ways?

- Is learning in your general education program assessed, and have you made improvements in the program based on assessment findings?

- Does the campus routinely analyze the retention and success of students who vary in systematic ways, such as age, ethnicity, gender, or income, to identify groups of students who require special assistance?

- Do faculty and staff accept a shared, mutually respectful responsibility for helping general education students meet your standards?

Alignment Through Course Certification

In the past, most campuses relied on individual faculty and departments to determine what was taught in general education courses, but we have moved to a learning-centered model that is based on a shared, campus-wide understanding of what students should learn. Individual faculty determine how they teach, what their students do, and how grades are assigned; but everyone who teaches a general education course is expected to help students meet agreed-upon criteria. Individual faculty and departments might augment the general education outcomes with some of their own. For example, a general education course might also serve as an introduction for majors, but it also includes the relevant general education outcomes.

The general education program and the array of approved courses sometimes has been stable on a campus for decades, and faculty who teach these courses may be accustomed to more freedom than this model provides. Substantial differences in stated or implied learning outcomes for the same course may be ignored, tolerated, or even encouraged. The time has come for colleges and universities to take collective responsibility for general education, its expectations, and its courses so that students experience a cohesive, integrated program. At the same time, campuses should respect faculty autonomy to manage their own courses in ways that meet student needs.

Alignment specifies which outcomes will be introduced and supported in each general education course. Many campuses also set additional criteria for general education courses. For example, the University of Montana (2002) sets outcomes and criteria for each general education segment. Here are the criteria for courses that meet their natural sciences requirement:

1. Courses should systematically develop principles for comprehension of a broad class of physical phenomena and should demonstrate the methods scientists use to gather, validate, and interpret data.

2. Lab courses should include specific examples of some typical activities, instruments, and materials used, and a description of the relationship of lab or field work to the course content for lab courses.

3. Applied and narrowly focused courses should include significant and coherent attention to basic principles and theory or the application should follow a prerequisite natural science course that has exposed those theoretical foundations.

4. Courses should not be mainly descriptive or have as their primary objective the development of a professional vocabulary. (Criteria for Courses in Perspective VI: Natural Sciences section)

Course Certification

Most campuses use a formal certification process to ensure course alignment with general education outcomes. A committee, generally composed of faculty, sometimes augmented by an administrative representative, usually reviews proposals to determine how well courses align with general education expectations. Campuses may have one committee or multiple committees, each charged with oversight of a segment of the general education program. Often this committee makes a recommendation to a relevant academic administrator, such as an undergraduate dean or provost, or to a council, such as an academic senate, for final course approval.

For example, San Francisco State University (1999) developed learning outcomes for its oral communication requirement, and any department wishing to offer a new or revised general education course to meet this requirement must petition the Segment I Committee that deals with basic skills. The petition includes a syllabus that has already been approved by the University Course Review Committee and discussion of how the course will meet the specified criteria, including the alignment of instruction, assignments, and grading with relevant learning outcomes. The proposal is reviewed by the Segment I Committee, which makes a recommendation to the General Education Committee, and the General Education Committee makes a recommendation to the dean of Undergraduate Studies for final determination. Departments can appeal to the General Education Committee if they are not satisfied with its recommendation.

San José State University takes the course certification process seriously, because it is the foundation for the embedded assessment of their general education program. With extensive collaboration, learning outcomes were developed for each general education requirement, course review criteria were created, faculty development and support mechanisms were implemented, and campus leaders reviewed hundreds of course proposals (Anagnos, Dorosz, & Wheeler, 2002). For example, courses meeting the upper-division Self, Society, & Equality in the U.S. requirement have four learning outcomes. Students who complete the course should be able to:

- describe how religious, gender, ethnic, racial, class, sexual orientation, disability, and/or age identity are shaped by cultural and societal influences in contexts of equality and inequality;

- describe historical, social, political, and economic processes producing diversity, equality, and structured inequalities in the U.S.;

- describe social actions by religious, gender, ethnic, racial, class, sexual orientation, disability, and/or age groups leading to greater equality and social justice in the U.S.; and

- recognize and appreciate constructive interactions between people from different cultural, racial, and ethnic groups in the U.S. (San José State University, 2000, Student Learning section)

In addition, instructors who teach these courses must help students develop writing skills by providing feedback on both in-class and out-of-class writing (at least 3,000 words), and they must require students to apply the basic skills developed earlier in the general education program (e.g., reading, speaking, critical thinking, information literacy, and mathematics). Faculty must not rely only on lecturing. They are required to use active learning techniques and to include primary sources among course readings (San José State University, 2000).

Procedures for reviewing course proposals are described on the campus web site (San José State University, 1998). Departments wishing to propose a general education course submit a Course Certification Request Form, a course description (syllabus, learning outcomes, topic list, prerequisites), a discussion of assessment plans (which have been approved by the Office of Undergraduate Studies), and discussion of planned instruction (pedagogy, general information on instructor qualifications for all who might teach the course, and course coordination plans to ensure consistency across sections). The required assessment plan describes the nature of the course assignments, examinations, and assessment strategies that faculty will use to assess and improve student achievement. Course certification requests are reviewed by the relevant college curriculum committee and dean, the relevant general education advisory panel, and the Board of General Studies. The board negotiates changes, if required, and makes a formal recommendation to the provost, who makes the final determination. Although the process seems complex, it guarantees that faculty, department chairs, administrators, and the Board of General Studies have a common understanding of how each course aligns with general education expectations for learning outcomes and embedded assessment.

Course Recertification

Courses, once approved, may drift from their focus. New faculty might be assigned to teach them, new department chairs may not be aware of the responsibility to oversee the department's contributions to the general education program, or faculty might revise courses and lose track of commitments they made during course certification. Most faculty know, through the student grapevine or other paths, how courses in their major are being taught; but the general education program generally is so spread throughout the institution that it is impossible for anyone to be aware of what is happening in every course.

Campuses might require annual summaries from departments offering general education courses, but this might degenerate into a checklist that is routinely ignored because of workload demands on faculty, department chairs, and general education committees. An alternative solution is periodic review and recertification of courses. The cycle may be regular, such as every four or five years; or the first recertification may be required in three years, with subsequent reviews less often. Committees generally examine a narrative summary that responds to specific questions, syllabi, exams, and assignments to verify that the course continues to meet general education criteria. They also might ask for samples of student work at varying levels of performance, such as sample A/B papers, C papers, and D/F papers to verify that student performance and grading criteria align with general education expectations.

Faculty must be aware of course recertification plans so they can save copies of needed documentation. The certification usually is of the course, not the instructor, so departments need to accumulate the appropriate array of documents from all course sections. This should not be an involved process, but a friendly reminder and verification that all is going well. If any problems are identified, they can generally be solved through negotiation. If serious problems emerge and negotiation fails, courses can be decertified, but normally this is a rare event.

Alignment Studies

A list of alignment questions were identified earlier in this chapter, and any of them could become the focus on an assessment study examining alignment in the general education program. For example, a research team might analyze syllabi to verify that course learning outcomes are specified and are consistent with general education expectations, or they might analyze transcripts to see if students take general education courses in the required order or to see if new prerequisites should be created. Student surveys, such as the National Survey of Student Engagement (NSSE; see http://www.indiana.edu/~nsse), might be used to examine student opinions about and experiences in general education courses. Campus records could be examined to see the range of faculty ranks among general education instructors. Focus groups could be used to investigate faculty perceptions of recognition and reward systems, the use of techniques to reach students who learn in different ways, or the degree of consensus on an overriding general education mission or philosophy. Surveys or interviews of campus professionals could identify how often student affairs and academic affairs representatives collaborate to support the general education program, and they also could examine perceptions of their effectiveness and support needs.

These alignment studies allow us to understand what is happening in our general education program, and results can be just as informative and transformative as assessing student learning. For example, uncovering curriculum alignment gaps can lead to curriculum improvements *before* student learning assessment data are collected. Discovering unreasonable course sequences can lead to a formalization of prerequisites within the program, and finding a lack of collaboration between academic and student affairs professionals can lead to finding forums for needed discussion.

Subsequent chapters in this book describe how to design and implement an assessment plan to examine the extent of student mastery of general education learning outcomes, but many of these same strategies could be used to focus attention on alignment. Systematic alignment of courses, pedagogy, grading, and institutional support should provide students the learning environment they need to succeed.

CHAPTER 4

The Assessment Plan

Developing an assessment plan for your general education program should save more time than it takes to create. It helps you and your colleagues stay focused and avoid costly mistakes, and it should lead to more effective assessment. As the plan develops, keep asking about the three criteria introduced in Chapter 1. Is the plan meaningful? Is it manageable? Is it sustainable? If any of the answers is negative, design a better plan.

Before you begin your assessment plan you should have your learning goals and outcomes articulated, and you should have considered the alignment of the outcomes with the curriculum, courses, and institution. Alignment studies and the refinement of course certification processes may be ongoing as you are developing and implementing the assessment plan, and all these processes should be considered holistically because they are interrelated. Changes in one might necessitate changes in another.

The purpose of assessment is to improve the general education program by identifying what is working well and what requires improvement. Assessment should have *impact*. It is not filling rooms full of data, and doing so is not assessment unless we reflect on the findings and make changes when they are required. It is better to do a series of small studies well than to try to do everything at once. The latter approach is more likely to exhaust and overwhelm us than to result in meaningful refinement of the program. The codirector and senior scholar at the Policy Center on the First Year of College, Swing (2004a), states this well:

> In a nutshell, high-quality assessment always leads to one of two outcomes: It either creates improvement or confirms existing practice. Notice what was not mentioned. Production of reams of "interesting data" or the identification of problems outside of institutional control (e.g., poverty, changes in demographics) are not hallmarks of effective

assessment. Stated in other words, assessment is not an end in itself but always a means to one of two desirable ends: (a) improvement of individual or program performance or (b) confirmation of existing practice. The measure of high-quality assessment, then, is best established by how, or if, the assessment results are used. It is not enough simply to fill book shelves with unread reports and undigested data even if these were produced by methodologically perfect assessment practices. (pp. xiii–xxvi)

Assessment is not designed just to reveal problems; it can help us identify what is working well. Unless there is reason to be concerned, I begin each assessment project with the assumption that things are going well and use a "trust, but verify" empirical approach—an honest look at evidence to confirm existing practice or to identify and implement changes to improve learning. General education programs and the associated cocurricular environment are complex systems, and virtually any complex system has aspects that are running well and flaws that can be identified and corrected. Assessment is the formal infrastructure for taking an honest look at the impact of the general education program, and, done well, it should lead to a series of incremental improvements to student learning.

Selecting Assessment Techniques

As will be discussed in the next two chapters, a variety of assessment techniques are commonly used, such as standardized or locally developed exams, embedded assignments, portfolios, and surveys. Assessment planning requires an awareness of the array of strategies, as well as their potential strengths and limitations. Criteria for selecting specific techniques include *validity, reliability,* having *actionable results,* efficiency, cost-effectiveness, and *engagement* of respondents and those who should act on results.

Validity

A measurement is *valid* if scores reflect what we are trying to measure. For example, if we are assessing how well students can write, a quick writing sample may not be sufficient because students are not given the opportunity to reflect on, develop, and edit their drafts. Results would not be valid because they are unlikely to show the extent of students' writing skills. On the other hand, if the purpose of the assessment was to see how well students can write quick drafts, the process could result in valid findings. Well-written outcomes allow us to know the type of learning we want to assess. Validity concerns how well assessments align with learning outcomes, and the most important kind of validity for assessment is *formative validity*—how well an assessment procedure provides information that is useful for improving what is being assessed.

Procedures may be valid for one purpose, but not another. For example, the Major Field Assessment Tests (Educational Testing Service [ETS], 2005; see http://www.ets.org/hea/mft) may be useful for assessing graduating seniors' understanding of concepts in their major, but these tests would not be valid for assessing general education outcomes.

Reliability

Reliability is conceptualized in many ways, but in general deals with score stability and precision. Reliable data are stable across time, across versions of the measurement instrument, within the measurement instrument, and across raters (Allen & Yen, 2002). *Test-retest reliability* involves checking how stable scores are across time. If individuals receive almost identical results each time they are assessed, scores have high test-retest reliability. On the other hand, if each time we test individuals we get very different results, the measurement lacks test-retest reliability.

Sometimes we develop multiple versions of an assessment instrument. For example, if a test is given to students in multiple sections of a course, we may develop several test versions because we are concerned that students in earlier sections will share information with students in later sections. *Parallel or alternate forms reliability* is high if scores on two versions of a test correlate highly, but low if they do not. This type of reliability asks if the various versions of the test yield equivalent results.

An alternative way to approach reliability is by asking how internally consistent a measurement tool is. For example, do the odd- and even-numbered items on a test generate scores that correlate highly with each other? The most common indicator of internal-consistency reliability is *coefficient alpha*, based on intercorrelations of all items with each other. *Internal consistency* is a reasonable approach to reliability if we are measuring a relatively homogeneous characteristic, but is less important if we are measuring something that is multidimensional. If we are measuring complex learning outcomes, parts of a test might reflect different dimensions and would not necessarily correlate highly.

Assessment often requires subjective judgments of students' work, and we want to be sure that these judgments are reliable. We investigate *interrater reliability* by comparing results from different raters. If ratings are consistent, we are comfortable with our findings, but if ratings are inconsistent, we cannot trust the results and must refine the data collection procedures.

Reliability and validity should not be confused. Reliability deals with the stability of results; validity deals with the meaningfulness of results. A very reliable assessment generates findings that are stable and precise, but these scores might be precisely wrong if the measurement lacks validity. In this case the findings, although reliable, do not reflect the outcome you are trying to assess. For example, a set of fact-based, multiple-choice questions may yield very reliable scores, but they may not produce a valid measure of deeper levels of understanding.

Actionable Results

Assessment studies are diagnostic, and, if results are disappointing, a more precise diagnosis helps us understand what needs to be fixed. For example, a global indicator that students' critical thinking skills are weak might not help us pinpoint reasonable changes, but if we discover that students are competent using some critical thinking skills, but not others, we can more easily address these deficiencies. These more detailed findings are *actionable* because we can determine what actions are required if results do not meet our expectations.

Efficiency and Cost-Effectiveness

Faculty often are invited to review student work in assessment studies, and time is one of the most important commodities in faculty lives. Assessment planners should respect faculty time and ensure that it is not wasted. If faculty will be expected to spend considerable time on a general education assessment project, they should find ways to "stop doing something else" (Suskie, 2004, p. 29), such as reducing their participation in other campus committees. Cost-effectiveness is important, too. No campus has unlimited resources, and funds should not be wasted on assessment studies that could be done in reasonable, less costly ways. A lot of waste could be prevented if assessment planners routinely pilot-test and refine procedures before moving into full-scale studies. In addition, campuses might begin with an audit of the information they already have. Institutional research offices and registrars often have an array of standardized test scores and re-

tention data that could be used i
reason to collect the same informatio

Engaging Procedures

When we ask students to demonstrate the exte
to be sure that they take the assignment seriously
this and find disappointing results, we are left with a
dents do poorly because they could not do the task or b
extend the effort? Similarly, if we interview or conduct fo
student volunteers or others, we want thoughtful, honest ansv
sential that the respondents in our assessment studies engag
process. In my experience, treating potential respondents with respe
providing information about the importance of the study usually allows
to avoid potential problems of respondent apathy.

Another group should be engaged in the assessment process, but at the receiving end of what was learned. Faculty and others who might be asked to make changes based on assessment findings should be interested in assessment results, and they should be flexible and creative when identifying solutions to problems. If they don't care about results, the assessment study might be wasted. It is important that assessment planners take into account those who will be affected by findings. One way to consider them is by thinking about possible results and asking colleagues what they would do if these were the findings. If their answers are "not much," regardless of results, then design a better study, perhaps by inviting your colleagues to contribute ideas that they really care about.

Three Levels for General Education Assessment

Campuses typically use one or more of three basic approaches to assessing the general education program. They focus on assessment at the course, program, or institutional level. *Course-level assessment* ascertains how well students have mastered learning outcomes associated with specific general education courses. Faculty who staff these courses routinely assess course outcomes, refine their courses based on results, and report findings and changes to an oversight committee. Assuming course outcomes are well aligned with program outcomes, results can be generalized to the program, as a whole.

general education
whole. For exam-
humanities learn-
student products
courses. The focus

nent in advanced
ell learning in the
ighout the institu-
(2004) complete a
irses in the major,
ave mastered gen-
eck that students
ped the marks of a

For assessment purposes, and there is no
... twice.

t of their learning, we want
If we cannot be sure of
uestion. Did the stu-
cause they didn't
s groups with
ers. It is es-
e in the
r and
us

125

Course-Level Assessment Example: San José State University

San José State University has a well-developed system for assessing the general education program at the course level, and this is a major undertaking. This campus has more than 200 general education courses that meet 18 general education requirements, and more than 500 general education course sections are scheduled each semester. Faculty who teach sections of the same general education course collaborate to assess student mastery of general education outcomes within their courses. In addition, they document other course certification requirements, such as using active learning techniques and helping students develop communication and critical thinking skills (Anagnos, Dorosz, & Wheeler, 2002). An example of their course certification requirements for the Self, Society, & Equality in the U.S. requirement is provided in Chapter 3.

Designated course coordinators submit a "Coordinator Summary" that:

- Summarizes the number of course sections that were offered and assessed

- Responds to any concerns expressed during the course certification review

- Lists the number of students who took the course and the number of students who achieved each learning outcome

- Briefly summarizes the kinds of activities that helped students develop each outcome

- Highlights results that demonstrate that students have exceeded expectations

- Highlights results that demonstrate that students have not met expectations

- Describes course modifications based on assessment findings

- Summarizes what has been learned about effective ways to meet additional course requirements (e.g., providing effective feedback to develop writing skills)

- Describes the course coordination process, including faculty discussion of assessment findings

- Describes changes in the assessment plan for subsequent offerings of the course

A Coordinator Summary for the Self, Society, & Equality in the U.S. requirement is available online (David, 2001). This assessment approach results in continuing refinement of each general education course as well as ongoing collaboration among faculty who teach it.

Program-Level Assessment Example: California State Polytechnic University–Pomona

California State Polytechnic University–Pomona's (2003) Interdisciplinary General Education (IGE) Program is an impressive example of program-level assessment. Pomona students have the option of participating in the IGE Program to meet most of their lower division humanities and social sciences general education requirements. Students complete this innovative program in cohorts, taking one course each quarter starting in their freshman year; the eighth and last course is a capstone course in which students create integrative projects that are expressed in a 15-page paper and through an alternative medium, such as a poster or work of art. About six to eight sections of each required course are offered each quarter, and about 80–100 students complete the program each year.

Tenured and tenure-track faculty, as well as adjunct faculty, offer IGE courses, and many have participated in the program for years. Around 12 faculty offer IGE courses each year, and they share responsibility for assessing the program. IGE faculty, including adjunct faculty, meet regularly to discuss the program and its assessment; each quarter the program hosts a "torch passing" in which faculty who have just taught the students "pass" them into the hands of the next instructors by sharing what they have done and what they have learned through the ongoing assessment program.

Alignment of the IGE program is planned through an alignment matrix and is made explicit during the torch passing. In addition, many of the courses are team taught, and involved faculty carefully orchestrate their courses to meet program and course outcomes. Throughout the year faculty meet to discuss how their courses help students build the skills necessary for the capstone project, including attention to fostering the required information competence, critical thinking, and communication skills. IGE faculty also meet for an annual retreat each June to review progress and establish goals for the next academic year.

The IGE program is assessed in multiple ways, including both direct and indirect assessment. Students accumulate a portfolio of their work as they proceed through the program, and they evaluate their own learning each quarter. Faculty survey current students as well as alumni, and they conduct student interviews at the end of the first year, the middle of the second year, and the end of the program. Faculty obtain their major direct evidence by assessing the portfolios and capstone projects, and an outside evaluator is periodically invited to visit courses and review student work.

IGE faculty consider themselves part of an ongoing learning community, and they routinely review assessment results and reflect on their implications. Over the years they have refined the capstone assignment, revised the curriculum and learning outcomes, developed effective relationships with staff at the campus library and student affairs offices, and monitored the impact of their changes on student learning (N. P. Fernandez, personal communication, July 1, 2005).

Institution-Level Assessment Example: Truman State University

Truman State University assesses its general education program at the institutional level by embedding portfolio requirements in capstone courses taken in the majors. In 2003 approximately 83% of the graduating class submitted portfolios, and they reported spending about four or five hours developing them. Faculty who teach capstone courses assign and collect the portfolios, and some departments augment the assignment to collect additional data for assessing majors. The assignment may change slightly from year to year, but during the 2002–2003 academic year, faculty required students to submit work demonstrating critical thinking, interdisciplinary thinking, historical analysis, scientific reasoning, and aesthetic analysis, as well as work that the student felt was most personally satisfying; a reflection on their growth while at Truman State; and anything the student would like to share about their university experience (Truman State University, 2005a).

Students receive explicit instructions for each segment of the portfolio. For example, the Spring 2005 assignment for Critical Thinking and Writing asks students to submit the best example of their writing that demonstrates critical thinking:

> Please include an example of your best writing that demonstrates your critical thinking skills. As stated in Truman's LSP [Liberal Arts and Sciences Program] outcomes, good writing is a reflection of good thinking. Thus, as a result of an intellectual process that communicates meaning to a reader, good writing integrates ideas through analysis, evaluation, and synthesis of ideas and concepts. Good writing also exhibits skill in language usage and clarity of expression through good organization. (Truman State University, 2005c, p. 1)

Students identify the course from which the writing sample was drawn and their academic status when taking the course (freshman, sophomore, etc.). They specify if the writing was individual or collaborative, describe the assignment that elicited the paper, reflect on the kinds of thinking demonstrated in the writing sample, and comment on their growth in critical thinking. Faculty assess the writing samples by focusing on critical thinking, organization, style, and mechanics (Truman State University, 2005c).

Although paper portfolios were required originally, Truman State University began requiring electronic portfolios in 2005. Students go to the portfolio web site (http://assessment.truman.edu/components/Portfolio) for instructions, and they submit portfolios on disks, CDs, or other media. The assessment coordinator suggests that faculty review instructions in class and encourage students to work on different sections of the portfolio every two weeks, so that work is not done at the last minute. Students in courses requiring the portfolio must complete their portfolios before graduation, and this is certified during the graduation check process (Truman State University, 2005b).

Many portfolios are collected each year. For example, the portfolio director received nearly 1,000 portfolios in 2003–2004, and they were reviewed by 45 faculty and two staff members over a three-week period. Most faculty spent one week, working daily from around 8:00AM–4:30PM, and approximately 20 readers worked each week. Readers apply standards specified in rubrics to classify products into one of four categories: No Evidence, Weak Competence, Competence, and Strong Competence (Truman State University, 2004).

Results are reported at the department, division, and university level, although only division and university results are made public in the annual *Assessment Almanac*, as well as at various events, such as planning workshops and faculty development luncheons (Truman State University, 2005a). The *Assessment Almanacs* are available online (http://assessment .truman.edu/almanac/), allowing anyone to see the rubrics, the detailed analyses of each year's data, and qualitative analyses of the students' feedback about their learning and the campus.

Combining the Three Approaches

Campuses may assess at one or all levels. For example, faculty may use course-level assessment to assess each course in the college writing sequence to verify that it results in the learning required for entry into the subsequent course. Faculty may use program-level assessment to examine science outcomes by analyzing lab reports drawn from a variety of general education science courses, or a four-year institution may examine the impact of the general education science curriculum by collecting student work in upper division, general education science courses. In addition, some outcomes may be assessed at the institution level. For example, information literacy may be introduced in general education courses, but the campus might expect further development within the majors. In this case, the combined impact of all courses might be assessed by examining student products in advanced courses.

Comparison of the Three Approaches

Course-level assessment puts control in the hands of those most affected by the assessment—the faculty who staff each general education course— and it has strong potential for improving the program because every general education course is affected. Because assessment planning is done by the faculty who execute the assessment, studies are likely to be time- and cost-efficient. Most of San José State University's general education courses are offered by multiple faculty, and they are required to share ideas for promoting student learning. These ongoing conversations about teaching and learning are a best practice in assessment.

The campus, though, has the responsibility to ensure that the assessment is of reasonable quality. For example, San José State University leaders developed detailed expectations for each course, review course assessment plans during the course certification process, and monitor course coordinator reports. Implementing and managing course-level assessment programs takes considerable effort. It is likely that the assessment varies in quality across courses, and it may be difficult for the leadership team to monitor every course in sufficient detail to identify and correct weak assessment efforts. Studies for individual courses may lack reliability and validity, may not result in actionable findings, and may not be taken seriously by all faculty involved. This approach might be accused of focusing on the trees, rather than the forest. Unless leaders are proactive, broad campus conversations about general education program outcomes may not occur, connections between courses may not be refined, and student affairs professionals may not become involved. San José State requires considerable detail in the course coordinator's report, and reviewing these reports from hundreds of courses takes considerable time. Campuses might be tempted to reduce the course reports to very brief summaries or checklists, and this might undermine some of the strengths of this approach.

Program-level assessment focuses attention on the program, as a whole. Assessments probably are more likely to identify needs to improve connections between courses, and attention can focus on broader program-level outcomes, not just course-level outcomes. Student affairs professionals may be more likely to participate in the process, and multi-disciplinary conversations about assessment results are more likely to occur. For example, general education humanities faculty in multiple disciplines may review student work together and discuss effective pedagogy for meeting program-level expectations. If the assessment plan cycles through the program learning outcomes over a few years, fewer people do assessment each year, reducing the burden on faculty who staff general education courses. In addition, if fewer studies are conducted each year, more attention could be given to their quality, so studies may generate more uniformly valid and reliable results. Compared to the course-level approach, though, assessment results may be less actionable because they are one step removed from individual courses so closing the loop may be more difficult. Strong leadership is required to collect assessment data, coordinate its assessment, and promote conversations that lead to improvement.

Institution-level assessment probably is most likely to result in campus-wide, multi-disciplinary conversations about general education learning outcomes. Effective assessment at this level requires central coordination and the cooperation of professionals from throughout the campus. Like program-level assessment, fewer studies may be done, and they may be more uniformly valid and reliable than when course-level assessment is used. Because so many factors might affect results, including the effect of transfer students who have completed general education courses elsewhere, closing the loop may be more difficult, but if faculty and staff development personnel and professionals work together, significant campus improvements can occur.

Developing the Assessment Plan

The assessment plan itself can be relatively simple. It should answer the basic journalist's questions: Who? What? When? Where? How? The major elements of an assessment plan describe:

- How each outcome will be assessed

- Who will collect and analyze the data

- Where and how data will be collected

- When and how often each outcome will be assessed

- Who will reflect on the results and close the loop, when needed, by implementing appropriate changes

- How results and implications will be documented

It is not necessary to assess every outcome every year. You can cycle through the outcomes to keep the assessment manageable, with plans to assess each outcome periodically, such as every fourth year. In addition, plans should be flexible. For example, if the results in year one resulted in significant changes, then it might make sense to do a follow-up study in year three to verify that the changes have had the desired effect.

Multiple Measures

No assessment technique is perfect, but if multiple approaches to examining an outcome lead to the same conclusion, we have more confidence in that conclusion. If results are consistent across multiple measures, they *triangulate*. Inconsistent results are ambiguous because we cannot be sure which conclusion is accurate, although we generally have more confidence in conclusions from direct assessment studies than from indirect assessment studies. We should try to use multiple measures when we assess an outcome so we can check for triangulation. For example, we could assess students' understanding of the scientific method by reviewing research proposals, laboratory reports, and responses to exam questions focusing on this topic.

One relatively simple way to get multiple results is to supplement direct assessment with indirect assessment. For example, you might investigate critical thinking by examining the quality of students' arguments in a debate and their ability to deal effectively with complex case studies (direct assessment); you could also conduct a survey, interview, or focus group to obtain students' opinions about their own ability to think critically and their perceptions about how they learned these skills (indirect assessment). In general, evidence from direct assessment studies is more convincing because perceptions can be wrong, but if both approaches lead to the same conclusion, we can respond with more assurance. In addition, the indirect assessment data might provide information that will be useful if we are disappointed in the direct assessment results, such as ideas for course activities and assignments that students believe help them learn about critical thinking. Another nice thing about collecting both direct and indirect data is that discrepancies can be important. For example, if direct evidence suggests serious critical thinking problems and self-reports suggest that students believe they have excellent critical thinking skills, faculty have two problems to solve. They have to help students make more realistic self-appraisals, and they have to help students expand their critical thinking skills.

Sample Size

A geologist does not have to study every rock formation, and a developmental psychologist does not have to study every child. Both researchers draw samples when they do research, and they generalize from the samples to the populations from which the samples are drawn. We can use the same strategy when doing assessment. We can examine a sample of students chosen to *represent* the population. Representativeness is important because we want to avoid biased findings. For example, we should not just sample honor students or students who need developmental assistance, unless the population of interest is one of these subsets of students. A random sample might be drawn, but this often is difficult. However, if all students are required to take a course and if there is no reason to expect biased samples if we examine students in several sections of that course, we can sample classes of students. This *cluster sampling* should result in a representative sample. It is best to sample from more than one instructor because we want to generalize to all students, not just those in a particular teacher's section; and we want to be sure that we're focusing on the program, not an individual faculty member.

How many students should be in the sample? The answer depends on the needed measurement precision and the variability among students. Assessment often comes down to two questions: What proportion of students meets our criteria, and is that proportion acceptable? If the proportion is acceptable, we have confirmed present practice, but if it is not, we have identified an issue that requires further attention.

If you like thinking statistically, you will enjoy the discussion in the next three paragraphs, but if not, you can scan through them and jump to the summary.

To think about sample size, consider the distribution of the number of successes you would observe if you took all possible samples of the same size from a population (statisticians call this a *sampling* distribution). For example, if 80% of students do meet the criteria for the learning outcome being assessed, and we take a sample of size 25, the mean of the sampling distribution is 20 (80% of 25). That is, on average, we expect 80% of the 25 students to be successful if we take random samples. Of course, not all samples will have 20 successful students; there will be some variability (*sampling fluctuation*). The variance of the number of successes for a dichotomous variable based on n subjects when the proportion of successes is p and the proportion of failures is q is npq. In the situation where n is 25, p is .80, and q is .20, the variance of the number of successes we would observe is 4.00, and the standard deviation, its square root, is 2.00. Estimating using a normal distribution, we would observe 20 successes +/- (2.00)(1.645) 90% of the time. This is the estimated middle 90% of the sampling distribution of the number of observed successes, and the 1.645 comes from a normal distribution table. (About 90% of scores are within

1.645 standard deviations of the mean in a normal distribution.) If we took all possible samples of size 25 from the population of students, then 90% of the time we would observe about 17 to 23 successes, leading to estimates of the percentage of successes ranging from about 68 to about 92. (Because our data are counts of the number of successes, I rounded to whole numbers.) Bring the sample size up to 50, and we would have a variance of 8.00 [(50)(.80)(.20)], a standard deviation of 2.82, and a 90% range from about 35 to about 45 successes [40 +/- (2.82)(1.645)], with estimates of the percentage of successes ranging from 70 to 90. Figure 4.1 shows the results of these calculations for a number of different situations, including the two just discussed. The last column in Figure 4.1 is the range of expected proportions—the difference between the two entries in the previous column.

What is the pattern in Figure 4.1, and what does it tell us about sample size? First, as shown in the last column, estimates of the percentage of successes are less variable when larger samples are used, regardless of the actual proportion of successes. Most of us know this intuitively. Estimates of statistics are more stable when we study larger samples. That is why we are more confident when generalizing from larger random samples. This does not mean, however, that assessment studies must examine huge samples. Notice that doubling sample sizes does not double the potential accuracy of the estimate. Even moderate sample sizes can be useful if all we need is an estimate of the percentage of students who meet our expectations. In addition, although we may state that we want at least 80% of our students to meet our criteria, most of us would not panic if we only found 78 or 79%, so exacting precision is not essential. Also notice that variability (npq) is highest when $p = .50$. That is, if half the students meet our criteria and half don't, sample estimates are the most variable. But, even in this case, moving to very large samples (e.g., 500 or 1,000 cases) does little to improve the accuracy of the estimate. If most of our students meet our criteria (e.g., $p = .95$), even small samples are sufficient to identify this, and the same is true if very few students (e.g., $p = .05$) meet our criteria because the variance of the sampling distribution (npq) is the same [$npq = nqp$].

Using the data summarized in Figure 4.1 and imagining that we require at least 75% of our students to meet our standards, we see that any of the summarized sample sizes would be reasonable if $p = .30$, .50, and .95 because they are unlikely to lead us to the wrong conclusion. When $p = .30$ and .50, none of the estimated percentages exceed 75%, and when $p = .95$, all of them

Figure 4.1

Analysis of Sampling Distributions

n	p	q	npq	Mean	90% range	Estimates of the population percentage	Range
15	.95	.05	.71	14.25	13–15	86–100	14
25	.95	.05	1.19	23.75	22–25	88–100	12
50	.95	.05	2.38	47.50	45–50	90–100	10
100	.95	.05	4.75	95.00	91–99	91–99	8
15	.80	.20	2.40	12.00	9–15	60–100	40
25	.80	.20	4.00	20.00	17–23	68–92	24
50	.80	.20	8.00	40.00	35–45	70–90	20
100	.80	.20	16.00	80.00	73–87	73–87	14
15	.60	.40	3.60	9.00	6–12	40–80	40
25	.60	.40	6.00	15.00	11–19	44–76	32
50	.60	.40	12.00	30.00	24–36	48–72	24
100	.60	.40	24.00	60.00	52–68	52–68	16
15	.50	.50	3.75	7.50	4–11	27–73	46
25	.50	.50	6.25	12.50	8–17	32–68	36
50	.50	.50	12.50	25.00	19–31	38–62	24
100	.50	.50	25.00	50.00	41–58	41–58	17
200	.50	.50	50.00	100.00	88–112	44–56	12
500	.50	.50	125.00	250.00	232–268	46–54	8
1000	.50	.50	250.00	500.00	474–526	47–53	6
15	.30	.70	3.15	4.50	1–7	7–46	39
25	.30	.70	5.25	7.50	4–11	16–44	28
50	.30	.70	10.50	15.00	10–20	20–40	20
100	.30	.70	21.00	30.00	22–38	22–38	16

do. When $p = .60$, we are likely to reach the correct conclusion when samples are over 25 students, and when $p = .80$, the odds against making an incorrect conclusion are very low if we use a sample of over 50 students. Overall, we need larger samples when the actual percentage of successes is near our criterion percentage, and smaller samples are sufficient when the actual percentage is quite different from our criterion percentage. This makes sense because we need greater precision to make fine distinctions.

In summary, if you are assessing one outcome and want to estimate the proportion of students who meet or exceed your standard:

- If almost all your students are doing well or poorly, small samples (e.g., 25 students) are sufficient to identify this result.

- Very large samples (over 100) are rarely needed. Keep the process manageable and sustainable by not doing more work than necessary. Adding more cases to your sample probably will not generate much more useful information.

- If you're looking for a rule of thumb, moderate samples (about 50 to 75 students) generally are sufficient for assessment work when assessing one outcome.

- Consider creating confidence-interval estimates of the population proportion, rather than point estimates (e.g., rather than estimating that the population proportion is 84, conclude with, say, 90% confidence that the percentage is between 77 and 89). This makes clear the degree of imprecision in your estimate and allows reviewers to make fully informed judgments concerning how well students are doing.

- It is more important that the sample be representative than that it be huge. If the sample is biased, even large samples may lead to inaccurate conclusions.

Of course, there are times when larger samples are reasonable. The above discussion concerned the case of making a dichotomous decision about a single outcome. We need larger samples if we want to be confident about multiple decisions. For example, if we want accurate estimates of the proportion of students who are at each level of a four-point analytic rubric, we should use larger samples. Survey researchers also generally use larger samples. The marginal cost is low, they want to see the full range of responses to open-ended questions, and they are examining a number of variables simultaneously. If data are extracted from student records, collecting data from larger samples or from the entire population may require no added expense, so it makes sense to use larger samples. We also should collect larger samples if measurement precision is important. For example, campus leaders might decide that they need to estimate the campus mean to within a fraction of a point. In this case, the campus might have to sample several hundred students.

We also need larger samples when we intend to disaggregate the data. For example, Truman State University summarizes findings for the university, each division, and each department, so a reasonable representative sample of students must be assessed for every department. You might want to examine results separately for other groups, such as older and younger students, athletes and non-athletes, native and transfer students, or students with different types of entrance exam scores. To do this, you must have a sufficient number of students representing each group so you can trust the estimates. This might require systematic oversampling of some groups because a random sample of all students may not include enough of some groups. For example, if international students are a small fraction of your general education students, you might have to collect their data in special ways. You might distribute surveys at a campus event that is particularly attractive to them. If surveys are mailed, you can send them to *purposeful* samples. For example, you might send surveys to random samples of 5% of some groups of students, but to 50% of groups that are less represented in the student population. Your campus is likely to have a sampling expert, perhaps in your institutional research office, and it is always wise to identify local talent and make use of their expertise.

Organizing the Plan

Much of the assessment plan can be organized into a matrix, with columns identifying the outcome (or sets of outcomes clustered together) and assessment details (e.g., how, when, who, how often?). For example, the plan might specify that:

- Writing Outcomes 1 and 3 will be assessed every third year starting in 2007–2008 by collecting student writing samples from at least five sections of courses meeting these outcomes and at least three senior capstone courses, as well as by asking students to respond to surveys in which they report their campus writing experiences and self-confidence as writers. An interdisciplinary committee will develop an appropriate rubric and analyze the writing samples, and the assessment center will develop and analyze the survey in consultation with the campus Writing Council. All results will be considered by the Writing Council, and they will make recommendations concerning changes.

- Social Science Outcomes 1, 2, and 4 will be assessed every fourth year starting in 2008–2009 by assessing student lab reports and by embedding relevant questions in an exam in upper-division general education social science courses. In addition, at least two focus groups will be conducted in upper-division social science courses to analyze student self-perceptions and obtain their feedback on the general education social science courses. An ad hoc committee of social science general education faculty will be appointed by social science department chairs. They will develop and score the test, and they will develop and apply a rubric to analyze the lab reports. Focus groups will be conducted by faculty development center staff, who will work in consultation with the ad hoc committee. The ad hoc committee will review all findings, share them at the social science chairs' meeting, and file a summary report with the General Education Assessment Committee with recommendations based on the results.

If you began with many goals and outcomes associated with general education requirements and clustered them, you can plan the assessment at the outcome, requirement, or cluster level. If you didn't form clusters, you could develop your plan at the requirement or outcome level, perhaps looking for opportunities to cluster similar outcomes in the same year. The main advantage of working at the requirement or cluster level is that assessment can be tied to periodic campus-wide conversations about each requirement or cluster, focusing faculty, staff, and administrators on a common issue.

The plan can have a mixture of strategies. For example, humanities faculty may prefer to work among themselves to examine outcomes associated with the humanities requirement, rather than join colleagues to assess outcomes at the cluster level. Usually general education assessment leaders face the problem of getting volunteers to participate in the assessment, so why not take advantage of their interest? The goal of the assessment plan is not necessarily to push everyone into a common mold, but to establish how and when outcomes will be assessed and to ensure assessment quality.

Assessment leaders may plan for the humanities faculty to work independently, but their assessment could be concurrent with others examining the cluster, allowing them to participate in campus-wide conversations about related outcomes.

Assessment plans might also include alignment studies. For example, the plan for assessing the science courses might include an analysis of syllabi, exams, and assignments to verify alignment with relevant outcomes. Periodic course recertification might be timed to correspond with alignment and assessment cycles, spreading this workload over a number of years.

Assessment Ethics

Although federal guidelines exempt data collected for the sole purpose of improving instructional programs from Institutional Review Board (IRB) review, faculty do not have a license to exploit students to obtain assessment data. Most agree that campuses should respect the usual guidelines for human-subjects research. Ethical concerns include:

- *Anonymity.* Results cannot be associated with individuals. For example, before assessing student essays, faculty can remove students' names from the products being assessed.

- *Confidentiality.* Respondents' names are known to the researcher, but they are not disclosed.

- *Privacy.* Respondents determine what personal information they will disclose.

- *Data security.* Data are stored in such a way that confidentiality is protected.

- *Informed consent.* Respondents agree to participate after they learn the purpose of the project, the expected use of the data, their rights not to participate and to withdraw from the study, and if their responses will be anonymous or confidential.

For example, Truman State University includes an informed consent form in their portfolio assignment. The 2005 form acknowledges that individual data will be safeguarded:

> Your portfolio will be read and evaluated by faculty members after spring graduation. One or more of the works you submit might be used in the future, without your name attached, as examples to help train faculty readers. Samples of student commentary, mostly from cover letters, are quoted anonymously in the portfolio written for Truman's *Assessment Almanac*. The data that is [sic] generated through portfolio readings is [sic] reported collectively, with no names attached. There are several other potential uses of items in your portfolio that we would employ only with your permission. Please read about these below and check the appropriate box for each of the specific purposes described below. (Truman State University, 2005d)

Students can decline or agree to let the campus post non-anonymous quotes to the portfolio web site, post or put in the library all or parts of the portfolio as a model for subsequent students with all identifying information removed, or post or put in the library all or parts of the portfolio with identifying information to serve as a model for subsequent students.

Campuses collecting embedded assessment data might include a general informed consent form with syllabi, allowing students the opportunity to decline participation in assessment studies. Informed consent is especially important if faculty might use any of the assessment data in research that is presented or published. (For a more thorough discussion of ethical principles relevant to assessment, see Allen, 2004.)

Characteristics of Effective General Education Assessment Programs

Most effective general education assessment programs have a number of characteristics in common. Effective programs engage the campus in conversations about important general education outcomes, and these conversations occur in multiple environments, such as within the general education assessment committee, between the committee and faculty who staff the program, among the faculty who staff the program, and within faculty and staff development programs. Findings may have implications for student affairs units, librarians, advisors, and those who organize the cocurricular environment or who support campus technology initiatives; representatives of these groups should be invited to participate. This focused attention should improve institutional support for general education outcomes and should create a more cohesive learning environment and increase learning. In addition, effective assessment should provide opportunities for faculty and others to contribute to the growing literature on teaching and learning. (See http://www.indiana.edu/~libsalc/SOTL/ for a list of journals on this topic.)

As you consider your own assessment plan, ask:

- Do you have a quality-assurance process to verify that assessment studies are conducted in a reasonable way?

- Do you focus on learning outcomes that faculty value?

- Do you generate valid, reliable, actionable results?

- Do you assess outcomes in multiple ways so you can check for triangulation?

- Do you use direct assessment and supplement these findings with indirect assessment?

- Is your plan efficient in the use of time and money?

- Does your plan engage those who provide data and respond to results?

- Does your plan have potential for refining a cohesive general education program with supportive links between courses and between courses and the cocurricular environment?

- Does your plan encourage communication about teaching and learning—among faculty, students, staff, and administrators?

- Do faculty and staff development professionals provide needed follow-up support?

- Is there a process for follow-up when assessment results have implications for funding or for developing a stronger campus infrastructure to support learning?

- Does your plan include documenting findings and the impact of each assessment study?

- Does your plan provide faculty and others opportunities to contribute to the scholarship of teaching and learning?

Assessing First-Year Experience Programs

A number of variables are commonly assessed when examining first-year experience programs. The major indicators of success are usually increases in student retention and graduation rates, as well as achievement of the learning outcomes associated with the program. Campuses sometimes also examine grade-point averages, student satisfaction, and student engagement. Examples of first-year experience learning outcomes were provided in Chapter 2.

Analyses of the effect of first-year experience courses on retention rates and grades generally involve comparing students who completed the course to historical data or, if the course is optional, to a control group of students who did not complete the course. The first approach is reasonable if the student body has not changed in important ways, but might not make sense if the student body makeup has changed. For example, the admission of more part-time students or returning adult learners may affect retention, as well as grades. A similar problem occurs when comparing students who did and did not take an optional first-year experience course. Positive results might suggest positive impact of the course, but it is possible that students who will persist and succeed are more likely to enroll in this course because they understand its value.

Some campuses use statistical controls to analyze the impact of the course or compare matched groups of students. For example:

- Northern Illinois University used an analysis of covariance with ACT composite scores as a covariate to examine the impact of the first-year seminar on grades, and they found significant, positive results (House, 2005).

- Northern Kentucky University compared retention rates for three types of students: regular admits, stipulated admits (those requiring developmental work in writing, reading, or mathematics), and restricted admits (those requiring developmental work in at least two areas or who have not completed college prerequisites). They found that their optional first-year seminar course had statistically significant impact on the graduation of stipulated and restricted students, but not on regular students, with stronger impact for stipulated students. For example, the seven-year graduation rates for regular, stipulated, and restricted students who took the seminar were 47%, 41%, and 21%, respectively, and 43%, 28%, and 14%, respectively, for those who didn't (Stieha, 2005). This information can help advisors identify students who are most likely to benefit from the course and can lead to course changes to better serve other students.

- Occidental College compared students who took two types of first-year seminars. While some students took stand-alone seminars, dorm residents took their seminars together as a "Living and Learning Community." To ensure that comparisons were not biased, students were matched on gender, race/ethnicity, and verbal SAT score. Comparisons revealed strengths for the community approach. Those students reported statistically higher academic and social engagement with peers in their seminar and a greater sense of belonging to a campus community. In addition, while the next semester's grades dropped for students in stand-alone sections, this did not occur for students taking the course with dormitory peers. (Nakamoto, 2005)

- Southeastern Louisiana University has offered "Freshman Seminar 101" as an elective course since 1997. To assess its impact on retention rates, students who took the course were matched with other students on race, gender, ACT composite score, and full- versus part-time status. Comparisons revealed that students who opted to take the seminar were more likely to return after one year, two years, and three years, and they earned more units each year. Results led campus leaders to expand the program. (Wood, 2005)

Correlation does not imply causation—just because two variables are correlated, we cannot conclude that one necessarily caused the other. For example, freshman grades might predict sophomore grades, but both are probably caused by study habits, motivation, and preparedness. Nonetheless, correlational data are easy to obtain and may provoke important discussions about promoting learning. For example, Southwest Missouri State University correlated grades with students' responses to a survey asking about variables such as course load, study hours, employment, and use of campus resources. They found many significant relationships. For example, grades were higher for students who completed at least 15 units per term; who reported studying at least two hours outside of class for every hour of class time; who worked less than 20 hours a week; who had zero or one absence from courses during each term; who slept seven to eight hours a night; who ate three good meals a day; who reported good experiences with academic advisors; who reported using campus computer labs, the library, and the writing center; who regularly participated in a religious center; who participated in campus activities and events; and who were committed to graduating within five years. Faculty used this information to refine their freshman seminar, "Introduction to University Life" (Casady, 2005).

One possible indicator of the success of an optional first-year seminar is increasing enrollments. For example, the University of Texas–El Paso has a three-unit freshman elective, "Seminar in Critical Inquiry." Enrollment increased from 1,265 students in 1999–2000 to 2,957 students in 2002–2003, representing 44% and 70% of first-time freshman enrollments, respectively. Perhaps this can be attributed to the seminar's success. An analysis of covariance controlling for ethnicity, gender, and SAT scores revealed that participation in the seminar was significantly related to GPA. For example, fall seminar students' average GPA exceeded other students' average GPA by .39 to .91 each year from 1999 to 2003. In addition, most students reported on surveys that "their academic survival skills, sense of comfort, campus participation, and use of essential student services improved as a result of the seminar" (Ward, 2005, p. 182). Word of mouth among faculty, advisors, staff, administrators, *and* students can contribute to an optional course's success.

CHAPTER 5

Direct Assessment of
General Education Learning Outcomes

Direct assessment involves an analysis of products or behaviors that demonstrate the extent of students' mastery of learning outcomes. A variety of strategies can be used, including the use of standardized tests, locally developed tests, embedded assignments and activities, and portfolios.

Faculty can use two approaches when directly assessing skills. They can ask students to respond to questions about those skills (e.g., Which of the following pull-down menus can be used to add page numbers to a Microsoft Word document?), or they can ask the students to demonstrate the skill, itself. The latter approach is called *performance assessment*—we evaluate how well students can perform a skill. For example, we can watch them conduct library searches, ask them to edit a document with built-in errors, observe them manipulating a laboratory apparatus, or assess their skill on the tennis court. On the assumption that the instructions are clear and students are motivated to do well, these performance assessments provide very convincing evidence concerning the extent of student learning. We become more concerned about validity when we move away from performance assessment. For example, a student may be able to explain all the movements a tennis player should make, but still be unable to compete in a tennis game.

Direct assessment often involves subjective analyses of complex products or behaviors, and inter-rater reliability is a concern. Carefully developed scoring guides or rubrics generally are used to ensure that all reviewers apply the same criteria and standards. Rubrics will be described at the end of this chapter, after a review of techniques commonly used for direct assessment. (For a comprehensive discussion of the assessment of online programs, see Comeaux, 2005.)

Standardized Tests

Professional test publishers, such as the Educational Testing Service (ETS) and the College Board, have developed a variety of instruments that might be useful when assessing general education programs:

- The Academic Profile (http://www.ets.org/hea/acpro) measures college-level critical thinking, mathematics, reading, and writing, and its items were designed to reflect content typically included in lower-division general education humanities, social sciences, and natural sciences curricula. Scores are organized into three proficiency levels ranging from basic knowledge (Level 1) to sophisticated understanding (Level 3). The standard form can be administered in two hours, and an abbreviated 40-minute version is also available.

- ACCUPLACER (http://www.collegeboard.com/highered/apr/accu/accu.html) is an online test designed to measure incoming students' competence in reading, writing, and mathematics. ACCUPLACER is a *computer-adaptive test.* Each student is given an array of test items selected to most efficiently determine his/her competency level. ACCUPLACER assesses writing samples with sophisticated software that "knows" when it can generate a score and when it should refer a test to a human for scoring. Research shows that its computer-generated scores correlate highly with scores generated by human readers, but sophisticated test takers can generate meaningless answers that can fool the software (Holst & Elliott, 2002).

- ASSET (http://www.act.org/catalog/asset.html) is designed to assess reading, writing, mathematics, and student information related to advising and placement decisions. It is locally scored, so results can be known immediately. Additional options include the measurement of clerical speed, mechanical reasoning, and space relations.

- The California Critical Thinking Skills Test (http://www.insightassessment.com/test-cctst.html) is a 32-item multiple-choice test designed to measure critical thinking based on a definition developed by the American Philosophical Association. Subscores include inductive and deductive reasoning, analysis, inference, and evaluation.

- The College Basic Academic Subjects Examination (College BASE or CBASE; http://arc.missouri.edu/collegebase) is a state-wide test in

Missouri designed to assess general education English, mathematics, science, and social studies. The test has 180 multiple-choice questions and an optional essay question. Eleven cluster scores reflect different segments, such as reading and literature, writing, general math, and algebra. The entire test is administered in about three hours, plus 40 minutes if the essay is used; but test segments can be given to different students if testing time is limited. The CBASE can be given to incoming freshmen to provide information on their entry-level knowledge and skills, and a second testing provides opportunities to demonstrate value-added learning (Humphreys, 2004).

- The Collegiate Assessment of Academic Proficiency (CAAP; http://www.act.org/caap/index.html) is used by hundreds of institutions to document student learning in general education programs and to certify student readiness for advancement and upper-division coursework. CAAP consists of six 40-minute tests, and institutions can decide which to use. The six tests assess reading comprehension (deriving meaning, interpretation), writing skills (usage, mechanics, and rhetorical skills), writing essays (ability to formulate and support an idea effectively), mathematics (algebra, geometry, and trigonometry), science (understanding, analyzing, and generalizing science topics), and critical thinking (analyzing, evaluating, and extending arguments). Five of these tests are in multiple-choice format, and one requires an essay. ACT provides reports on individual students and institution-wide summaries of results. (Lutz, 2004)

- The Collegiate Learning Assessment (CLA; http://www.cae.org/content/pro_collegiate.htm) is designed to be given to freshmen and seniors to assess value-added growth in student achievement, and it is offered to participants in a project sponsored by the RAND Corporation's Council for Aid to Education. Scores reflect critical thinking, analytic reasoning, and written communication skills; all questions are open-ended, rather than multiple-choice. Students respond to relatively complex tasks set in the context of the sciences, social sciences, and the arts and humanities, such as analyzing an interview transcript or newspaper article, and they write essays in which they state and defend a position. (Benjamin & Chun, 2003)

- COMPASS (http://www.act.org/compass) is an online test designed as a placement test in writing, reading, mathematics, and English as a second language. Like ACCUPLACER, this test uses artificial intelligence to provide immediate, electronic scoring of writing samples.

- The Watson-Glaser Critical Thinking Appraisal (http://harcourt assessment.com/haiweb/Cultures/en-US/Products/Product+Detail.htm ?CS_ProductID=015-8191-056&CS_Category=BrowseByProduct& CS_Catalog=TPC-USCatalog) was designed for use in career advising and personnel selection, and its 40 items require demonstration of critical thinking skills, such as defining a problem, recognizing assumptions, and developing and testing hypotheses.

Strengths and Limitations of Standardized Tests

Standardized tests are professionally developed, have established reliability and validity, and generally provide multiple comparison groups. For example, you could compare your students' results to national samples of community college freshmen or students in research universities. Depending on how many copies you buy, tests might cost from less than one dollar to more than $20 per student.

One of the biggest problems with the use of standardized tests is that scores may not align with your learning outcomes or curriculum. If this occurs, they provide little direct evidence for assessing the efficacy of your general education program. Most of these tests rely heavily on multiple-choice items, so they may not assess outcomes at the depth of processing stated in your outcomes. In addition, the scores themselves may be too broad to be actionable. Campuses might find a test occasionally useful to see how their students compare to students at other institutions, but the marginal gain from annual testing may be low. A last problem with the use of standardized tests is that campuses might find it difficult to motivate students and faculty to take them seriously. If low scores are found, faculty might wonder if student motivation was a problem, and faculty might not be willing to make major changes in courses or curricula based on the results of such findings.

Professional organizations have expressed some concerns about the use of standardized tests. For example, the Conference on College Composition and Communication's (1995) Committee on Assessment's policy statement on the assessment of writing skills criticized standardized exams, especially those that do not examine writing samples: "... *choosing a cor-rect response from a set of possible answers is not composing*" (p. 3). In addi-tion, they warn that reliance on such tests might mislead students into thinking that good writing is accomplished quickly and conforms to stylis-tic and grammatical rules without concern for meaning. They suggest that writing assessment funds are better spent compensating local readers than by purchasing published tests, and there are many fine scoring rubrics al-ready developed for this purpose.

The Association of American Colleges and Universities (2002) shares their concern about multiple-choice exams. "Multiple choice tests, in par-ticular, provide little evidence of the analytical power, creativity, resource-fulness, empathy, and abilities to apply knowledge and transfer skills from one environment to another that students will need for college success" (p. 13). Wiggins (1998) agrees: "Conventional test questions, be they from national tests or the teacher down the hall, do not replicate the kinds of challenges that adults face in the workplace, in civic affairs, or in their per-sonal lives" (p. 22). He argues that faculty should embed more authentic testing in courses to provide ongoing, formative feedback on students' aca-demic progress.

Advice for Using Standardized Tests

If you are considering using a standardized test, be sure to do your home-work. Critical reviews of tests are available in the *Mental Measurements Yearbook,* and its publisher, the Buros Institute, provides useful advice and an index of all test reviews on its web site (http://www.unl.edu/buros/). Get a *specimen set* from the publisher (a copy of the test and relevant man-uals that describe the test's development and use) and verify that the items and scores are reasonable for your purpose. A test may have proven validity for another purpose, but may not be valid for your assessment. For exam-ple, a placement test designed to assess incoming freshman skills may not include items at a level appropriate for students who have completed the general education curriculum.

If you decide to use a standardized test, be sure to motivate students to take the test seriously. Your campus might use an orientation to convince stu-dents of the importance of the test, provide individual feedback to students on their scores, embed the test as a graded component in a relevant course, host a lottery to award prizes to students who have exceeded a specified score, or provide an award to the class or student club with the highest average score.

Examples of Campus Use of Standardized Tests

Many campuses have integrated standardized tests into general education assessment programs, and here are a few examples:

- Boise State (Office of Institutional Assessment, Boise State University, 2002) administered the Academic Profile to approximately 1,000 students in three lower-division English courses. As expected, the majority of students were proficient in Level 1 tasks in reading and writing, but fewer than 30% of the students were proficient in Level 2 tasks, and only 2% were proficient at Level 3 tasks. They concluded that their students are stronger in reading than in writing, and they anticipate retesting some of the students later in their academic careers to verify curriculum impact.

- Eastern New Mexico University (2005a) gives the Academic Profile to all second semester sophomores. Previously, they used the CAAP, but switched in 1999 because leaders decided that they preferred the criterion-based interpretations provided for the Academic Profile.

- The University of Wisconsin–Green Bay (2004a) requires participation of all students who have completed between 54 and 72 units in the UW–Green Bay General Education Assessment Program. It begins with a one-hour orientation in which students learn the value of their participation, then students take the three-hour College BASE exam. All students receive individual feedback on their scores.

- In Spring 1996 the South Dakota Board of Regents (2004) began requiring state-wide testing, and after two years of pilot studies, they selected the CAAP as the required test and set minimum standards in writing, reading, science reasoning, and quantitative reasoning. Students and their advisors at Dakota State University receive individual score results, and the campus receives institution-wide results. Based on their findings, Dakota State faculty changed assignments in the reading development course (Dakota State University Assessment Office, 2000).

- Mercer University (2005) uses the CAAP Mathematics Test to assess the mathematics segment of their general education program. This test yields an overall score as well as subscores in basic algebra and college algebra/trigonometry. They administered the test to 268 students in

2003–2004, and they set as their criterion the standard that 70% of their students should exceed the national median for college students on all three scores. Although their students' mean exceeded the national mean on two of the three scores, they found that fewer than 70% met their standard. Campus leaders decided to reconsider their criterion, perhaps specifying different standards for students in different majors.

Locally Developed Tests

Rather than purchase a standardized test, faculty might decide to develop their own test. Although this requires time, they can construct tests that align precisely with campus general education outcomes. Because such tests can be hand-scored or observed by faculty, they can include authentic assessment, performance assessment, and questions that reveal depth of understanding; they can also be conducted as oral competence interviews.

Faculty should create a *test blueprint* before writing the questions by carefully planning what the test is supposed to measure (Suskie, 2004). They should determine the knowledge, skills, or values that will be addressed, their relative priority on the exam, and the appropriate depth of understanding. Well-developed learning outcomes help test developers focus precisely on what faculty want students to learn. Test developers should verify that exam questions align with the learning outcomes being assessed, and they should consider the curriculum that students have experienced. The test might be invalid if students have not been given opportunities to practice and develop the knowledge, skills, and values that the test is measuring, or, alternatively, low scores might indicate problems with curriculum alignment.

A number of item formats commonly are used in paper-and-pencil tests, including completion, matching, multiple-choice, and true-false questions. These objective questions generally have right and wrong answers, and they usually require either recall or recognition. For example, students must *recognize* the correct alternative in a multiple-choice question or *recall* a term for a completion (fill-in-the-blank) question. Creating objective questions that assess deeper levels of understanding requires considerable skill, and most locally developed objective tests assess surface-level learning.

Essay questions can provide authentic assessment of higher levels of learning. For example, faculty might assess ethical decision-making by asking students to resolve a campus controversy, they might assess quantitative reasoning by asking students to interpret some graphs and statistical reports, or they might ask students to analyze case studies to demonstrate their multicultural understanding or their ability to apply scientific reasoning. Faculty also could include performance testing, such as asking students to edit a computer document, create a spreadsheet, or translate a passage.

Competence interviews (oral exams) also could be used to assess general education learning outcomes. Usually interviewers work in pairs or small teams and use prescribed scripts and scoring guides. One strength of this approach is that interviewers can ask questions to determine the depth of students' thinking. When reading essays, faculty must make judgments about students' levels of understanding based on limited information, but when conducting oral exams, they can test hypotheses concerning students' skills by probing for more information.

Calder and Carlson (2004) recommend the use of *think alouds* to assess deep understanding. They argue that traditional written exams and competence interviews tend to overestimate the learning of verbally fluent students and underestimate the learning of less fluent students, but think alouds allow us to understand the sophistication of our students' thinking as they apply what they've learned. Faculty train students to verbalize their thoughts, then ask them to think aloud as they do tasks.

Calder and Carlson (2004) used think alouds in a freshman history course that was recently revised to focus on big issues and critical thinking, rather than historical facts. Students in an earlier section of this course completed eight identical assignments, and faculty analysis of their work showed little growth in the quality of the products across the semester. Both faculty and students, though, believed that students had learned a great deal in this course. Calder and Carlson recruited a dozen students in a new section of this course and paid them $10/hour to think aloud as they completed the first and last of the eight assignments. Using a five-point scale (ranging from high school–level to professional-level historical thinking), researchers assessed six types of thinking in the think-aloud transcripts. Results demonstrated increases in students' ability to think historically, that reading skills were a serious barrier to course mastery among students who did not do well, and that some C students actually had significant growth in their thinking skills, but were not able to express this learning in writing.

Calder and Carlson concluded that "the real roadblocks to learning histori-cal thinking, we discovered, are poor reading comprehension and prose writing" (p. 37).

The use of locally developed tests requires a test-taking context. Tests might be embedded in courses, or students may be required to take tests on designated assessment days. If students will not be graded, problems con-cerning motivation could emerge, just as they did with standardized exams.

Strengths and Limitations of Locally Developed Tests

Locally developed tests can be mixtures of objective and essay questions, and they can require performances or oral responses, allowing faculty to explore a wide variety of learning outcomes. Questions can be aligned with campus curricula, ensuring that students have had relevant learning oppor-tunities, and well-chosen questions can provide authentic assessment of higher-order learning outcomes. Competence interviews offer faculty the opportunity to probe for the breadth and depth of students' knowledge, and faculty also can use them to assess oral communication skills, critical thinking, and problem-solving. If students take exams as graded compo-nents of courses, they are motivated to demonstrate the extent of their learning, and faculty create the exams so they are likely to be interested in results and willing to act on them. Well-written tests should align well with the outcomes and the curriculum so they should have strong validity.

Unlike standardized tests, most locally developed exams have un-known reliability and validity, and they lack *norm groups* for comparison. In addition, they are not usually machine-scored, so faculty time is re-quired to analyze results. Developing a quality exam and scoring guide takes time, but this time is well spent because it helps faculty agree on how to operationalize their learning outcomes. Competence interviews require careful development of the *interview protocol* and interviewer training, and faculty must be careful or they will intimidate students, undermining stu-dents' ability to show the extent of their learning.

Campuses with similar missions could agree to share a common locally developed exam, allowing campuses to develop reasonable comparison groups for interpreting scores, but for most assessments, criterion-referenced interpretations are more important. The question usually is: "Did students meet our criteria?" rather than "How did our students do compared to students elsewhere?" The value of *benchmarked* results is that they allow faculty to verify that their standards and student work also meet criteria established at other institutions.

Advice for Using Locally Developed Tests

Although it is tempting to rely only on objective test items, locally developed exams may more clearly target learning outcomes when students are required to develop more complex answers. If outcomes focus on skills or the ability to apply learning, faculty should consider asking students to respond to case studies or other authentic tasks. Faculty should also seriously consider using performance exams to generate assessment results with obvious validity.

As with any assessment technique, it is wise to pilot-test exams and scoring guides before the assessment project is fully implemented. For example, faculty may invite a few students to think out loud as they respond to exam questions. This allows faculty to verify that items unambiguously lead students in the appropriate direction. If insufficiently tied to the outcome being assessed, the assessment is likely to be unproductive. Faculty might consider drafting possible responses to open-ended questions. This allows them to check for alignment between exam questions and what faculty want students to do and helps them clarify how data will be interpreted.

Examples of Campus Use of Locally Developed Tests

Faculty routinely write tests in their own courses, so it is not surprising that they create tests to assess general education outcomes. Here are a few examples:

- Faculty at Kansas State University conduct General Education Senior Interviews to assess general education outcomes. Teams of faculty work together during three weeks of interviews, and each interview is scheduled for 45 to 50 minutes. Students are randomly selected, and they receive $25 for their participation. They are asked to consider their response to a broad question as they prepare for the interview: "Please discuss a topic that you find personally interesting or important and that is not related to your major. Identify two that you would like to discuss. Although usually there is only time to talk about one topic, you can discuss the second if time allows" (IDEA Center, 1998, p. 8). Faculty follow a structured interview protocol and ask clarifying questions to allow them to assess responses using 13 rating scales, such as how well students communicate and demonstrate critical thinking skills (IDEA Center). About 120 graduating seniors are interviewed each year (Kuh, Kinzie, Schuh, & Whitt, 2005).

- Mesa Community College assesses general education areas using locally developed tests, and they compare results for incoming freshmen to results for students completing general education requirements. Each spring they host an assessment week during which they invite students in selected courses to take an exam during one class period. For example, in 2005 more than 3,000 students in 173 course sections completed exams. The Office of Research and Planning analyzes results and publishes a report each fall. (Mesa Community College Office of Research and Planning, 2005)

- Students at Old Dominion University (State Council of Higher Education for Virginia, 2002) must pass the Exit Examination of Writing Proficiency before they graduate. A passing score indicates that their essay is well written and demonstrates critical thinking about a complex topic. Students must receive at least a rating of "satisfactory" on each of five scales. Papers must have a clearly stated objective, supporting evidence, effective sentence structure and word choice, logical organization, and "reasonable freedom from mechanical errors" (Standards of the Competency section). Because passing is a graduation requirement, this test guarantees that all graduates demonstrate effective writing and critical thinking. During the 2001 testing, 94% of students passed the exam, and the others must retake the exam before they can graduate.

- Faculty at the University of Pennsylvania (2002) developed a 24-item science literacy test that emphasizes university-level scientific concepts and scientific reasoning, and they refined it based on pilot-test data. In addition, they decided to add additional items to assess attitudes toward science and students' ability to understand the nature of science.

- Faculty at the University of Virginia (State Council of Higher Education for Virginia, 2002) developed a performance exam for the use of technology (e.g., setting up a personal computer, using a word processor, searching the Internet, setting up a database). Students take the test in a computer lab, and scoring is done by trained graduate students who monitor individual students' work.

- The Quantitative Assessment Committee at the University of Wisconsin–Madison designs tests for instructors to use as pre-tests in their courses to verify that students have assumed mathematical skills. Graduate students score the tests within a week so that faculty *and* students learn about discrepancies between faculty expectations and student skills. Mathematics faculty use feedback from these tests to refine general education mathematics courses. (Alvarez-Adem & Robbin, 2003)

Embedded Assessment

The assessment of general education programs frequently relies on embedded assessment, and entire assessment programs, such as the course-embedded model at San José State University, rely on this technique for their direct assessment data. Remember the alignment matrix that maps outcomes onto courses? (See Chapter 3.) This matrix can be used to identify where potential embedded assessment data can be found within the general education program.

Embedded assessment data may be based on a variety of activities, such as community service-learning and other fieldwork activities, exams and parts of exams, homework assignments, oral presentations, group projects and presentations, and in-class writing assignments and learning journals. General education capstone courses often require capstone projects in which students integrate and reflect on what they have learned in the program, and these projects can be assessed for content, as well as communication and critical thinking skills. When designing embedded assessment, the task usually becomes selecting from a wide variety of options, rather than searching for a rare opportunity.

Campuses with learning outcomes related to civic engagement often require community service in the general education program, and student reflections on their experiences can provide direct evidence of their growth in understanding the community, their ability to tie academic learning to real-world experiences, and their interest in subsequent activities. In addition, fieldwork supervisors can provide feedback on students' demonstration of their learning.

Whole exams can be dedicated to the assessment of general education outcomes, as described in the last section, and faculty also can make use of parts of exams. For example, faculty who help students achieve an outcome may agree to embed in their exams a question directly related to that outcome. Faculty would grade their exams, as usual, but student responses to the common question would be collected and assessed. Although it may be difficult to embed a whole exam in a number of courses, many faculty would not object to including a single essay question or a small number of objective questions in their exams.

Homework assignments, unlike most in-class exams, give students time to edit, reflect on, and document their thoughts. Faculty who teach courses supporting an outcome may agree to include a similar assignment in their courses, perhaps adapting it to the specific content of each course. For example, faculty who assign term papers might agree to ask students to summarize how they located and selected their sources so that information competence skills can be assessed, or faculty may agree to assign a similar laboratory report so that scientific reasoning can be assessed.

Oral presentations offer faculty opportunities to assess content, as well as process. Outcomes related to oral communication skills might be assessed through the application of a common grading rubric, or perhaps faculty or others, such as trained graduate students, could attend oral presentations to assess oral presentation skills. Similarly, the content and the process of group projects and presentations could be assessed. For example, learning outcomes such as collaboration or leadership skills could be assessed using peer feedback or faculty observations of group discussions and presentations. Some faculty require students to submit minutes of their team meetings, providing opportunities for faculty to understand how productively student teams functioned.

In-class writing assignments or learning journals offer other opportunities for embedded assessment. For example, students could be asked to write brief papers that demonstrate their ability to integrate learning across disciplines or to apply new concepts to real-world problems. General education course instructors might ask students to do the same writing assignment twice, at the beginning and end of the term. For example, students in critical thinking courses might be asked to analyze the same argument twice, and a rubric could be used to assess growth in the sophistication of their reasoning. *Reflective essays* allow us to assess values and predispositions. For example, we might ask students to discuss how they might handle a sensitive interpersonal situation or to describe how they changed as a result of a course activity. This writing also could be done as a series of assignments in learning journals—requiring students to reflect on and apply what they are learning.

Strengths and Limitations of Using Embedded Assessment

Embedded assessment offers opportunities for authentic and performance assessment within the teaching-and-learning context. Both students and faculty are engaged in these activities. Students are motivated because they will be graded or because the activities tie directly into courses they are taking, and faculty care because the assessment is integrated into their teaching. Data collection is unobtrusive and requires little or no additional workload for students and faculty, other than time to coordinate the assessment and accumulate results. Out-of-class assignments offer opportunities for students to demonstrate their learning without the time constraints imposed on in-class activities or timed tests. Course activities allow faculty to assess content, as well as process, such as communication and collaboration skills. In addition, as faculty develop embedded assessment projects, they are probably increasing the alignment between their courses and re lated learning outcomes, creating a more cohesive curriculum.

Embedding the same assessment in multiple courses requires coordination, as well as concerted effort to develop and apply standards in a uniform way. Faculty must agree on a grading scheme that can be used for grading and assessment, or they can assess the accumulated products at some other time. The reliability and validity of embedded assessment activities is not known, but probably adequate for assessment purposes. Because data can be tied to specific faculty, safeguards must be in place to guarantee that the assessment focuses on the program, not individual faculty.

Advice for Using Embedded Assessment

Faculty already assign many tasks that could be used as embedded assessment activities, but most discover that these tasks require some tweaking to be effective assessment tools. Usually the assignment needs some minor restructuring to focus student attention on the targeted learning outcome.

Faculty should try to embed the assessment in more than one course taught by more than one instructor so that information can be generalized to the program as a whole. As with locally developed exams, faculty should pilot-test embedded assessment assignments and scoring guides to ensure that the learning outcome being assessed is appropriately targeted.

Some of the best assessment projects I've participated in involve groups of faculty reviewing student work together. As will be discussed later in this chapter, group assessment using rubrics can be a powerful assessment technique because faculty who have just assessed the students' work can immediately discuss what they learned and the implications of results.

Examples of Campus Use of Embedded Assessment

Embedded assessment is probably the most common way to assess student learning because students already generate relevant products and behaviors that are suitable for assessment. Here are a few examples of campus embedded assessment activities:

- Students at California State University–Bakersfield must satisfy an upper-division writing competency requirement, and they can do this by satisfactorily completing a designated upper-division writing course or by passing a challenge exam. The challenge exam's coordinator, in consultation with the assessment director, embedded an assessment of critical thinking in the challenge exam by asking students to write on a topic that required them to demonstrate their critical thinking skills, as well as their writing skills. Essays were evaluated for writing to assess students' ability to meet the upper-division writing requirement, and another group of faculty assessed general education critical thinking outcomes by reviewing a sample of the essays. (Noel, 2000)

- Mount Mary College's first-year seminar, "Leadership for Social Justice," has a number of outcomes related to understanding social justice. At the beginning of this course, faculty required students to respond to two scenarios dealing with social justice and a want ad containing implicit assumptions concerning gender. They repeated the assignment at the end of the term. Data were analyzed using three-point rubrics that give credit for recognizing multiple perspectives, social justice issues, and implicit messages. Faculty found statistically significant improvement on all three measures, verifying that the course had had its intended impact. Gratified with these results, faculty in many departments are expanding explicit teaching of social justice and leadership within their majors. (End, 2005)

- Students at Virginia State University (State Council of Higher Education for Virginia, 2002) take an online, self-paced technology training program, and embedded in it is a series of exams that assess their ability to use Microsoft Word, Excel, PowerPoint, and FrontPage. Students must pass all tests with a minimum score of 75% to complete the course, and they may retake exams until they pass. This mastery-learning approach guarantees that all students meet minimum expectations.

- Faculty at Winthrop University (Office of Assessment, Winthrop University, 2002) embedded the assessment of general education oral communication outcomes in freshman- and senior-level courses by videotaping required oral presentations. Faculty who were trained on the use of a locally developed oral communication rubric assessed the videotaped speeches using three dimensions (content, organization, and delivery), and they documented significantly better presentation skills among seniors.

Portfolios

Most portfolios are student-created collections of their academic work. Two types of student-created portfolios are common: showcase portfolios and developmental portfolios. *Showcase portfolios* are collections of the student's best work. *Developmental portfolios* contain work early and late in the student's academic career and are designed to document growth. Sometimes developmental portfolios are integrated into the advising process. For example, Alverno College requires students to develop a diagnostic portfolio that advisors use to help students select appropriate coursework (Loacker, 2002). The portfolios are used for *developmental assessment*, tracking the progress of individual students.

Most faculty require students to organize portfolios around the learning outcomes, and students usually are required to write a reflective essay in which they explain how the evidence in the portfolio demonstrates their mastery of each outcome. In addition, students may be asked to respond to other questions, such as:

- Which item is your best work? Why?
- Which item is your most important work? Why?
- Which item is your most satisfying work? Why?

- Which item is your most unsatisfying work? Why?

- In which item did you "stretch" yourself the most, taking the greatest risk in exploring new territory?

- List three things you learned by completing this portfolio. (Suskie, 2004, p. 194)

On some campuses, the portfolio is a collection of all general education course products, without required analysis.

Portfolios are collected in many ways. Campuses might require all students to create general education portfolios, usually as a graded component of a capstone course, or they may collect them from a subset of students. In addition, campuses may require portfolios for a limited set of outcomes. For example, portfolios for assessing written communication skills are common, and they may be developed within a single course or over the sequence of general education writing courses. Hard-copy portfolios are common, but increasingly popular are *webfolios,* or *digital portfolios,* that students place on web sites or CDs. The use of digital portfolios greatly reduces storage and access problems for the assessment team.

To avoid confusion, faculty should carefully specify expectations for portfolio content, length, organization, and format. For example, students may want to know if they can include evidence from courses outside the general education program or materials in various formats, such as videotapes. If the assignment is not clear, students will receive different advice from individual faculty members, creating confusion. Sometimes students are given considerable discretionary power over the content of their portfolios, and sometimes required portfolio-designated assignments are embedded in the general education curriculum.

Faculty have other decisions to make (Allen, 2004):

- How and when will students learn about portfolio requirements?

- What are the expectations for transfer students or students who, for legitimate reasons, have lost crucial assignments?

- Why should students take the portfolio assignment seriously?

- When and how will portfolios be collected?

- If portfolios will be graded, how will grades be determined?

- Who will have access to portfolios and for what purpose?

- How will student privacy and confidentiality be protected?

- Who owns the portfolios—students or the campus?

- Will portfolios be returned to students?

- How and when will portfolios be assessed?

An alternative type of portfolio is a *collective portfolio*. In this case, faculty create a single portfolio by selecting various students' work relevant to a learning outcome. For example, faculty who teach a variety of courses may submit examples of student papers that reflect their understanding of science or their ability to make ethical decisions. Rather than examining dozens (or hundreds) of student portfolios, faculty assess the evidence in a collective portfolio for a limited number of students focusing on one outcome. While the student-created portfolios require student effort, collective portfolios impose no additional demands on student time.

Strengths and Limitations of Portfolios

One of the strengths of student-created portfolios is that they require students to take responsibility for their learning and reflect on it—characteristics of the intentional learners described by the Association of American Colleges and Universities (2002) in *Greater Expectations*. Assembling the portfolio over the course of the general education program encourages students to monitor their own learning and recognize the impact that education is having on their lives. Developmental portfolios can be integrated into advising, helping each student select appropriate courses. Faculty who review portfolios develop insights about student learning, and they also have a window into other instructors' courses, assignments, and expectations so productive discussions about course alignment and teaching and learning are likely to occur.

Faculty in some institutions assign student portfolios without carefully thinking through the entire process. They end up with shelves full of thick binders, but don't know what to do with them; or they face student resentment because instructions aren't clear or time demands are excessive. Preparing the portfolio assignment and collecting, storing, and assessing the portfolios takes effort. If portfolios won't be graded, it may be difficult to motivate students to take the task seriously, but grading portfolios takes time. Most students require assistance as they develop portfolios, and faculty will have to integrate this support into their courses or office hours. In addition, some feedback from the students may not be trustworthy. For example, students, in their reflections, may avoid criticizing courses or faculty because portfolios usually are not anonymous.

Collective portfolios are a variation on embedded assessment and share its strengths and limitations. They can provide excellent data for the assessment of particular outcomes, and they require much less work than student portfolios—for students, as well as faculty. Sampling of student work must be done carefully so that results can be reasonably generalized to the program. Biased samples would undermine the validity of the assessment study.

Advice for Using Portfolios

If you are considering requiring students to create general education portfolios, be sure that you and your colleagues agree on the questions raised above, such as what materials can be included and what format is required. With faculty cooperation, portfolios could be integrated into general education capstone courses, a separate portfolio course, or senior-level courses in the major, as is done at Truman State University; or they could be accumulated as routine submissions to a paper or electronic warehouse each semester.

Portfolio grading should be fair to students and should not require extensive faculty time. Because most of the work in the portfolio has already been graded, faculty often grade based on the quality of the reflective essay, organization, and conformity to formatting requirements. This rewards student effort and encourages them to reflect on their own academic and personal development.

When it is time to assess the portfolios, use rubrics. They make the assessment manageable because they focus reviewers on the outcomes and their associated criteria. In addition, if you have a large number of portfolios, consider assessing a random sample of them. Your assessment plan should specify the number that will be reviewed each year, as well as the outcomes that will be examined. Of course, if these portfolios will also be used to provide feedback to departments on their students' development of basic skills and other general education outcomes, a sufficient number will have to be analyzed for each department.

Consider requiring portfolios from a subset of your students. The marginal gain from collecting a thousand portfolios, rather than 100, is probably low if you are just focusing on assessing the general education program, but the workload could be ten times as high. You might consider inviting some freshmen to develop portfolios over their first two years. If your two-year attrition rate is 40% and you want to have 100 portfolios, you should invite at least 170 freshmen. You might offer these students an incentive for turning in their course products at the end of each semester, such as a bookstore credit, tickets to campus events, or a unit of independent study.

The ongoing use of portfolios allows you to track student learning across time. For example, if significant changes have been made in some segments of the general education program, you could compare results from before the change to results after the change to document impact. If you keep the portfolios, you could look back at earlier student work using revised assessment rubrics, ensuring that comparisons across the years are reasonable. It is easier to accumulate portfolios if they are in electronic form because storage is relatively simple, but don't forget to back up the collection or a computer crash could lose years of data.

If you opt for collective portfolios, keep the process manageable by limiting the amount of data you collect. For example, you might collect writing samples from a variety of courses, but you might ask each faculty member to submit only a few students' work. Representativeness is important, so be sure that faculty don't contribute only their best students' products. Perhaps you could use a random process to select the students from each class whose work will be included, or you might consider asking faculty to submit two of the best papers, two "average" papers, and two of the weakest papers they collect in the designated course. These two sampling schemes will result in data that should be interpreted differently. If students and courses are selected randomly from the relevant population of students and courses, the quality of the collected work can be generalized to the entire program. On the other hand, if you collect the strongest, weakest, and in-between papers, you and your colleagues could ask how well these groups of students mastered characteristics of the outcomes being assessed. Are there some aspects of the outcome that weaker students mastered or that challenged stronger students?

Examples of Campus Use of Portfolios

Portfolio requirements and effective warehousing of portfolios provides broad opportunities for faculty to assess student work, including the ability to develop new scoring schemes and reanalyze older data to examine trends. Here are some examples of campuses that have used this approach:

- Each student at New Century College (2002a) creates a comprehensive graduation portfolio: "In these portfolios, students assess critically their academic knowledge and practice, and communicate through extensive self-reflection the value of their undergraduate work, their understanding of their learning process and their goals for the future" (p. 1). Portfolios include a self-assessment of nine core competencies, and each student selects a faculty reviewer who assesses the portfolio, conducts an exit interview, and certifies the portfolio requirement so the student can graduate. Detailed portfolio guidelines are available online. (New Century College, 2002b)

- Students at the University of Wisconsin–Superior (2002) develop a portfolio as an "electronic briefcase" that is stored on a campus server, and they are required to place their work into folders corresponding to their general education courses each semester. In addition, they evaluate each course and their work in each course by updating a preprogrammed spreadsheet each semester. Students who do not actively maintain their portfolios are blocked from registering for subsequent coursework.

- Faculty at the College of William and Mary (State Council of Higher Education for Virginia, 2002) accumulated a collective portfolio of student papers from five departments, and they used a five-point rubric to assess writing quality. They found that 73% of the papers displayed "strong" writing, and all of the others displayed "adequate" writing.

Rubrics

You have probably already noticed repeated mention of rubrics in this book, and if you have never used one, I hope this section will convince you of their value. Rubrics specify criteria for classifying products or behaviors into categories that vary along a continuum. The lowest category is used for products or behaviors that are inadequate, that fail to meet expectations, or that represent naïve or unsophisticated thinking. The highest category is reserved for products or behaviors that are exemplary, that exceed expectations, or that represent sophisticated thinking. Intermediate categories may have labels like marginal, developing, satisfactory, meets minimum expectations, or competent.

Rubrics explicitly describe the criteria to be used. For example, when assessing students' understanding of the scientific method, a product may be classified as *marginal* if it suggests only limited understanding of how scientists form and test hypotheses. Faculty who use the same well-written rubric should agree on the classification of each reviewed product.

Rubrics can have two categories (satisfactory and unsatisfactory), but they usually have from three to five categories. Category labels vary with the outcome being assessed, but these are typical:

- Developing, Acceptable, Exemplary

- Unacceptable, Competent, Accomplished

- Unacceptable, Marginal, Meets Expectations, Exceeds Expectations

- Novice, Developing, Proficient, Expert

- Weak, Developing, Acceptable, Exceeds Expectations, Excellent

Alternatively, some campuses just use numbers for the categories, such as scores ranging from 1 to 5, with larger numbers indicating greater achievement.

Notice that words like "average" or "above average" are not on these lists. When we use rubrics to assess student learning, we want to do *criterion-referenced interpretations*. We ask what portion of our students satisfied our criteria. *Norm-referenced interpretations* ask how well each student performed compared to other students. Knowing that about half our students are below the student average and about half are above the student average does not provide useful assessment information, but learning that 95% of our students satisfied our criteria is a valuable assessment finding.

How many categories should a rubric have? The final conclusion of an assessment study is generally dichotomous; we are either satisfied or unsatisfied with results. This might suggest that all we need are dichotomous rubrics. In practice, though, dichotomous judgments are hard to make because many student products are in the middle—marginally competent or barely meeting expectations. In my experience, it is easier for faculty to do assessment if intermediate categories are available, and three- and four-point rubrics are common. For example, the Association of American Colleges and Universities Board of Directors (2004) suggests four levels: below basic, basic, proficient, and advanced.

Holistic and Analytic Rubrics

There are two basic types of rubrics: holistic and analytic. *Holistic rubrics* describe how to make a single judgment about the product or behavior. When using a three-point holistic rubric to assess student essays, our only question is, "Is this essay a 1, 2, or 3?" We set aside our red pens because we will not write comments in the margins or mark grammatical errors. We make the judgment, then we pick up the next essay to be assessed. Experienced raters, using a holistic rubric like the example in Figure 5.1, can analyze dozens of papers effectively and efficiently. Sometimes products demonstrate aspects of multiple categories, and the judge must decide which of the category descriptors best fits the document being reviewed. Faculty are accustomed to making grading decisions, and they quickly become accustomed to applying rubrics.

Figure 5.1
Holistic Rubric for Assessing Student Essays*

Inadequate	The essay has at least one serious weakness. It may be unfocused, underdeveloped, or rambling. Problems with the use of language seriously interfere with the reader's ability to understand what is being communicated.
Developing Competence	The essay may be somewhat unfocused, underdeveloped, or rambling, but it does have some coherence. Problems with the use of language occasionally interfere with the reader's ability to understand what is being communicated.
Acceptable	The essay is generally focused and contains some development of ideas, but the discussion may be simplistic or repetitive. The language lacks syntactic complexity and may contain occasional grammatical errors, but the reader is able to understand what is being communicated.
Sophisticated	The essay is focused and clearly organized, and it shows depth of development. The language is precise and shows syntactic variety, and ideas are clearly communicated to the reader.

*Source: Allen (2004), p. 139.

We use *analytic rubrics* when we assess multiple outcomes simultaneously or when our outcomes are multidimensional and we want to rate each dimension separately. Instead of a single judgment about each product or behavior, we make multiple judgments. The analytic rubric describes the criteria for each of those judgments. Analytic rubrics may provide more actionable data than holistic rubrics because they allow us to identify both potential strengths and weaknesses in the products we're reviewing. Figure 5.2 is an analytic rubric that might be used to assess aspects of information

Figure 5.2

Rubric for Assessing Aspects of Information Literacy in Term Papers

	Below Expectations	*Meets Expectations*	*Exceeds Expectations*
Range of relevant materials	The paper cites only web sites, has too few primary sources, or frequently cites sources only marginally related to the topic.	The paper cites reasonably relevant web sites, journals, and books, although too few sources are used or key materials that should have been cited were missing	The paper cites a rich array of relevant web sites, journals, and books, including classic materials related to the topic.
Citations	The paper fails to cite sources using a consistent, formal citation style (e.g., APA or MLA style).	Most of the citations follow a consistent, formal style, although occasionally citations contain minor errors or provide incomplete information.	All citations are complete, accurate, and consistently conform to a formal style.
Use of sources	Cited materials are poorly integrated into the paper and connections between sources (such as consistencies or inconsistencies) are not noted.	Cited materials generally are integrated into the paper, but some important connections between sources are not explored.	Cited materials are well-integrated into the paper and connections between sources are explicitly discussed.
Plagiarism	The student fails to cite sources when using others' ideas or fails to include necessary quotation marks or page numbers for direct quotations.	The source of information is generally clear, but occasionally may be ambiguous. Quotations are properly indicated.	The source of all ideas is carefully documented and quotations are properly indicated.

literacy when reviewing term papers. Notice that the rubric focuses just on information literacy, pointing reviewers toward evidence related to the outcomes being assessed and encouraging them to ignore aspects of the papers irrelevant to this assessment, making the assessment a focused, efficient process.

Sometimes analytic rubrics are presented without all the details, as in Figure 5.3. If faculty are able to generate reliable ratings using this rubric, it serves its purpose; but if ratings are unreliable, more detailed explanations of the criteria are necessary.

Figure 5.3
Rubric for Assessing Portfolios

	Unacceptable: *Evidence that the student has mastered this outcome is not provided, unconvincing, or very incomplete.*	Marginal: *Evidence that the student has mastered this outcome is provided, but it is weak or incomplete.*	Acceptable: *Evidence shows that the student has generally attained this outcome.*	Exceptional: *Evidence demonstrates that the student has mastered this outcome at a high level.*
Learning Outcome 1				
Learning Outcome 2				
Learning Outcome 3				

*Adapted from Allen (2004), p. 142.

Strengths of Rubrics

Imagine doing an assessment of information competence by reviewing term papers without a rubric like the one in Figure 5.2. You and some colleagues review the term papers and have to decide if students are developing sufficient information competence skills. Each of you reviews the papers, and each might have his/her own set of standards, so disagreements are likely. At some point, though, you probably would come to the conclusion that you need to develop a set of explicit criteria and that you should share them with your students when you assign the papers. This is learning-centered teaching. We tell students what we want them to learn, we provide support for that learning, and we hold students responsible for acquiring that learning.

Rubrics are frequently used to assess embedded assessment data, portfolios, and collective portfolios. They have many strengths for assessment projects:

- Developing an assessment rubric helps faculty clarify their expectations. For example, faculty may agree that students should develop critical thinking and communication skills, but they are likely to have different conceptions of what these skills are.

- Assessment using well-designed rubrics is likely to be reliable, valid, and actionable.

- Complex products or behaviors can be assessed efficiently using rubrics.

- Once the criteria for assessing outcomes are clear, faculty can better align their courses to help students meet these expectations. This should increase the cohesiveness of the curriculum.

Faculty can share rubrics with students to communicate their expectations. This should help students focus their efforts and increase their learning. Rubrics may be especially helpful for first-generation college students who don't have family members who can tell them what college faculty expect. In addition, rubrics can be integrated into courses in other ways to promote learning (Allen, 2004). You might:

- Use a rubric for grading student work and return the rubric with the grading on it. Faculty save time writing extensive comments; they just circle or highlight relevant segments of the rubric. Some faculty include room for additional comments on the rubric page, either within each section or at the end.

- Develop a rubric with your students for an assignment or group project. Students can then monitor themselves and their peers using agreed-upon criteria that they helped develop. Many faculty find that students create higher standards for themselves than faculty would impose on them.

- Have students apply your rubric to some sample products before they create their own. Faculty report that students are quite accurate when doing this, and this process should help them evaluate their own products as they are being developed. The ability to evaluate, edit, and improve draft documents is an important skill.

- Have students exchange paper drafts and give peer feedback using the rubric, then give students a few days before the final drafts are turned in to you. You might also require that they turn in the draft and scored rubric with their final paper.

- Have students self-assess their products using the grading rubric and hand in the self-assessment with the product; then faculty and students can compare self- and faculty-generated evaluations. (p. 144)

Using Rubrics for Grading and Assessment

Most faculty grade by assigning points to course components. For example, the oral presentation to be graded using the rubric in Figure 5.4 is worth up to 30 points, and up to 8 of those points can be earned for organization, up to 13 points can be earned for content, and up to 9 points can be earned for delivery. Rubrics tied to learning outcomes can be designed so that faculty collect assessment information while they're grading.

Faculty who want to collect assessment data using the rubric in Figure 5.4 have considerable flexibility, as long as they leave the assessment-related components intact. For example, an instructor may decide that the oral presentation in her course is worth up to 50 points, and 45 of them are for the quality of the content. Another instructor might add a fourth dimension that will be graded, such as how well students integrate their community service experiences into their presentation. Other instructors may decide to add a comments section at the end of the rubric. The numbers are used for grading; the categories are used for assessment. When the grading is completed, each instructor who uses the rubric reports how many below expectation, satisfactory, and exemplary ratings were given to organization, content, and delivery. The accumulated results allow faculty to assess students' oral communication skills.

Many general education faculty are expected to teach outside of their area of expertise. For example, faculty who teach humanities, social science, and science general education courses are frequently expected to help students develop basic skills (such as critical thinking, information literacy, speaking, and writing). A rubric like the one in Figure 5.4 can be an invaluable aid to faculty without primary expertise in oral communication. They can share the rubric with students before they develop their presentations,

Figure 5.4

Analytic Rubric for Grading Oral Presentations*

	Below Expectation	Satisfactory	Exemplary	Score
Organization	No apparent organization. Evidence is not used to support assertions. (0–2)	The presentation has a focus and provides some evidence which supports conclusions. (3–5)	The presentation is carefully organized and provides convincing evidence to support conclusions. (6–8)	
Content	The content is inaccurate or overly general. Listeners are unlikely to learn anything or may be misled. (0–2)	The content is generally accurate, but incomplete. Listeners may learn some isolated facts, but they are unlikely to gain new insights about the topic. (5–7)	The content is accurate and complete. Listeners are likely to gain new insights about the topic. (10–13)	
Delivery	The speaker appears anxious and uncomfortable, and reads notes, rather than speaks. Listeners are largely ignored. (0–2)	The speaker is generally relaxed and comfortable, but too often relies on notes. Listeners are sometimes ignored or misunderstood. (3–6)	The speaker is relaxed and comfortable, speaks without undue reliance on notes, and interacts effectively with listeners. (7–9)	
Total Score				

*Source: Allen, 2004, p. 141

provide effective formative feedback to each student, and grade efficiently and effectively.

When I used to grade oral presentations, each student gave a brief presentation, and I scrambled to write some quick feedback as the next student came forward. Imagine, instead, grading with an underliner and an oral presentation rubric. You could underline to emphasize key descriptive language in the criteria, assign points to each category, and easily generate the grade. Rubrics like this allow faculty to describe important characteristics of each student's presentation, and a student who is not performing at the exemplary level is given explicit instructions on how to improve. For more information on grading with rubrics, useful resources are available (e.g., Stevens & Levi, 2005; Walvoord & Anderson, 1998).

Using Rubrics for Assessment

An alternative to assessing while grading is to collect student work, such as responses to exam questions, lab reports, learning journal entries, or portfolios. These can be assessed by faculty working alone or in groups. Individual faculty may assess the students' work in the room in which materials are stored, they may be given a packet of materials to review, or they may review materials that are available online. Alternatively, a group of faculty could assess the materials simultaneously. For example, they may spend an afternoon assessing student work together.

Usually two raters independently assess each student product, and sometimes a third rater resolves discrepancies. For example, a third reader may review the document if the first pair of judgments differ by more than a point. If the original reviewers give scores of 1 and 3, and if the third rater gives a 3, the outlier judgment (the rating of 1) is discarded.

An alternative group data collection strategy is to have raters work in pairs. Each is given the same set of documents, and they coordinate the assessment of each product. Each member of the pair assigns a score to each document, then they compare their ratings and reach consensus. For example, if both first assign a rating of 3, they record a 3 on the score sheet; but if they begin with different ratings, they discuss the ratings until they agree on the appropriate score. Although data collection may take a little longer, faculty are very confident in the scores because two professionals have agreed that each score is correct.

If comparisons between groups will be made, raters should do *blind reviews*—they should not know individuals' group membership while assessing their products. For example, if the critical thinking of sophomores will be compared to the critical thinking of seniors, raters should review all documents using the same rubric without awareness of the class level of the student being reviewed. This allows us to avoid biased ratings.

Training in the Use of Rubrics

Training is important to ensure that all reviewers understand the rubric and apply it in the same manner. This is usually accomplished by preselecting exemplars of different levels of student performance, such as a quality product, a marginally acceptable product, and an inadequate product. Individual raters review the products and compare their ratings to predetermined judgments by experts or, if they are working in a group, to each other. Discrepancies are discussed with the goal of calibrating all readers so that inter-rater reliability will be high. Skipping this *calibration* is not advised because we want to generate quality data and make effective use of faculty time.

Two other concerns should be included in the training. First, faculty should be aware of the halo effect if they will be using analytic rubrics. Many people have the tendency to let holistic judgments cloud their ratings, and this is the *halo effect*. For example, if three characteristics will be assessed and the student's work is exceptionally strong or weak on the first category, there is a tendency to assume the student will receive similar scores on the other two categories. Faculty should be encouraged to make each judgment independently of the others. A student might score in the top category on one dimension and in the bottom category on another.

Second, some faculty must be reminded that assessment is criterion-referenced, not norm-referenced. We are not "grading on a curve." We might find that all students demonstrate exemplary skills, or we might find that none of them do. The purpose of the assessment is to discover how many students meet our standards, not to compare students to each other. You will know that this part of the orientation is important the first time one of the reviewers asks, "About how many threes should I give?" This question suggests a misunderstanding of the assessment process. It is best to systematically ensure that none of the reviewers begins the assessment with an assumption about how many students should receive each score so results reflect student performance rather than a preconceived distribution.

Examining Inter-Rater Reliability

If rubrics are developed, pilot-tested, and refined and if raters are appropriately trained, inter-rater reliability should be high. Most campuses routinely check for inter-rater reliability by having two independent raters assess each student product. When this is done, inter-rater reliability can be examined in two ways. The correlation between the two sets of ratings indicates the extent of their agreement, and it is commonly calculated. This statistic, though, can underestimate the extent of agreement if ratings are not sufficiently variable. For example, if most ratings are twos and threes, the correlation will be attenuated (reduced) due to restriction of range.

An alternative is to consider discrepancies between the pair of raters. How often do they give identical judgments, ratings that are one point apart, two points apart, etc.? For example, Noel (2001) examined the reliability of ratings during the assessment of two arts and humanities outcomes: students' ability to describe major historical trends and to write critical reviews. Correlations between faculty ratings were .81 and .82, respectively. When assessing students' ability to discuss historical trends reviewers gave identical ratings 68% of the time and gave adjacent ratings 32% of the time. These percentages were 75 and 25, respectively, for the ratings of critical reviews. None of the ratings were more than one point apart. Faculty discussed the reliability of the findings and agreed that it was acceptable before asking if students met their criteria for these outcomes.

Establishing Standards

Say you assessed a representative sample of student work using a 4-point holistic rubric and find that 31% of the products are exemplary, 67% are competent, 2% are marginal, and none are unacceptable. Would you be satisfied with these results? Most faculty would be elated with such findings because 98% of their students have met or exceeded competence standards, and none generated unacceptable work.

What if 3% of the products are exemplary, 65% are competent, 20% are marginal, and 12% are unacceptable. Is this satisfactory? Results indicate that 68% of the students meet basic competence standards, but faculty probably will be sufficiently concerned about the other 32% that they will be disappointed in the results.

When results are discussed, faculty eventually come down to a conclusion. Are results satisfactory, or are they so disappointing that changes are necessary? Faculty frequently adopt a general standard. For example, they will be satisfied with results if:

- at least 80% of the ratings are threes or fours and no more than 5% are ones, or

- at least 10% of the ratings are fours, at least 85% are threes or fours, and no more than 5% are ones.

Of course, standards can vary across outcomes. For example, faculty might take particular pride in the writing skills of their students, and they would only be satisfied if 95% of their students receive ratings of 3 or 4.

Available General Education Rubrics

Thanks to generous colleagues, a number of general education rubrics are available on the web. Although your outcomes and criteria may differ, you may find it easier to adapt someone else's work than to start from scratch. Consider the following college and university web sites:

- *Bowling Green State University* (http://www.bgsu.edu/offices/assessment/Rubrics.htm). Links to six general education rubrics for assessing connection, investigation, leadership, participation, presentation, and writing

- *California State University Information Competence Initiative* (http://www.calstate.edu/LS/1_rubric.doc). An analytic information competence rubric based on the Association of College and Research Libraries' (2000) *Information Literacy Competency Standards for Higher Education*

- *California State University–Long Beach* (http://www.csulb.edu/divisions/aa/personnel/fcpd/resources/ge/). A holistic and an analytic writing rubric

- *California State University–Fresno* (http://www.csufresno.edu/cetl/assessment). Links to four general education rubrics for assessing critical thinking (CTScoring.doc), integration (ICScoring.doc), integrative science (IBScoring.doc), and writing (WritingScoring.doc)

- *California State University System* (http://www.calstate.edu/acadaff/sloa/links/rubrics.shtml). Links to a wide variety of rubrics that could be adapted for general education assessment

- *Johnson County Community College* (http://www.jccc.net/home/depts/ S00015/site/plan/). Links to rubrics for culture and ethics, mathematics, modes of inquiry, problem solving, speaking, and writing

- *Northeastern Illinois University* (http://www.neiu.edu/~neassess/ gened.htm#rubric). Links to a writing rubric and long and short versions of a critical thinking rubric

- *Palomar College* (http://www.palomar.edu/alp/benchmarks_for _core_skills.htm). Links to holistic rubrics assessing communication (listening, speaking, reading, and writing), cognition (problem solving, creative thinking, quantitative reasoning, and transfer of knowledge and skills to a new context), information competency (technical competency), social interaction (teamwork), and personal development and responsibility (self-management and respect for diverse people and cultures)

- *State University of New York–Geneseo* (http://gened.geneseo .edu/pdfs/assess_tools_revised.pdf). Rubrics for assessing numeric and symbolic reasoning, critical writing and reading, humanities, social science, fine arts, basic research, U.S. history, non-Western traditions, natural science, and oral discourse outcomes

- *University of Arkansas–Fort Smith* (http://www.uafortsmith.edu/ Learning/GeneralEducationCompetenciesAndRubrics#Bookmark Rubrics). Links to rubrics assessing analytical skills, communication skills, computer literacy, creativity, global and cultural perspectives, information literacy, personal responsibility, quantitative reasoning, scientific and technological literacy, and social interaction

- *University of California* (http://www.sdcoe.k12.ca.us/score/actbank/ subja.htm). A holistic writing rubric

- *University of South Carolina* (http://ipr.sc.edu/effectiveness/assess ment/criteria). Links to seven general education rubrics for assessing electronic, humanities/cultural, math, oral communication, science, social/behavioral sciences, and writing outcomes

- *Washington State University* (http://wsuctproject.wsu.edu/ctr.htm). An analytic critical thinking rubric

In addition, a handy rubric for assessing rubrics is available online (Mullinix, 2003).

Creating Rubrics

Faculty can create a rubric by adapting one that someone else already developed, or they can use an analytic or expert-systems approach to create one from scratch. Faculty are excellent critical thinkers, and as they look at some of the examples given above, they are likely to find opportunities to adapt a rubric that aligns with their outcomes, saving themselves considerable effort.

The *analytic approach* to creating a rubric begins, of course, with analysis. Faculty identify what they are assessing and analyze its characteristics. For example, if they are developing a critical thinking rubric, they might decide that its major dimensions are the appropriate use of evidence and the recognition of logical fallacies. An effective way to do the analysis is in discussion with colleagues. The major criteria and standards will emerge as faculty talk about how they recognize strong and weak critical thinking in student products or behaviors. These criteria become the dimensions in an analytic rubric, or they form the basis for the category descriptions in a holistic rubric. Many people find it easiest to develop the criteria in each cell of the rubric by beginning at the extremes. Using the characteristics developed through analysis, they describe exemplary and unacceptable or marginally acceptable student work, then they describe the remaining categories.

The *expert-systems approach* begins by recruiting a small number of experts. For example, a few general education humanities faculty might be invited to develop the rubric for assessing relevant general education outcomes. They review a sample of student products and sort them into piles varying in quality. The number of piles and their labels (e.g., unacceptable, developing, competent, exemplary) may be preset, or the experts may determine them. Once the products are sorted, the descriptions of each category in the rubric are the characteristics that discriminate between adjacent piles. For example, the experts determine what distinguishes exemplary from competent work, and these criteria are entered into the rubric to guide others in subsequent classifications of student products. If they are developing an analytic rubric, the experts would sort the documents multiple times, once for each dimension.

Regardless of how the rubric is developed, the last step is to pilot-test it by ensuring that other faculty understand the criteria and can reliably use them to assess actual student products or behaviors. This allows the rubric developer to fine tune the rubric before it is put into practice.

CHAPTER 6

Indirect Assessment of General Education Learning Outcomes

Indirect assessment of learning outcomes involves people's opinions, and these opinions can richly supplement what is learned in direct assessment studies. Campuses can use surveys, interviews, or focus groups to collect self-assessments by students, as well as the opinions of others, such as alumni, employers, and fieldwork supervisors. In addition, students and alumni can provide important feedback on their satisfaction with the general education program, their ratings of its quality and personal usefulness, experiences that supported or interfered with their development, and suggestions for improvement. Alignment studies frequently use indirect assessment to obtain student, alumni, faculty, or staff opinions concerning the general education curriculum and related cocurriculum and support services.

Creating Survey and Interview Questions

Two kinds of questions are generally used when collecting indirect assessment data: close-ended and open-ended. *Close-ended questions* present choices from which respondents choose a response, such as Yes/No or Agree/Disagree. *Open-ended questions* require respondents to generate a response, such as describing course characteristics that helped them learn. Surveys generally have a preponderance of close-ended questions, and interviews and focus groups rely more on open-ended questions.

Close-Ended Questions

Close-ended questions might focus on the learning outcomes or on the general education support environment. For example, students might be invited to rate the extent of their learning for each general education learning outcome, using a 1 to 5 rating scale. Sometimes students also are asked to rate the personal importance of each learning outcome, so researchers can determine whether students mastered the outcomes they valued. When rating scales are used, such as the 1 to 5 scale, they should be *anchored* by key, explanatory phrases. Examples of anchoring formats are provided in Figure 6.1.

Figure 6.1

Examples of Rating Scale Anchors

Type of Anchor	Example
List	Please use the following scale: 1 = I didn't learn anything. 2 = I learned a bit, but not much. 3 = I learned a fair amount. 4 = I learned a lot. 5 = I learned a great deal.
Linear	Not much 1 2 3 4 5 A great deal
Linear	1 2 3 4 5 Not Important Neutral Very Important
Unnumbered	Unsatisfied __|_|__|__|_|_|_|__|_|_ Satisfied

Sometimes close-ended questions are only partially closed because they provide an "other" category that requires an explanation, for example:

Please indicate where you spent your freshman year of college.

____ At this institution.

____ At a community college.

____ At a four-year college other than this institution.

____ Other. Please explain:

A common item type asks respondents to use a *Likert scale* to indicate their degree of agreement, such as:

> The general education program helped me understand global politics.
>
> strongly disagree   disagree   neutral   agree   strongly agree

Checklists are also common, and they allow respondents to select multiple responses, such as:

> Which of the following general education goals helped prepare you for your major? (Check all that apply.)
>
> ___ Critical thinking
>
> ___ Information literacy
>
> ___ Problem solving
>
> ___ Quantitative reasoning
>
> ___ Reading
>
> ___ Speaking
>
> ___ Understanding cultural diversity
>
> ___ Writing

Close-ended questions are most common on surveys, but they can also be integrated into interviews and focus groups. Interviewers often ask respondents to respond to a series of items using a rating scale or Likert scale. For example, the interviewer might ask respondents to rate how well they achieved each of the general education learning outcomes or how strongly they agree with a series of statements about the quality of courses and support services.

Allen (2004) offers the following suggestions for writing effective close-ended questions:

- Avoid compound items. *(Did you like the courses and instructors? What about people who like the courses but not the instructors, or vice versa?)*

- For close-ended questions, be sure to include all possible response categories. (This may require the use of an "Other" category.)

- Avoid vague questions. *(Did you learn because of your efforts or the efforts of the instructor?)*

- Avoid confusing wording. *(I rarely use the library. True__ False__.* Does a "False" answer mean that the person never, often, or always uses the library?)

- Sometimes you have to allow respondents to not answer questions. *(How often do you use your home computer to access online course materials?* How should students without a home computer respond?)

- Avoid wording that might bias responses. *(We expect students to study at least three hours outside of class for each hour in class—please estimate the number of hours you study outside of class for each hour in class.)*

- Avoid questions that threaten or alienate your respondents. *(How concerned are you that our efforts to increase campus diversity threaten academic quality?)*

- Be careful of order effects, when the response to one question influences the response to a later question. *(Have you ever plagiarized a source when preparing a paper or assignment?* followed by *To what extent have you followed departmental ethical guidelines while completing your degree?)*

- Consider specifying a time frame. *(How many books have you read in the past six months that were not required for a class?)*

- Avoid negative wording. *(I received ineffective career advice. True__ False__.* Some respondents become confused about what their answers mean.)

- Remember cultural differences. *(If you had a personal problem while a student here, did you use the counseling center or did you consult a professional, such as a priest or therapist?* What about a rabbi, minister, parson, elder, mullah, or other representative of a religion?) (pp. 107–108)

Open-Ended Questions

Respondents create their own response to *open-ended questions,* and their responses can help us uncover unanticipated perspectives. Open-ended questions should be broad enough to capture the full range of relevant ideas, but not so broad that irrelevant information is collected. In addition, open-ended questions should not be too narrow. For example, sometimes open-ended questions are really close-ended questions in disguise, such as, *Were you satisfied with the general education advising process?* If you are really interested in students' opinions about advising, you could ask, *Tell me about your first general education advising session. What did you learn? What questions remained unanswered?* Some respondents will give detailed replies, and others will provide sketchy answers, and this is where interviews and focus groups have an advantage over surveys because the interviewer can repeat questions and probe for details.

When creating open-ended questions, carefully determine what you want to learn and be sure that the question elicits this information. For example, if you want to examine students' opinions concerning general education advising, are you interested in:

- The affective impact *(Did you feel welcome and supported? Describe what your advisor did to welcome you to the campus. How did your advisor help you make personal and academic decisions? How might the advising process be improved to better welcome and support new students?)*

- The cognitive impact *(Did you learn the requirements and how to register? What questions about general education requirements remained after your first advising session? Describe the quality of your first registration experience.)*

- The social impact *(Did your advisor suggest that you join a learning community or take a linked course in the general education program? What kinds of questions about these opportunities remained after your advising session?)*

- The developmental impact *(Describe how your advisor helped you clarify your long-term goals. How did your advisor help you understand options and opportunities, such as choosing courses to explore majors or using the Tutoring Center? What do you know now about the campus and the GE program that you wish you had learned from your general education advisor?)*

Open-ended questions should avoid biasing respondents' answers, and should seek information that they can legitimately provide. For example, respondents generally are more accurate when describing their own experiences than the experiences of others. Providing a little structure in the question allows you to focus answers on the target issues. For example, rather than, *What do you think about our GE program?*, you could ask students to describe how the program contributed to their understanding of science or how well lower-division courses prepared them for upper-division work.

Questions for Interviews and Focus Groups

Interviews and focus groups generally begin with a *warm-up question* that is relatively non-threatening and easy to answer. This is particularly important in focus groups because you want everyone to feel free to contribute opinions and to agree or disagree with others' comments. For example, the focus group might begin by asking respondents to briefly describe where they took their general education courses or to provide a simple, one-word summary of their overall view of the general education program.

These interviews generally end with a *closing question* that invites additional comments from respondents. For example, a focus group might end in this way: *We've covered a lot of ground today, but we know you might still have some other input about the general education program. Is there anything else you'd like to say about the program that hasn't been discussed already?* Interviews might end with a similar open-ended query, such as, *Any other comments about the general education program?*

Interview and focus group protocols generally include some optional questions. For example, if students don't provide full answers, interviewers might ask for more details (e.g., *Tell me more . . .*), or they might paraphrase what they're hearing to check for accuracy and probe for more details (e.g., *You're saying that your advisor was helpful. Can you give me some examples of the kind of help she provided?*).

Finalizing Survey Questions and Interview Scripts

You can save a lot of wasted effort if you routinely pilot-test survey questions and interview scripts before actual data collection. Ask a few students to think out loud as they respond to questions to verify that questions unambiguously lead students to the topics you want to assess. Do some pilot interviews using the interview script. Sometimes what sounds good on paper sounds awkward or artificial when you say it out loud, and you want to ensure that respondents are informed, relaxed, and comfortable sharing their personal opinions with you. In addition, be sure that data collection forms are easy to fill out and well organized.

The most important advice, though, is to avoid writing too many questions. Sometimes surveys are written by committees, and any question that anyone suggests is included. Imagine you are a busy student and you receive an 18-page survey in the mail or you are invited to participate in a two-hour interview. Wouldn't you be more likely to participate if you received a one-page survey or were invited to a 15-minute interview? How about a quick email or online survey, a survey you could fill out in class, or a focus group during a class session?

Surveys

Surveys have been used for decades in higher education, and they allow us to obtain opinions from students, alumni, employers, and other stakeholders, such as faculty, staff, and community members. Because they can be mailed, emailed, or placed online, surveys allow us to reach respondents asynchronously and at a distance—a major advantage over interviews and focus groups. Surveys can examine opinions about learning, as well as the context for learning.

Figure 6.2 is an example of a short survey that might be used in general education science courses. This survey is short enough that data could be collected in class near the end of the term, and it was designed to assess several aspects of science learning outcomes—how well the course was designed to support the learning of each outcome, how well each outcome was learned, which assignments or activities promoted the learning, and what could have been done to improve learning.

Surveys generally collect demographic information (e.g., class level), especially if researchers anticipate doing analyses for separate groups. For example, using the survey in Figure 6.2, faculty might investigate differences in opinion between lower- and upper-division students or between students who are taking the course to satisfy a general education requirement and students who are taking the course for other reasons. Notice how all the other questions in the survey directly relate to the outcomes. Every question on the survey fills a purpose, and none are there just because someone was curious. If faculty were concerned about the effect of gender, age, or some other variable, questions acquiring this information would be added.

Figure 6.2
General Education Science Course Survey

We are assessing aspects of our General Education (GE) program, and we would appreciate your honest feedback on the science course you are taking. Please do not put your name on this survey. All responses will be combined to reach general conclusions about our GE program, and results will not identify individual respondents. Your instructor will be able to review responses from this course only after course grades have been submitted.

1. Why are you enrolled in this science course? (check all that apply)
   ___ general interest/personal reasons
   ___ to satisfy a GE requirement
   ___ to satisfy another requirement (e.g., a requirement in your major or minor)

2. Your class level:
   ___ Freshman   ___ Sophomore   ___ Junior
   ___ Senior   ___ Graduate Student

3. Please indicate your degree of agreement with each of the following statements:

   A. Assignments and activities in this course were well-designed to help me understand how scientists test theories.

1	2	3	4	5
strongly disagree		neutral		strongly agree

   B. Assignments and activities in this course were well-designed to help me understand the role science plays in everyday life.

1	2	3	4	5
strongly disagree		neutral		strongly agree

   C. I have learned a lot about how scientists test theories.

1	2	3	4	5
strongly disagree		neutral		strongly agree

   D. I have learned a lot about the role science plays in everyday life.

1	2	3	4	5
strongly disagree		neutral		strongly agree

4. Please describe some assignments or activities from this course that promoted your learning about science.

5. What might have occurred in this course to improve your learning about science?

Thanks for your help!

Results from this survey can complement results from direct assessment studies. If the direct assessment demonstrates that students are mastering the outcomes well, the survey allows researchers to verify that students' self-perceptions are accurate and to identify students' perceptions concerning aspects of their courses that should be preserved. On the other hand, if direct assessment results are weak, the survey provides information on the types of assignments and activities that students believe are effective and that they recommend. Individual faculty can see results for their own courses, and aggregated results can be used for program assessment, providing opportunities for course as well as program improvement.

Alumni, employers, and community members can provide feedback on learning, the campus's reputation for learning, campus engagement in the community, or the desirability of possible learning outcomes. Faculty and staff might be surveyed to examine their beliefs about student attainment and general education learning outcomes, interactions with students, satisfaction with the general education program, suggestions for improving the program, their use of active learning techniques, and support needs.

Although it is relatively easy to generate a survey and most campuses have a long history of dependence on surveys, one should not do a survey just out of habit. Leaders should determine which questions are worth asking and if surveys, interviews, or focus groups would be the best approach for gathering the answers.

Questions about general education programs can be included in longer surveys. For example, the University of Wisconsin–Green Bay (2004b) conducted a survey among seniors. Many of the questions involved their majors, but a segment of the survey asked students to rate—using a 3-point scale (low, medium, high)—how well the general education program contributed to a variety of characteristics, such as critical analysis, problem-solving, and written communication skills, as well as their knowledge of a number of areas, such as science, technology, Western civilization, and contemporary global issues and problems. Students also rated their proficiency in each of these characteristics, using the same 3-point scale (low, medium, high). Results were reported in two ways: the percentage of students indicating each response and a mean for each item. Overall, the students indicated that the general education program contributed to their learning to a moderate degree (averages ranged from 1.9 to 2.2), and that their learning was moderately strong (averages ranged from 2.0 to 2.7).

Surveys are popular tools for assessing first-year experience programs. For example, Bristol Community College used surveys to assess its College Success Seminar. Survey results from 2001 indicated that 98% of students reported using study skills learned in the seminar in other courses, and 97% reported investigating career goals. Students who took this course in 2002 reported that they gained confidence in asking for help (89%) and began to understand the general education program (94%; Korn, 2005).

Asking students to report opinions about their learning or campus experiences can help faculty understand students' perspectives, but results could be misinterpreted. Suppose students reported that the campus provides weak support for community service learning. Students may not see this as a problem if they aren't interested in community service placements. One way to examine this is to ask students to provide importance ratings. For example, students at the State University of New York–Brockport rated the importance and accomplishment of a number of variables associated with their first-year seminar (Fox, 2005). Overall, we hope that students value what they have accomplished and that student and faculty opinions align—that they value similar things. Discrepancies allow faculty to understand student resistance to some aspects of their education and point out the need for faculty to work more diligently to convince students that undervalued learning outcomes are important.

Sometimes surveys can be embedded in the curriculum. For example, the Freshman Year Experience group at Virginia Commonwealth University learned a great deal about their freshmen using a "Prompts Project." Students in a required freshman writing course did weekly 10-minute writings on a series of writing prompts, such as questions concerning campus social life, grades, relationships with instructors, and academic honesty. They obtained about 700 responses each week, about 10,000 essays in all. Teams of volunteer campus professionals analyzed responses to each question. They began with a preliminary reading to identify themes, then coded the essays and looked for interesting unique perspectives. They collected student demographic information with the essays, so they were able to analyze findings for subgroups of students; they finished their work by summarizing conclusions and making recommendations for institutional change. Although the workload was high, campus professionals who served as reviewers found the experience gave them new perspectives about their freshmen, and many of their recommendations resulted in campus improvements, including major efforts to engage students in large freshman courses (Hodges & Yerian, 2004).

Surveys can also be used to ask students' opinions about proposed changes in courses or programs. For example, Eastern Connecticut State University invited students in their first-year seminar course, Resources, Research, and Responsibility, to respond to proposed changes, and they expressed strong support (76%) for creating discipline-specific sections (Lashley, 2005).

Locally developed surveys, like the example in Figure 6.2, can explicitly target local learning outcomes. A variety of professionally developed surveys are also available, and they give campuses the opportunity to use questions that have already been tested and to compare local findings to results from other campuses.

National Survey of Student Engagement and the Community College Survey of Student Engagement

The National Survey of Student Engagement (NSSE; http://www .iub.edu/~nsse) and its community college version, the Community College Survey of Student Engagement (CCSSE; http://www.ccsse.org), although less than a decade old, have become very popular assessment instruments. Based on decades of research on the importance of student engagement, these surveys ask students to report their engagement in a number of activities, such as participating in study groups and visiting faculty during office hours. These surveys also collect information on aspects of the college environment, such as being challenged by exams and developing positive relationships with peers, and they obtain student self-assessments on their personal growth in a number of areas, such as developing a personal code of ethics.

NSSE campuses learn how their students responded to each question, and they receive overall scores for five key clusters: level of academic challenge, student interaction with faculty members, active and collaborative learning, enriching educational experiences, and supportive campus environment.

Some NSSE results have caused national concern. For example, findings based on responses from 163,000 full-time students representing 472 four-year institutions indicated that most students spend less time studying than faculty expect. Almost half of them (44%) reported studying less than 10 hours a week, in spite of their full-time status. Results also provide some pleasant news. For example, about 90% of students classified their college experience as "good" or "excellent," and about 60% of seniors and 37% of freshmen reported doing volunteer work (Students Study, 2004). Annual reports are available on the NSSE web site.

To encourage the use of the NSSE for general education assessment and accreditation reviews, NSSE staff developed "toolkits" for each regional accrediting body. For example, the *Accreditation Toolkit* for the Western Association (NSSE, 2004) notes that NSSE results are actionable because they identify specific characteristics of the undergraduate experience that can be strengthened. If the survey is repeatedly administered, campuses can track improvements in student engagement across time and can examine relationships between increased engagement and student learning. Campus results can be compared to benchmarks for similar or *aspirational* comparison groups. For example, leaders at a four-year public college can compare results to other four-year public colleges; but they also might *aspire* to be more like private liberal arts colleges, so they can compare local results to that comparison group, too. Faculty are sometimes pleased with these comparisons, and sometimes embarrassed and surprised that their students rate them lower than expected.

The *Accreditation Toolkit* for the Western Region maps NSSE items onto specific WASC standards and provides seven "accreditation tips." For example, the first tip is, "Student engagement results provided by NSSE are one direct indicator of what students put into their education and an indirect indicator of what they get out of it" (NSSE, 2004, p. 10). The *Toolkit* also provides examples of campuses that have used NSSE as evidence in accreditation reviews. For example, the University of California–Santa Cruz used NSSE results to demonstrate that their students spend more time reading and studying, and they develop stronger relationships with faculty than students at comparison institutions. Other campuses have responded to NSSE findings productively, and this can be used as evidence of an effective, ongoing cycle of assessment and improvement. For example, Lawrence Technological University students reported doing less writing than students at comparison institutions, and this finding led the campus to enact a major, university-wide writing initiative; faculty at Southern Utah University used NSSE results to revise their general education curriculum and its outcomes, including the addition of a new first-year success program.

Campuses must decide which NSSE items and scales are of local interest. For example, Indiana Wesleyan University has "an evangelical Christian
commitment" that "permeates the programming and culture and comple-
ments the campus focus on life purpose" (Pattengale, 2005, p. 67). Campus
professionals were pleased with their students' average rating of 3.10 (on a
4-point scale) on "Participated in activities to enhance spirituality," compared to 2.11 for the Council of Independent Colleges and 2.08 for the
NSSE national norm group (Pattengale, 2005). The University of
Arkansas–Fort Smith (2003–2004) used specific NSSE items that corre-
sponded to their general education learning outcomes as supplements to
their direct assessment findings. For example, to analyze students' ability to
read well, they used results from the reading section of the CAAP exam,
local reviews of the reading program, and the NSSE question concerning
the amount of reading students do compared to other institutions. Belcheir
(2003) analyzed the responses of Boise State University freshmen and seniors on selected NSSE items and scales. She identified strengths, such as student reports of growth in critical thinking and writing skills, and areas of
concern, such as the need to increase instruction in information literacy and
the understanding of diversity.

The Community College Survey of Student Engagement (CCSSE)
became operational in 2001, and its major use is as a diagnostic test for
identifying specific opportunities to improve the level of student engagement. The publishers recommend that CCSSE results be analyzed
separately for students varying in age, ethnicity, gender, and income.
Combining these findings with similar analyses of student success in developmental and general education courses, grades, and progress toward
graduation allows campuses to identify groups of students who require
special attention.

CCSSE institutions receive feedback on each item and on five benchmark scales that reflect active and collaborative learning, student effort, academic challenge, student-faculty interaction, and support for learners.
Benchmark scores have a mean of 50 and a standard deviation of 25, so
campuses can easily tell how their students' opinions compare to students
at other community colleges.

Annual reports on findings are available on the CCSSE web site
(http://www.ccsse.org). The report on the 2004 findings (CCSSE, 2005)
analyzes results for more than 92,000 students from 152 community colleges, and it identifies 31 campuses as "top performers" with high rankings

on at least three of the five benchmark scales. Authors suggest that the most important comparison, though, is not external, but internal. Campuses should use their own CCSSE results as a benchmark and work toward their own definition of where they want to be.

The report provides many examples of community college efforts related to the benchmark scales. For example:

- To promote active and collaborative learning, the library at Santa Fe Community College provides indoor and outdoor space for students to work together, including a café.

- To increase student effort, James A. Rhodes College requires students to use stated criteria to self-assess papers, and their self-assessments are later compared to assessments by a peer or faculty member.

- Tallahassee Community College provides student rosters with photographs and email addresses to each instructor to promote student-faculty interaction.

- Sinclair Community College annually requires all full-time employees to participate in 16 hours of "customer service training" to ensure that student support is given priority.

The First-Year Initiative Survey

The First-Year Initiative (FYI; http://www.webebi.com/University/FYI) benchmarking survey was piloted in 2001 and is designed to assess ten types of learning outcomes typically fostered in first-year experience seminars:

- Study strategies

- Academic/cognitive skills

- Critical thinking

- Connections with faculty

- Connections with peers

- Out-of-class engagement

- Knowledge of campus policies

- Knowledge of wellness/spirituality

- Management of time/priorities

- Knowledge of wellness (Swing, 2004b, p. 119)

In addition, it collects demographic information (e.g., gender, age, living arrangements, alcohol use) and assesses campus satisfaction and some aspects of course delivery (e.g., effective readings, engaging pedagogy). Developers recommend that colleges administer the survey in the last week of the first-year seminar, that institution-wide results be compared to those from similar campuses, and that each local section be compared to a composite of other on-campus first-year seminars so that systematic strengths and problems can be identified. In addition, campus data can be analyzed to examine relationships between characteristics of the seminar, demographic, and outcome variables to determine which aspects of the course appear to have positive impact on student learning and which do not appear to be working effectively for some or all students (Swing, 2004b).

Campuses are finding the FYI useful. For example, Cardinal Stritch University used the inventory in 2003, and they found considerable variability in scores across sections of their first-year experience seminar. Although some of the differences made sense (e.g., a seminar focusing on writing, *Writing Your Own Story*, had unusually high scores on developing writing skills), faculty were concerned about some unusually low ratings. They decided to hold annual discussions of FYI results so that faculty can learn from their experiences and each other, and they developed a workshop for faculty who teach this course to help them better align their courses with campus expectations (Meuler, 2005).

Rollins College used the inventory in 2002 and 2003, allowing them to track changes and to see if identified goals had been reached. For example, they made changes to improve student interactions and found evidence for the desired impact. The campus percentile rank for the item "Course improved efforts to get to know students in my classes" increased from 44 to 73, and "Course improved ability to meet new people with common interests" increased from 35 to 61 from 2002 to 2003. Like many other campuses, Rollins College found that living-learning communities based in residence halls were particularly effective (Edge, 2005).

Other Professionally Developed Surveys

The Cooperative Instructional Research Program (CIRP) at the Higher Education Research Institute at the University of California–Los Angeles (www.gseis.ucla.edu/heri/freshman) manages the CIRP Freshman Survey for new students and Your First College Year (YFCY) survey for students about to move into the sophomore year. The CIRP Freshman Survey has been around since 1966, and it is administered to more than 350,000 students at more than 650 campuses each year. Questions deal with demographic characteristics (e.g., age, gender, religion, parental occupations), high school background (e.g., grades, courses), financial support (e.g., scholarships, jobs), college planning (e.g., reasons for going to college, expectations about college), student aspirations (e.g., planned major and career goals), and attitudes and values (e.g., attitudes toward social issues). Campuses can use this survey to understand incoming students, plan activities that meet their needs, compare findings to similar campuses, examine relationships between scores and student success indicators, and assess the broad impact of general education programs. For example, some scores are known to be correlated with freshman retention and success in science and mathematics courses (House, 2004).

Colleges began using the Your First College Year survey in 2000, which was designed for use in concert with the Freshman Survey to document changes. About a third of the items overlap with the CIRP Freshman Survey, and other items are designed to collect information on students' grades, campus experiences, satisfaction with the curriculum and cocurriculum, and self-confidence. Campuses can compare results found in the two surveys, and they can compare local findings with national norms (Sax & Gilmartin, 2004).

Alternative freshman surveys also exist, such as the Perceptions, Expectations, Emotions, and Knowledge about College survey (PEEK; http://www.hhpublishing.com/_assessments/PEEK). This 30-question survey assesses incoming students' expectations about their upcoming personal, social, and academic college experiences. It is designed to help student affairs staff and freshman faculty identify issues that should be addressed, such as discrepancies between student and faculty expectations for study time outside of class (Weinstein, King, Hsieh, Acee, & Palmer, 2004).

The College Student Experiences Questionnaire (CSEQ; http://www.indiana.edu/~cseq) and a shortened version, the College Student Expectations Questionnaire (CSXQ; http://www.indiana.edu/~cseq/csxq_generalinfo.htm), can be used separately or together. The CSXQ is designed to assess expectations among incoming freshmen (Gonyea, 2004), and the CSEQ is designed to assess experiences as students are about to complete the freshman year or to begin their sophomore year (Siegel, 2004). Common items deal with a variety of topics, such as information technology, student-faculty interactions, faculty expectations for reading and writing, and the cocurriculum. The CSEQ includes questions on the "quality of effort" expended in the first year, student perceptions of their own learning, and satisfaction with aspects of their first year in college. Used alone, the CSXQ can be used to identify areas of concern that require intervention, and the CSEQ can be used to understand student self-perceptions concerning their experiences and the relationship between those experiences and their learning. Used together, they allow researchers to compare expectations with reality, and this information can be integrated into freshman orientations or first-year experience courses.

Designed for community college students, the Community College Student Experiences Questionnaire (CCSEQ; http://coe.memphis.edu/CSHE/CCSEQ.asp), like the CSEQ, focuses on student "quality of effort" in their first year of college. Students report how often they participated in academic and social learning activities, such as interactions with faculty and peers, writing, and developing computer skills. In addition, students estimate their learning gains in six areas, such as career preparation, communication skills, and personal and social development. As with the CSEQ, analyses of results show positive relationships between reported effort and learning gains (Murrell, 2004; Siegel, 2004). Students who are engaged in their learning learn more, which supports the movement in higher education toward more active and collaborative learning models.

The Noel-Levitz Student Satisfaction Inventory (SSI; http://www.noellevitz.com) measures student satisfaction and priorities. Students rate their satisfaction with and the importance of a variety of campus characteristics, such as the adequacy of the library, bookstore, tutoring services, and computer labs. The survey report identifies campus strengths (items with high importance and satisfaction ratings) and challenges (items with high importance and low satisfaction ratings); the publishers recommend that results be used for strategic planning, improving student retention efforts, accreditation evidence, institutional marketing, and assessing progress toward campus-defined goals. The *National Student Satisfaction and Priorities Report* (Noel-Levitz, 1998–2005) summarizes findings for more than 675,000 students at more than 860 colleges and universities.

Students need to learn how to learn well and how to exploit their strengths when they study. A number of inventories related to learning and studying styles have been around for years, and they are based on a variety of theoretical models. Faculty can use these inventories to help students become more aware of how they learn, to help students improve learning skills, and to tailor assignments to specific learning strengths among students in their courses.

Suskie (2004) reviews a number of learning style inventories, including those based on the field independence/dependence model (ability to overcome contextual distractions), Jungian theory (e.g., the Myers-Briggs Type Indicator), sensory models (e.g., students might learn best by seeing, rather than by hearing), social interaction models (related to collaborative learning), multiple intelligences theory (e.g., differential development of musical or linguistic skills), and deep learning models (e.g., surface vs. deep learning). Although most of the instruments are not well validated, they may be useful to students and faculty for provoking ideas. Faculty might develop better understanding of the variety of students in their courses, and they might develop a greater appreciation of the differences between students' and their own approach to learning. In addition, learning styles may be useful as assessment tools when considering the alignment between course instruction and student needs (Suskie, 2004).

Two examples of such instruments are the Learning and Study Strategies Inventory (LASSI; http://www.hhpublishing.com/_assessments/LASSI/index.html) and the Study Behavior Inventory (SBI). The LASSI is based on cognitive and metacognitive models for learning and thinking, and results are summarized in ten scores related to skill, will, and self-regulation components of learning. Items ask students about studying characteristics, such as exam preparation skills, attitudes about studying, and time management. In addition, the LASSI web site provides tutorials to help students improve their study habits, test-taking skills, and motivation to succeed academically (Weinstein, Julie, Corliss, Cho, & Palmer, 2004). The LASSI can be used to document improved study strategies. For example, Southeastern Louisiana University students took the LASSI at the start and finish of their "Freshman Seminar 101" course, and analysis revealed significant increase in study skills in all areas, except for scales related to motivation and attitude, prompting campus leaders to consider additional course changes to address these issues (Wood, 2005).

The Study Behavior Inventory (SBI; http://www.sbi4windows.com/) focuses on student self-reported study behaviors—what they actually do rather than what they know how to do. Three scores were derived through factor analysis: Academic Self-Efficacy; Time Management for Preparing for Routine, Short-Term Academic Tasks; and Time Management for Preparing for Specific, Long-Range Academic Tasks. Students indicate how often they engage in a variety of behaviors, such as getting anxious during exams, routinely preparing for class, and planning long-term projects. Faculty can use this instrument to identify potential problems and intervene early to prevent academic catastrophes (Bliss, 2004).

Strengths and Limitations of Surveys

Surveys are very flexible tools that can easily collect opinions about a variety of issues. They can be given to large samples, so data can be separately analyzed for subgroups, if desired. Of the three techniques in this chapter, surveys are by far the least expensive way to collect indirect data, so it is not surprising that they are used more frequently than interviews and focus groups. Responses to close-ended questions are easy to tabulate, and visual displays can effectively communicate results. Responses to open-ended questions tend to be short and relatively easy to analyze. Surveys do not require face-to-face contact, so they can be administered via mail, email, or web sites, and respondents can fill them out at their convenience. Short surveys also can be conducted within classes, so responses from many individuals can be collected quickly. A variety of popular, professionally developed surveys are available, and they provide norms so campuses can compare local results to national benchmarks.

The validity of survey data depends on the quality of the questions and respondent willingness to carefully read and respond to them. Researchers generally consider the *response rate*, the proportion of surveys that are returned. Mailed surveys often have fairly low response rates, under 30%, so the representativeness of the sample often is questionable, making it problematic to generalize results to the entire population of interest. For example, if students who have strong feelings, either positive or negative, are more likely to complete surveys, opinions may appear more divided than they really are. A last problem with surveys is a problem for any indirect assessment technique: What people say they do or know may be inconsistent with what they actually do or know.

Interviews

Researchers can interview students, alumni, employers, faculty, staff, and others to collect indirect assessment data. These interviews are oral surveys, but with two advantages. Respondents have the opportunity to ask for an explanation if they don't understand a question, and interviewers can probe for details and ask questions to clarify responses. The data collection process is more dynamic than for surveys, and open-ended questions are likely to elicit more complete answers.

The cost for this more dynamic process is time. While surveying a few hundred people is relatively easy, interviewing the same number would require a lot of time, so interviews are generally done with small, representative samples.

Recruiting interview participants can be tricky. Students may be invited in selected classes, or they may receive phone, letter, or email invitations. Campuses frequently pay a nominal stipend or offer other incentives, such as bookstore credit, to make it more likely that students will show up for scheduled interviews, but usually this payment is so low that the no-show rate interferes with interview schedules. Spontaneous, on-campus student interviews might be conducted in public places, such as cafeterias or libraries; faculty and staff interviews could be scheduled during their office hours, increasing the chance of data collection.

Although interviewing, done well, looks simple, it requires interpersonal skills, and some training is essential. In addition, interviews are best done by neutral parties, rather than general education insiders, to convince the eventual audience for the report that results are unbiased. If the campus has an assessment center or faculty development center, center professionals might conduct interviews for the general education program, or they might train students who conduct interviews under their direction. The use of student interviewers benefits everyone. Student respondents are likely to be comfortable talking to another student, the interviewers gain practical skills and experiences, the campus benefits from the results, and campus professionals' time is spent supervising, rather than conducting the interviews.

Interviews should be conducted to elicit complete, honest opinions and to protect the privacy and confidentiality of respondents. Allen (2004) provides some tips for effective interviewing:

- Conduct the interview in an environment that allows the interaction to be confidential and uninterrupted.

- Demonstrate respect for the respondents as *participants* in the assessment process rather than as *subjects*. Explain the purpose of the project, how the data will be used, how the respondents' anonymity or confidentiality will be maintained, and the respondents' rights as participants. Ask if they have any questions.

- Put the respondents at ease. Do more listening than talking. Allow respondents to finish their statements without interruption.

- Match follow-up questions to the project's objectives. For example, if the objective is to obtain student feedback about student advising, don't spend time pursuing other topics.

- Do *not* argue with the respondent's point of view, even if you are convinced that the viewpoint is incorrect. Your role is to obtain the respondents' opinions, not to convert them to your perspective.

- Allow respondents time to process the question. They may not have thought about the issue before, and they may require time to develop a thoughtful response.

- Paraphrase to verify that you have understood the respondent's comments. Respondents will sometimes realize that what they said isn't what they meant, or you may have misunderstood them. Paraphrasing provides an opportunity to improve the accuracy of the data.

- Make sure you know how to record the data and include a backup system. You may be using a tape recorder—if so, consider supplementing the tape with written notes in case the recorder fails or the tape is faulty. Always build in a system for verifying that the tape is functioning or that other data recording procedures are working. Don't forget your pencil and paper! (pp. 116–117)

Strengths and Limitations of Interviews

Interviews are flexible in format, and they can include a mix of close-ended and open-ended questions to target an array of issues. Interviewers can encourage respondents to provide more complete answers and explanations, so responses to open-ended questions are likely to be richer in detail and more complete than responses to similar survey questions. In addition, respondents can ask for clarification about questions, so they are likely to understand what is being asked.

Scheduling one-on-one interviews can be challenging, and interviewers are likely to experience some frustration when scheduled interviewees fail to show up. Under most circumstances, data are collected from a limited number of respondents, so it may not be possible to disaggregate data for subgroups of students. The quality of the data depends, in part, on the quality of the interviewers. If they fail to connect with respondents, misread or inappropriately rephrase questions, incorrectly answer questions, fail to probe for needed details, or let personal biases affect results, the study is likely to lack validity.

Focus Groups

Focus groups provide the dynamic interchange available through interviews, and they usually are used to uncover more in-depth responses to fewer issues. In addition, participants can hear each other's ideas and respond to them, allowing the facilitator to check for consensus. Imagine that you did ten interviews and one respondent generated a wonderful idea. Your report would summarize your findings, and you might note that one person had an idea worth sharing. On the other hand, if you had the same ten individuals in a focus group, you could check for agreement and might be able to report that participants unanimously endorsed the idea.

Like interviewers, effective focus group facilitators have strong interpersonal skills. In addition, they have to understand group dynamics. "Facilitators must be able to establish rapport with participants and generate their trust; and they must manage the discussion to engage all participants, elicit the full range of opinions, and keep the process focused on project goals" (Allen, 2004, p. 119). They must juggle process and content to ensure effective data collection.

Although we use the term *focus group*, most assessment projects involve structured group interviews. *Traditional focus groups* are conducted by highly skilled facilitators who subtly guide open discussions toward targeted issues (Morgan & Krueger, 1998). Groups are small (usually six to ten people), all members fully participate in the discussion, and the facilitator does not follow a tightly structured script. Participants in heterogeneous groups may not share opinions if they feel intimidated or out-of-place in the discussion, so multiple focus groups are conducted with homogenous groups, such as older women students, athletes, or international students. Traditional focus groups are usually tape-recorded and transcribed, and the facilitator may spend days analyzing the transcripts from a series of focus groups to prepare an in-depth report.

Structured group interviews are more tightly scripted, and they are frequently conducted with larger groups, such as classes of students. Although facilitators need good skills, they do not have to have the expertise required for traditional focus group leaders. Facilitators generally follow a strictly defined protocol, with all questions prepared in advance, including some optional questions that might be used if answers seem incomplete. Sessions might be audiotaped, but interviewers generally take notes and periodically verify that the notes are accurate summaries of the opinions being expressed. These notes, augmented by listening to the tape, generally form the basis for the report.

Facilitators routinely check with respondents to ensure that they are correctly interpreting what is said and that all opinions are expressed and considered. For example, the focus group facilitator might say, "It seems that many of you agree that . . . Is this accurate? Please raise your hand if you agree with this statement. Now raise your hand if you disagree with it. Lily and Paul, I notice you raised your hands. Can you explain why you disagree? . . . What do the rest of you think about their ideas?"

Facilitators can integrate short surveys and other activities into group interviews. For example, Noel (personal communication, June 11, 2005) and his colleagues at California State University–Bakersfield, adapting work done at the United States Air Force Academy (Millis, 1999, 2001, 2004), conducted structured group interviews to assess academic programs, and they included several short exercises. After a brief welcome and orientation to the exercise:

- Students fill out a brief survey that summarizes their demographic characteristics and long-term goals.

- Students write a word or short phrase on an index card that characterizes their attitude toward the program being assessed, and they rate the quality of the program using a 1 to 5 rating scale.

- As a warm-up for the group interview, each student, in turn, shares his/her rating and word or phrase.

- The facilitator asks the group several pre-determined questions and encourages everyone to contribute ideas.

- Students work in small groups to develop short lists of the program's strengths and areas that should be improved, then, within their small groups, they rank order entries on the two lists.

- Students fill out a short survey that asks them to comment on the group interview experience and to indicate if they felt free to contribute their ideas.

The report summarizes each component, beginning with a description of the process and a summary of the participants (based on the first brief survey). The second short exercise is presented in a histogram that includes students' comments and ratings. (See Figure 6.3) The report summarizes the major ideas that emerged during the group interview and the extent of agreement with them. The rank-ordered lists are shared verbatim, so that readers can see the extent of student agreement about program strengths and areas that need improving. The last short survey is summarized, and, if all went well, student feedback indicates that the expressed opinions were honest and complete. At the end, an executive summary highlights the major findings concerning the program.

Figure 6.3
Index Card Histogram

1	2	3	4	5
				Great foundation
				Interesting
		Good		Engaging
	Too many required papers	Well-organized		Great core courses!
Too many required courses	Too much to learn	Learned a lot		Informative
Some courses were dull	Could use more interaction	Satisfied		Opened my eyes to new ideas

1	2	3	4	5
Not at all Satisfied	Slightly Satisfied	Moderately Satisfied	Very Satisfied	Extremely Satisfied

*Adapted from Allen (2004), p. 123.

Although this seems like a lot of work, Noel and his team routinely completed the whole interview process in approximately one hour. Noel and his professional colleagues at the Assessment Center trained and supervised students who worked in pairs to facilitate the group interviews, and interviews were conducted during regularly scheduled class periods. Small classes were interviewed together, but if the enrollment exceeded 25 students, the class was split in half and two structured group interviews were conducted simultaneously.

Strengths and Limitations of Focus Groups

Focus groups and structured group interviews allow campuses to collect in-depth perspectives concerning a few issues, rather than brief responses to a large number of questions. Interviewers can probe for details about the reasoning underlying respondents' beliefs and attitudes, and these details can be crucial when campuses respond to direct assessment findings. Participants can respond to each other's ideas, so rich information becomes available, and the facilitator can check for consensus and the reasons underlying differing opinions. Short surveys and other activities can be used in conjunction with structured group interviews to collect a great deal of information in a limited amount of time.

Focus groups are the most time-intensive of the three strategies discussed in this chapter, and focus group leaders must have strong interpersonal skills and knowledge of group dynamics. The validity of results depends on the quality of the questions, facilitator skills, and data interpretation skills when preparing the report. Like interviews, focus groups are best conducted by neutral parties who are unlikely to bias responses or their interpretation. Recruiting and scheduling focus groups can be difficult, but conducting student groups within classes can solve this problem.

Analyzing Data from Surveys, Interviews, and Focus Groups

Responses to close-ended questions are fairly easy to summarize, and results generally are presented in tables or charts. Although some people can easily interpret tables of numbers, others might require visual displays to understand what was found. Visual displays also have the potential to ignite enthusiasm, especially if results strongly confirm or disconfirm expectations. For example, Figure 6.4 presents the percentage of responses to two survey items for two groups of respondents. Before you look at the next two figures, determine the pattern of results. Then take a look at Figures 6.5 and 6.6. Do they lead you to the same conclusion? If your answer is "yes," you might not require visual displays, but if your answer is "no," you'll appreciate the value of alternative data summaries.

Figure 6.4
Percentage of Responses to Each Item

Group	Strongly Disagree	Agree	Neutral	Agree	Strongly Agree
Item A: *I learned to write well in my GE courses.*					
1	45	55	0	0	0
2	0	5	20	40	35
Item B: *I learned to think critically in my GE courses.*					
1	20	40	25	10	5
2	25	35	20	15	5

Figure 6.5
Results for Item A: *I learned to write well in my GE courses.*

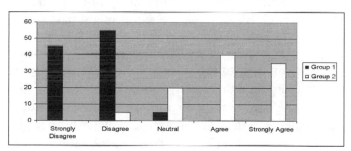

Figure 6.6
Results for Item B: *I learned to think critically in my GE courses.*

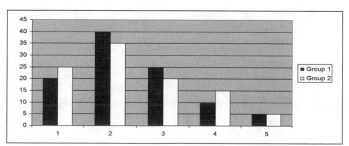

If too many questions have been asked, summary tables are usually produced. I have seen three-inch thick binders of summary tables from campus studies, with so much information and so many variables that most people don't even look at them or only give them a casual glance. To be effective, fewer, more focused questions should be asked, and those who review results should care about the answers to each question.

Making sense out of responses to open-ended questions requires more effort. Usually responses to survey questions are relatively short, so the task is not as difficult as reviewing tapes or transcripts from long interviews or focus groups. The goal of the *content analysis* is to accurately report what was learned, focusing on the issues that were to be explored.

Reviewers usually begin the content analysis by scanning the responses to identify recurring or important themes, although sometimes the themes are predetermined. For example, if students are reporting how well they mastered each outcome, basic categories might be *weak*, *moderate*, and *strong*. But, if students are identifying the types of learning experiences that were productive or if they are making suggestions to improve the learning environment, the reviewer creates conceptual groupings. Once themes are known, the reviewer creates a *coding scheme* to guide the review of each response so that judgments are made consistently and the degree of agreement can be examined. For example, the report might state:

> Forty-eight of the 64 students offered suggestions for improving the learning environment to foster information literacy. Almost half of them (46%) suggested that faculty more clearly explain their expectations, 42% suggested that instructors spend more class time in computer labs helping students develop these skills, 25% suggested that librarians be better informed about faculty expectations for particular courses, and 17% suggested that faculty provide more explicit formative feedback to help them develop these skills.

Notice that this summary is objective. It lets readers know how many students offered ideas, and it communicates how frequently each idea was expressed. The goal is to accurately summarize what respondents said, without imposing your own "spin" on results.

Reviewers generally are more effective in explaining what was heard when examples of verbatim comments are included, and these comments are likely to have a more emotional impact on readers. For example, a report might state:

Twenty-seven of the interviewed students worked during the day and took evening classes. All of these students had concerns about the availability of courses and campus services to evening students, such as:

- "I was never able to see an advisor because none were available at night."

- "I really wanted to take a different GE science course, but I had to take the only one that was offered at night this year."

- "I never get to know my teachers. They run home right after class, and they hold office hours while I'm at work. I'd like to do some independent study research, but I guess that's just not possible."

- "I heard that day students got to substitute some community service for a paper in that course, but we didn't get that option. I would have loved to do some weekend volunteer work instead of another paper."

- "I got a letter from the financial aid office asking me to come in to discuss my application, but they're only open during the day. My job is an hour from campus; there's no way I can pop over for something like this. It took several phone calls to get this resolved—what a run-around."

Making sense out of qualitative data is an art, as well as a science. It requires a willingness to hear what respondents are telling us, without introducing our own biases. Well-done qualitative studies can provide essential information about student experiences in our general education programs, as well as the opinions of others. Surveys, interviews, and focus groups can be effective tools in our assessment programs, and they can provide crucial information on the links between teaching and learning.

CHAPTER 7

Bringing It All Together

Geneneral education is the foundation of undergraduate education, and the assessment of general education can focus an entire institution on student learning. General education assessment is more challenging than the assessment of single-discipline programs. Classes are distributed throughout the campus, and they are taught mostly by faculty whose primary allegiance is to their discipline. Adjunct faculty offer many general education courses, and it is essential that they be actively involved in the assessment program. Faculty hiring and course assignments generally are controlled by department chairs and deans, and the general education committee relies on department chairs and other colleagues to ensure that courses match their expectations. General education leaders often must advocate for the support of their program, and they may feel that they have all the responsibility, but none of the authority for this program, with the exception of their ability to certify and recertify courses. As campuses move toward being more learning-centered, conversations about the effectiveness of the general education program become easier.

Learning-Centered Institutions

Most campuses claim to be learning centered, although they may not share a common definition of this term. Here are some characteristics that most would endorse:

- Assessment is an essential process. Faculty ask if students master learning outcomes and staff assess their impact on students, and they are flexible and creative when developing solutions to identified deficiencies.

- Faculty and staff see institutional effectiveness as a goal, contribute to it, and work collegially to promote student success.

- Campus recognition and reward systems recognize and reward contributions to student learning.

- Campus policies and procedures, including program reviews and budgeting, support learning and rely on empirical evidence for decision-making.

- Faculty and staff development programs provide ongoing support for the development of effective strategies and the collegial sharing of ideas.

- Campus professionals are accustomed to routine campus conversations about the general education program and student learning in it.

- General education programs, including first-year experience seminars, acculturate students to college life, including discussion of faculty expectations for their active participation as intentional learners. Institutions do more than provide access to higher education; they help students develop the tools they need to succeed.

- Faculty collaborate to create a cohesive curriculum that systematically helps students develop increasing sophistication within the general education program and beyond. Students are given repeated opportunities to practice, receive feedback, and reflect on their learning, as well as to integrate what they are learning in different courses.

- Faculty systematically align assignments, activities, and grading procedures with course outcomes; engage learners; and encourage their development as intentional learners.

- Faculty recognize that students come with different backgrounds and learn in different ways, and they develop a repertoire of teaching and course-design strategies to address diverse students and learning outcomes.

- Staff who provide direct support to students and who design the cocurricular environment develop opportunities to enrich student learning.

Professionals at learning-centered institutions have institutionalized assessment and recognize its value for improving student learning and retention. Maki (2004) suggests one way to verify that assessment has been institutionalized: When she hears, "We were doing fine until our provost left," "Our director of assessment left so we haven't been able to sustain our commitment," or "We are waiting to hire a new president" (p. 171), she knows that campus professionals view assessment as being driven by individuals, rather than as being a long-term institutional commitment to improving student learning.

The pedagogy in learning-centered institutions is based on engagement and the idea that learning is a social and cognitive act—enhanced through discussion, reflection, practice, feedback, and authentic activities. Although many faculty have been moving toward increased use of active and collaborative learning over the last few decades, in earlier years they lacked benchmarking tools that are available today. For example, the NSSE and CCSSE make it possible for campuses to take a snapshot of their students' engagement and compare local findings to national norms. These surveys provide actionable feedback—campuses can pinpoint specific areas to address, and professionals receive the assistance they need to respond through active faculty and staff development programs. Tracking survey results over time provides a historical record of the impact of program changes.

Assessment Planning

Campuses generally use one of two basic models for general education goals and outcomes, and they use one or more of three basic models for assessing the program. Learning goals and outcomes can be:

- A short list of broad competencies, such as communication and critical thinking

- A longer list of more narrow competencies generally associated with specific segments of the curriculum, such as an understanding of social science principles or the scientific method

Both approaches have strengths. Assessment leaders might find it easier to engage the campus in multi-disciplinary discussions of a short list of broad outcomes. A short list is easier to remember, can be translated into a core program, and can define campus culture by summarizing the marks of a campus graduate. Outcomes might be so broad, however, that closing the loop can be difficult, and assessment requires strong, centralized leadership. Longer lists provide useful details for course certification and course-level assessment, but so many outcomes are being assessed that broad, campus-wide issues and connections between courses might not be addressed. Campuses with longer lists can consider clustering some outcomes together as they develop their assessment plan, increasing the chance of campus-wide engagement in the discussion of results and their implications.

Assessment can focus at the course, program, or institutional level. Course-embedded assessment is generally conducted by faculty in their own general education courses, who usually collaborate with colleagues who teach other sections of the same course. Campuses that rely on this approach generally require the ongoing assessment of general education courses for course certification and recertification. This approach, done well, is likely to improve individual courses, but it may be more difficult for campuses to assess the program as a whole, and to identify needed improvements in connections between courses or student support outside of the classroom. Program-level assessment generally focuses on specific segments of the program, such as the arts and humanities courses and their associated learning outcomes. This approach requires more centralized coordination and the cooperation of multiple departments, and it is likely to result in cross-disciplinary discussions about teaching and learning as well as considerations of program cohesion within the segment being examined. Institution-wide assessment generally focuses on broad learning outcomes and tends to embed assessment within upper-division courses so that transfer students are included in the assessment. This approach requires centralized planning and is likely to engage campus professionals, including non-faculty, in the discussion of results. As the assessment becomes more removed from individual faculty and courses, fewer assessment studies are done, each may be of higher quality, and closing the loop becomes more complicated. In addition, there is increased potential for institution-wide attention, reflection, and consideration of teaching and learning issues.

Most assessment studies focus on student learning, but they can also assess the context for learning, including the cohesion of the learning environment. Alignment matrices (see Chapter 3) are useful for promoting faculty discussion of the cohesion of the general education curriculum. Alignment studies also might examine the relationship of outcomes with pedagogy and grading, and they might focus on student support outside of the classroom, such as the quality of advising, tutoring, and the cocurricular environment. Researchers could examine syllabi and examinations, or they might survey or interview faculty, students, or others to verify that the learning environment supports student development.

Much attention has been paid to student engagement and retention, and institutions have access to a number of tools, such as the National Survey of Student Engagement (NSSE), the Community College Survey of Student Engagement (CCSSE), and the First Year Initiative (FYI). Institutions throughout the nation have developed first-year experience programs, and evidence suggests high potential for helping students develop successful academic careers. The accumulating literature offers many suggestions for providing quality support, such as the characteristics of DEEP (Documenting Effective Educational Practice) Project campuses and the suggested *Engagement by Design* (CCSSE, 2005) strategies.

The Assessment Report

Usually general education assessment projects are conducted by a variety of people, although an institution-wide assessment committee or assessment center staff may coordinate the efforts. For example, a team of mathematics faculty might take primary responsibility for the assessment of quantitative literacy and a team of social science faculty might take primary responsibility for the assessment of social science learning outcomes. Studies often have implications for others, and this might include dozens of adjunct faculty on large campuses, tutoring center staff, advisors, technology professionals, and faculty and staff development directors. Campuses have to find ways to document results, share them with colleagues, and collaborate on their implications. Campus email systems or web sites provide a conduit for assessment reports, and campus leaders might present assessment findings at department chair meetings, faculty and staff development events, in-service workshops, or assessment retreats.

Assessment reports serve other important functions. They record the ongoing assessment program and its impact. New general education faculty, department chairs, general education committee members, and administrators can review these records to understand what has been done, what has been learned, and why changes were made; they can use this record to revise assessment plans to verify that changes have had their desired impact. In addition, campuses can use the accumulating record as evidence that they are meeting accreditors' expectations.

Assessment reports should honestly summarize what was learned and should communicate sufficient detail about the study so that readers can understand how data were collected and interpreted. Research reports generally have the following components:

- *Introduction.* The introduction describes the outcomes being assessed, provides relevant history, and identifies how decisions were made as the study was conducted. It also identifies who was involved in the study, such as the names of faculty who assessed student products or the names of interviewers or content analysts.

- *Method.* The method section summarizes the sample and data collection procedures in sufficient detail so that readers can make judgments concerning them. Concerned readers will want to know how respondents were selected, how many there were, and any indications concerning the representativeness of the sample. This section reports response or participation rates (the proportion of invited respondents who participated) and summarizes respondents' demographic information, usually using counts and percentages for categorical variables (e.g., gender, ethnicity), and means and standard deviations for quantitative variables (e.g., age, GPA). The demographic breakdown of the sample may be compared to the breakdown among all students to verify that some groups were not systematically over- or under-represented. Verbatim oral instructions and copies of blank data collection forms, printed instructions, tests, and rubrics should be included.

- *Results.* The results section describes the data analysis and findings. If data were statistically analyzed, the report summarizes the tests that were conducted, and details are provided for significant findings. For example, the report might state: "The t test comparing the scores for freshmen and seniors was significant, $t(50)=1.84$, $p<.05$. Freshmen averaged 12.73 (*SD* [standard deviation] =2.14), and seniors averaged 14.69 (*SD*=1.61)." This tells the reader the statistical test that was used, the relevant descriptive statistics (means and standard deviations for the two groups), the calculated test statistic (1.84), and the significance level for the results (<.05). Non-significant results should be listed, but it is generally not necessary to report the other details for them, such as, "The *t* tests comparing freshmen to seniors on ABC and XYZ were not significant." The number and percentage of students classified into each level of a rubric or who responded to options for close-ended survey or interview questions are usually displayed in tables or figures, and sometimes confidence-interval estimates and means and standard deviations for these ratings also are provided. Qualitative results are generally summarized in a narrative that includes a brief description of the content analysis process.

- *Discussion.* The discussion section includes analyses and interpretations of results and implications for change. It also includes caveats concerning the study, such as warnings about non-representative samples or identified flaws in the procedures. The discussion section also might offer suggestions for subsequent studies, including improvements in the research methodology.

- *Executive Summary.* Not everyone who reads the report will be interested in all the details, and the executive summary (or abstract) may be all they read. It should briefly summarize the study, findings, and recommendations, and it may make use of bulleted or numbered lists.

The report author should take readers into account. Faculty and staff who feel insulted by the report are unlikely to eagerly seek solutions or volunteer to make needed changes. Identified strengths should be celebrated, and weaknesses should be addressed as challenges for the institution to solve. The goal is not to attribute blame; it is to move forward.

Academic institutions have a hierarchical administrative structure for many good reasons, and this structure should be respected. Assessment reports should flow from those who do the assessment through the general education committee to relevant faculty and staff, department chairs, shared-governance leaders, deans, provosts, and presidents. The level of relevant detail should shrink as the audience becomes more removed from the hands-on teaching and learning process, and usually only the executive summary or a more streamlined summary goes to the highest levels. Formal channels for this communication are established and routine on learning-centered campuses, as are forums for discussing results and planning for improvement.

Assessment is more than collecting and reporting data; impact is important. Faculty and other relevant stakeholders reflect on results and either confirm what they are doing or identify needed changes. The general education assessment committee might develop an annual report that summarizes assessment projects and provides follow-up information on the impact of earlier studies. For example, did only one instructor out of many revise a course, or did everyone? Did student affairs staff enact changes in response to results? Did administrators provide necessary release time, clerical or technical support, faculty or staff development support, and financial assistance to promote needed changes? What impact should the changes themselves have, and when will this be assessed? Impact summaries, tied to specific assessment findings, are crucial documents in effective assessment programs.

The Infrastructure for General Education Assessment

Assessment of the general education program will not happen without the coordination of faculty, staff, and administrators. Moving toward learning-centered instruction and a culture of evidence requires significant changes in most institutions, and this cannot be accomplished without the support of key administrators:

> While there are many reasons why some institutions are engaged in assessment and others are not, assessment practitioners and scholars have found that one factor predominates. If campus leaders are committed to assessment, assessment gets done and it gets done well. If campus leaders—especially the chief academic officer (vice president for academic affairs, provost, or dean) and the chief executive officer (president or chancellor)—aren't onboard, there may be pockets of assessment efforts across campus but assessment doesn't permeate campus culture. (Suskie, 2004, p. 36)

Suskie's conclusions are particularly true for general education assessment because it requires the attention of the entire institution.

Administrators

The researchers who conducted the DEEP Project note that "many institutions plod along without visionary executive leadership" (Kuh, Kinzie, Schuh, & Whitt, 2005, p. 49), but this is not true at the campuses they studied—campuses with exceptional student engagement and retention. Researchers found vocal, consistent support for student learning at the highest administrative levels. Sustainable movements in higher education require leaders who can inspire campus professionals to "pull in the same direction" and who recruit, socialize, and reward personnel who contribute to campus-wide initiatives. Effective assessment of any program, including general education, requires a campus culture that values contributions to the improvement of student learning.

Maki (2004) argues that high-level administrators, such as presidents and chancellors, have multiple responsibilities. They should:

- Communicate the value of assessment

- Make assessment a core process within the institution

- Ensure that assessment is integrated into "self-reflection, decision making, budgeting, and long- and short-range planning" (p. 6) within the institution

- Create a "neutral zone" (p. 6) for sharing and reflecting on results and suggesting changes

Several types of leadership are needed. Peterson and Vaughan (2002) report on a multiyear study supported by the National Center for Postsecondary Improvement. They found that four types of leadership are required for effective assessment:

- "Externally Oriented Leadership." A president or other leader advocates for institutional control of assessment with relevant funding agencies, governing bodies, and accrediting organizations and maintains positive relationships with these external groups.

- "Strategic Leadership." A chief academic officer or other administrator advocates for and integrates assessment into campus policies and procedures.

- "Process Leadership." A person or group provides training, consulting, and general support for effective assessment.

- "Technical Leadership." A person or group provides technical support in assessment methodology, data analysis, and data base management. (pp. 43–44)

Administrators control many campus incentives, reward systems, and resources. They demonstrate their support for the general education program by publicly promoting its importance, allocating necessary resources, recognizing and rewarding those who take the lead in general education assessment, and working with campus professionals to:

- Establish a person or committee with primary responsibility for overseeing the general education assessment program

- Provide externally oriented and strategic leadership

- Support the development of process and technical leadership

- Provide technical, clerical, and student assistance support for assessment projects

- Enable and support the participation of institutional research and student affairs professionals

- Support the dissemination of findings and provide the resources required for change

General Education Committee Members

Most campuses have general education committees that oversee the program and its assessment. Committee members:

- Work collaboratively with faculty to develop the goals and outcomes for the program

- Work collaboratively with faculty and academic leaders to develop policies for certifying and recertifying courses

- Use course certification and recertification as tools for negotiating alignment of courses, pedagogy, and grading with general education expectations

- Develop a system for assessing the general education program and a multiyear assessment plan that is meaningful, manageable, and sustainable

- Manage the assessment program, working collaboratively with relevant faculty, department chairs, administrators, faculty development and assessment personnel, and assessment teams

- Monitor the quality of assessment studies to ensure that findings are valid, reliable, and actionable

- Develop ways to share results, determine implications, and support needed changes

- Monitor the impact of the assessment program and intervene when necessary

Faculty and Staff Development Professionals, Assessment Personnel, and Institutional Research Staff

Faculty and staff development professionals, assessment personnel, and institutional research staff may accept the responsibility for process and technical leadership, or an assessment center or committee may have this charge. Although an occasional external expert may offer workshops or consultations, ongoing support requires local expertise. Campuses should provide a budget for professional time, clerical and technical support, books, software, supplies, and travel to assessment conferences, such as the Association of American Colleges and Universities annual general education and assessment conference. Whoever takes on this responsibility:

- Provides training for faculty and staff in assessment planning, the design of specific assessment studies, and analysis of assessment results

- May coordinate some or all of the general education assessment studies, working collaboratively with the general education committee and other relevant parties

- May provide direct support themselves, or may train and supervise student assistants or others who support assessment work such as drafting or reviewing surveys, conducting interviews, or collecting and analyzing data

- Provides developmental opportunities to faulty and staff in learning-centered approaches to teaching and supporting student development

- Provides support for implementing changes in response to assessment findings

Faculty

Faculty are in charge of the curriculum, and they are crucial in the general education assessment program. Faculty:

- Define the learning goals and outcomes for the program

- Align courses with the outcomes

- Use pedagogy that supports the outcomes and effectively engages individual learners

- Use assignments and grading to motivate and to provide formative feedback to students

- Use classroom assessment to monitor and improve the day to day operation of their courses

- Cooperate with assessment planners by providing advice and by collecting, assessing, and reflecting on assessment results and responding to findings

- Collaborate with student affairs professionals to promote institutional effectiveness in the support of the general education program

- Serve in leadership roles on the general education assessment committee and on teams that assess specific outcomes

Other Campus Professionals

Students learn in and out of the classroom, and they require support to succeed. For example, student progress will be hindered if campus bookstores don't have required books on the shelves, if financial aid checks arrive late, if parking lots are not accessible, if libraries aren't open, if technology support is unavailable, or if advisors encourage poor course choices. In addition, campuses can enhance learning outcomes by providing opportunities for students to interact with new ideas and to take on leadership positions. Campus professionals play important roles in the general education program and its assessment. They:

- Are aware of general education outcomes and provide support for student learning

- Provide a cocurricular environment that promotes general education outcomes

- Provide an infrastructure that allows students to concentrate on learning

- Collaborate with faculty to reflect on assessment results and implement changes designed to improve student learning

- Assess their impact on student success in the general education program and the rest of the curriculum

Selecting Assessment Techniques

Frequently used assessment techniques are described in Chapters 5 and 6, and many options are available. You want to select techniques that:

- Are valid

- Are reliable

- Generate actionable results

- Are efficient in the use of time and money

- Engage respondents and those who should act on results

In addition, assessment planners should primarily rely on direct assessment techniques (standardized tests, locally developed tests, embedded assignments and activities, and portfolios), and they should seriously consider supplementing this information with indirect techniques (surveys, interviews, and focus groups). Whenever possible, assessment planners should collect multiple measures so they can check for triangulation.

None of the assessment techniques is perfect, and each has potential strengths and limitations. *Direct measures* allow campuses to ascertain the extent to which students have mastered their learning outcomes, and it is important that the chosen technique motivates the engagement of students and has the confidence of those who will close the loop. *Indirect measures* can provide useful opinions about learning and the learning context. As with direct techniques, respondents should be engaged in the process so they will provide complete and honest opinions, and the study should provide information that interests those who will close the loop. Figure 7.1 summarizes some criteria for selecting among the direct assessment techniques, and Figure 7.2 summarizes some criteria for selecting among the indirect techniques.

Figure 7.1
Criteria for Selecting Direct Assessment Techniques

Technique	Selection Criteria: Consider this technique if:
Standardized tests	• Faculty have located a test that measures their learning outcomes. • Faculty want to compare their students' scores to national standards. • Faculty want to use a professionally developed test. • Faculty want to use a test with established reliability and validity. • Faculty have a budget to purchase tests. • Faculty can establish a context for administering the test.
Locally developed tests	• Faculty want the test to align precisely with their learning outcomes. • Faculty want to develop a test that is authentic, performance-based, or delivered orally in a competence interview. • Faculty can establish a context for administering the test. • Faculty are willing to plan the exam, write appropriate items, develop scoring criteria, pilot-test the exam, and score it.
Embedded assignments and activities	• Faculty want the assessment to align precisely with their learning outcomes. • Faculty prefer to use authentic or performance assessment. • Faculty want unobtrusive data collection that requires no add-on work for students. • Faculty are willing to embed relevant assignments or activities in their courses. • Faculty are willing to revise current assignments and activities to focus on specific learning outcomes. • Faculty are willing to create and pilot-test a rubric and use it to assess student products or behaviors.
Student-created portfolios	• Faculty want the assessment to align precisely with their learning outcomes. • Faculty want to promote student engagement and reflection on students' own learning. • Faculty want to use portfolios to track and assist individual students. • Faculty want access to a wide range of student work. • Faculty are willing to plan the assignment and help students develop portfolios. • Faculty are willing to create and pilot-test rubrics and use them to assess the portfolios. • Faculty can establish a context for collecting the portfolios.
Collective portfolios	• Faculty want the assessment to align precisely with a small number of learning outcomes. • Faculty want some of the benefits of student-created portfolios, but with much less work. • Faculty want to review a range of student work from a variety of courses. • Faculty want unobtrusive data collection that requires no add-on work for students. • Faculty can establish a reasonable sampling scheme for collecting student products. • Faculty are willing to assign and collect student products for the collective portfolio. • Faculty are willing to create and pilot-test a rubric and use it to assess the products.

Figure 7.2

Criteria for Selecting Indirect Assessment Techniques

Technique	Selection Criteria: Consider this technique if:
Professionally developed surveys	• Faculty have located a survey that allows them to answer important questions about the general education program. • Faculty are interested in collecting data from a relatively large, representative sample. • Faculty want to compare their students' results to national benchmarks. • Faculty want to use a professionally developed survey. • Faculty want to use a survey with established reliability and validity. • Faculty have a budget to purchase surveys. • Faculty can establish a context for administering the survey.
Locally developed surveys	• Faculty want information directly related to their learning outcomes or to questions that are uniquely local. • Faculty are interested in a variety of questions that can be answered by selecting options in close-ended questions or by briefly writing responses to open-ended questions. • Faculty are interested in collecting data from a relatively large, representative sample. • Faculty are interested in collecting data from people who are not easily available for face-to-face interviews. • Faculty can establish a context for administering the survey. • Faculty or others are willing to plan the survey, write appropriate items, pilot-test the survey, and summarize findings.
Interviews	• Faculty want information directly related to their learning outcomes or to questions that are uniquely local. • Faculty have a limited number of questions, and they want the opportunity to interact with respondents, to answer their questions, and to prompt for greater depth in their answers. • Faculty are interested in collecting more in-depth information from a smaller, representative sample. • Faculty have concerns that surveys will not be returned, will not be taken seriously, or will not be interpreted correctly by respondents. • Faculty can establish a context for conducting the interviews. • Faculty or others are willing to plan the interview protocol, write appropriate questions, pilot-test the interview, and summarize findings. • Someone is willing to train and supervise interviewers.
Focus groups	• Faculty want information directly related to their learning outcomes or to questions that are uniquely local. • Faculty have only two or three questions, and they want to have the opportunity to prompt for greater depth in respondent' answers and for participants to hear and respond to each other's ideas. • Faculty are interested in collecting more in-depth information through a thorough discussion of ideas and the reasoning behind them. • Faculty want to be able to check for consensus and points of disagreement. • Faculty can establish a context for conducting the focus groups. • Faculty or others are willing to plan the focus group protocol, write appropriate questions, pilot-test the interview, and summarize findings. • Someone is willing to train and supervise focus group facilitators.

Some Friendly Suggestions

As educators, we have the unique opportunity to develop the next generation's cultural, social, economic, and political leaders. We have the responsibility to help students develop a lasting foundation for lifelong learning, understanding, application, and appreciation of various approaches to understanding individuals, cultures, and the world we live in. Here are a few friendly suggestions for developing a meaningful, manageable, sustainable, and productive general education assessment program.

Don't skip steps. Remember the six steps in Chapter 1? It might be tempting to jump into assessment using a tool developed elsewhere, such as a standardized test, without thinking through your general education learning outcomes. In my experience, this generally results in scores that no one really cares about and that might have little to do with what faculty want their students to learn. Take the time to develop general education learning outcomes, to examine institutional alignment with the outcomes, and to develop a reasonable plan that will frame a sequence of assessment studies with the potential to improve student learning.

Don't try to do too much at once. Develop a multiyear assessment plan that allows you to do a series of well-conceived assessment studies. If you try to do too much at once, the assessment is likely to be trivialized or you will exhaust yourself and your colleagues, eventually leading to the abandonment of the effort.

Maintain quality controls. General education assessment may be conducted by a variety of ad hoc teams, but some individual or group has to take responsibility for quality control to be sure that studies result in valid, reliable, and actionable findings.

Pilot-test procedures. Pilot testing helps us avoid disasters. Be sure that assessment studies will result in actionable, valid, reliable findings before investing a great deal of time in them.

Close the loop. Just collecting data on the general education program is not assessment. Reflect on results, determine implications, identify and obtain needed support, and implement needed changes. As they say in the Midwest, "Weighing a pig doesn't make it fatter."

Take samples. You don't have to assess the work of every student. Having a representative sample is more important than having a huge sample.

Be professional. We are more likely to get quality data if our respondents understand the importance of their contributions. Effective assessment requires collaboration, respect, and collegiality among campus professionals. We should role model ethical research when collecting assessment data. Just as our children learn from what we do, as well as what we say, our students observe how we respect their privacy, confidentiality, autonomy, and time when we ask them to participate in assessment studies.

Get help. Most campus professionals haven't received special training in assessment methodology, but virtually every campus has experts in test development, survey research, focus groups, and data analysis. Many campuses have faculty development or assessment personnel who can save you time and effort. Why struggle when help is available?

Collaborate. General education is the responsibility of almost every person on campus, and solutions to identified problems may require the collaboration of faculty, administrators, and staff.

Don't forget alignment studies. Although the assessment of learning outcomes receives the most attention, learning occurs in a context. Alignment studies can lead to important improvements in that context, even before you begin directly assessing learning.

Don't seek perfection. Don't wait until everything is perfect, or you'll never begin an assessment study. You might get more precise estimates by testing 5,000 students or by using a 10-hour exam, but assessment only requires reasonable estimates of the proportion of students who meet your criteria.

Triangulate. No single assessment instrument is perfect, but we can have more confidence in results if findings are consistent when we use more than one data collection strategy.

Use rubrics. Rubrics help reviewers efficiently and accurately analyze student work, and they can also be effective tools in the teaching and learning process. As you develop more rubrics and begin integrating them into courses, you may find that you are collecting quality assessment data while you are grading, and these data can be aggregated to serve your assessment program.

Focus on what is important. Faculty can think of many desirable learning outcomes, but assessment should focus on learning outcomes that are universally valued so that faculty will care about results.

Do a data audit. Sometimes the information you're seeking already exists on campus. Institutional research and registrar's offices often have enormous amounts of information on students, including transcripts, test scores, surveys, writing samples, and data collected during the admissions process. Before you collect new data, make use of the data you already have.

Embed assessment. Avoid excessive, additional demands on student and faculty time and obtain data that are likely to show the extent of student mastery of learning outcomes.

Use authentic and performance assessment. General education helps students prepare for a future in a rapidly changing world, and the general education program should help them develop skills for meeting future challenges. Use authentic and performance assessment, when possible, to get results that indicate that students can use what they're learning.

Supplement direct assessment with indirect assessment. Students can tell us about their opinions, perspectives, and experiences in the general education program, and this information may be crucial as we determine how to respond to direct assessment findings. Sometimes it's best to *listen* to our students. We may not always like what we hear, but decisions should be based on understanding the whole picture.

Make time for assessment. Faculty never have enough time to do everything. Find ways to release assessment leaders from some other responsibilities so that assessment is not an additional burden in their busy lives.

Keep a written record. General education assessment is complex and involves volunteers from throughout the campus. Keep a written record of assessment studies and their impact to track progress and to accumulate evidence for accreditation reviews.

Get better at doing assessment. End each assessment study by asking how it might be improved and share what you've learned with colleagues so everyone becomes better at doing assessment.

Consider an annual general education assessment retreat. Engage the campus community in reviewing assessment results, interpreting what was learned, and brainstorming ways to improve learning. Then provide the support needed to implement the best ideas that were generated.

Glossary

Absolute attainment assessment. Assessment to see if students have mastered a learning outcome at an acceptable level.

Accreditation. Certification that programs or institutions have appropriate infrastructure, policies, and services to support their operations and that they are accomplishing their mission.

Actionable results. Results are actionable if they allow assessors to identify what needs to be changed to improve student learning.

Adaptive test. *See* **Computer-adaptive test.**

Add-on assessment. Assessment data collection occurs outside of classes. For example, students could be invited to take an exam or participate in a focus group on a campus assessment day.

Alignment. How well two systems converge for a common purpose; for example, how well the curriculum corresponds with program learning outcomes.

Alignment matrix. A matrix (table) that shows the relationship between two sets of categories, such as the relationship between courses in the curriculum and program learning outcomes.

Alternate forms reliability. *See* **Parallel forms reliability.**

Analytic approach to rubric design. Faculty analyze what they are assessing and use these characteristics to develop the rubric.

Analytic rubric. A rubric for making a series of judgments, each assessing a characteristic of the product being evaluated.

Anchor. Description of a rating scale level that help judges make decisions (e.g., 5 = very important).

Anonymity. Data elements cannot be associated with individual respondents.

Aspirational comparison group. A group that a campus would like to emulate.

Assessment. The collection and use of evidence to monitor and improve a product or process.

Assessment plan. An explicit identification of who, what, when, where, and how often each outcome will be assessed.

Assessment steps (for program assessment). Faculty develop learning outcomes, check for alignment between the curriculum and the outcomes, develop and implement an assessment plan, use results to improve the program, and routinely examine the assessment process and correct it, as needed.

Authentic assessment. The assessment process is similar to or embedded in relevant real-world activities.

Behavior. An alternative name for a learning outcome.

Benchmark. A criterion for assessing results compared to an empirically developed standard.

Bias. Systematic under- or over-estimates of what is being assessed.

Blind review. Reviewers who are evaluating products are not aware of the characteristics of the authors of those products.

Bloom's taxonomy. A popular scheme for defining depth of processing (Bloom, 1956).

Calibration (norming). Evaluators are *normed* or *calibrated* so they consistently apply rubrics in the same way.

CHEA. The Council for Higher Education Accreditation (CHEA) certifies American accreditation agencies.

Checklist. A survey format that provides a list of options that can be selected.

Classroom assessment. Assessment to improve the teaching of specific courses and segments of courses.

Close the loop. Professionals discuss assessment results, reach conclusions about their meaning, determine implications for change, and implement them.

Close-ended questions. Questions for which answer options are predetermined by the data collector.

Closing question. Interview or focus group question that brings closure to the process.

Cluster party. A process for combining outcomes into clusters that can be assessed simultaneously.

Cluster sample. Groups of participants are assessed together, such as embedding an assessment in several sections of a relevant course.

Coding scheme. A description of how to categorize responses in a content analysis.

Coefficient alpha. An indicator of internal-consistency reliability based on intercorrelations among test items.

Cohesive curriculum. A curriculum that systematically provides students opportunities to synthesize, practice, and develop increasingly complex ideas, skills, and values.

Collective portfolio. Collections of student work that are created by faculty for assessment purposes.

Competence interview. An orally administered test.

Competency. An alternative name for a learning goal or outcome.

Compound question. A question with two or more parts. Such questions might confuse respondents.

Computer-adaptive test. A test administered by a computer that is programmed to select the appropriate set of items to most efficiently and effectively measure each respondent.

Confidentiality. The person who conducts the assessment study is aware of who participated, but does not disclose this information.

Consensus. A decision-making process in which a group seeks to maximize the input and support of all participants.

Constructivism. A model for learning based on the assumption that learners actively process information and create cognitive models of reality.

Content analysis. Summarizing a set of communications by analyzing common themes and highlighting important issues.

Core curriculum. A general education program that usually has a focus on interdisciplinary coursework.

Course certification. A process for approving courses for the general education program.

Course diary. A record of the syllabus, assignments, exams, topics, handouts, and student performance in a specific course.

Course-level assessment. Conducting assessment within a specific course to monitor and improve learning in this course.

Course recertification. A process for renewing approval of courses for the general education program.

Criterion-referenced interpretation. Interpreting results by asking if each student satisfies the stated criterion (e.g., Is each student a competent writer?).

Curriculum map. *See* **Alignment matrix.**

Deep learning. Conceptual learning which makes knowledge personal and relevant to real-world applications.

DEEP project. The Documenting Effective Educational Practice (DEEP) project is focused on characteristics of campuses with higher than expected retention and student engagement.

Demographic characteristics. Individual characteristics, such as age and sex.

Depth of processing. Degree of command of what is learned, ranging from knowledge of facts to the ability to use information to solve problems, create new ideas, and evaluate relative merit.

Developmental assessment. Repeated assessment information on individual students is used to track, verify, and support student development.

Developmental portfolio. A portfolio designed to show student progress by comparing products from early and late stages of the student's academic career.

Differences between ratings. An indicator of inter-rater reliability.

Digital portfolio. *See* **Webfolio.**

Direct measure. Students demonstrate that they have achieved a learning outcome.

Distributed general education program. The general education program consists of a wide variety of options for each requirement.

Embedded assessment. Assessment activities occur in courses. Students generally are graded on this work, and some or all of it is also used to assess program learning outcomes.

Engagement. Active, rather than passive involvement.

Expert-systems approach to rubric design. Faculty sort student work into categories, then determine characteristics that distinguish between categories to develop the rubric.

First-year experience programs. Freshman programs generally designed to help retain students through focusing on the development of engagement, academic skills, and awareness of campus support services.

Focus groups. Planned discussions among groups of participants who are asked a series of carefully constructed questions about their beliefs, attitudes, and experiences.

Formative assessment. Assessment designed to give feedback to improve what is being assessed, or assessment of students at an intermediate stage of learning.

Formative validity. How well an assessment procedure provides information that is useful for improving what is being assessed.

Gateway course. A course that blocks students' progress because they are unable to pass it.

Generalizable results. Results that accurately represent the population that was sampled.

Goals. General statements about knowledge, skills, attitudes, and values expected in graduates.

Great books. A model for helping students develop through reading, reflecting on, and discussing classic books.

Halo effect. A problem that occurs when judgments are influenced by each other.

Holistic rubric. A rubric that involves one global, holistic judgment.

Impact. Assessment results in appropriate changes to improve what is being assessed.

Indirect measure. Students (or others) report opinions.

Informed consent. Participants agree to participate in assessment projects based on knowing the purpose of the project, the expected use of the data, the rights to not participate and to discontinue participation, and if data will be anonymous or confidential.

Institutional effectiveness. How well an institution promotes its mission.

Institution-level assessment. The general education program is assessed at the institution-wide level, usually in upper-division courses in the majors.

Intentional learning. Exhibited by students who are engaged, purposeful, and self-directive in their learning.

Intentional teaching. Designing learning experiences to help students develop mastery of specific learning outcomes.

Internal consistency reliability. A reliability estimate based on how highly parts of a test correlate with each other.

Inter-rater reliability. How well two or more raters agree when decisions are based on subjective judgments.

Interview protocol. A script and set of instructions for conducting interviews.

Learning outcome. A clear, concise statement that describe how students can demonstrate their mastery of a program goal.

Likert scale. A survey format that asks respondents to indicate their degree of agreement. Responses generally range from "strongly disagree" to "strongly agree."

Mission. A holistic vision of the values and philosophy of a program, department, or institution.

Norming. *See* Calibration.

Norms/norm group. Results that are used to interpret the relative performance of others, e.g., test results might be compared to norms based on samples of college freshmen or college graduates.

Norm-referenced interpretation. Interpreting results by asking how well each student compared to other students (e.g., Is each student above or below average compared to other students?).

Objective. An alternative name for a learning goal or outcome.

Open-ended question. A question that invites respondents to generate replies, rather than to pick a provided answer from among options.

Outcome. *See* **Learning outcome.**

Parallel forms reliability. A reliability estimate based on correlating scores from two versions of the procedure.

Partially close-ended question. A question that provides an "other" option in addition to specified options. Respondents are invited to describe the "other" category.

Performance assessment. Students exhibit how well they have achieved an outcome by doing it, such as using a computer program.

Pilot study. An abbreviated study to test procedures before the full study is implemented.

Placement test. A test designed to identify where students should begin in course sequences, such as sequences in mathematics, composition, or foreign languages.

Portfolio. Compilations of student work. Students are often required to reflect on their achievement of learning outcomes and how the presented evidence supports their conclusions. *See also* **Collective portfolio.**

Privacy. Research participants' right to determine what personal information they will disclose.

Program-level assessment. The general education program is assessed within the program, such as among social science general education courses, to monitor and improve student learning within the program.

Protocol. *See* **Interview protocol.**

Purposeful sample. A sample created using predetermined criteria, such as proportional representation of students at each class level.

Qualitative assessment. Assessment findings are verbal descriptions of what was discovered, rather than numerical scores.

Quantitative assessment. Assessment findings are summarized with a number that indicates the extent of learning.

Quantitative literacy. Understanding the process and application of mathematics.

Random sample. A sample selected in such a way that each member of the population is equally likely to be included.

Recall item. A test item that requires students to generate the answer on their own, rather than to identify the answer in a provided list.

Recognition item. A test item that requires students to identify the answer in a provided list.

Reflective essays. Respondents are asked to write essays on personal perspectives and experiences.

Reliability. The degree of measurement precision and stability for a test or assessment procedure.

Representative sample. An unbiased sample that adequately represents the population from which the sample is drawn.

Response rate. The proportion of contacted individuals who respond to a request.

Roadblock course. *See* **Gateway course.**

Rubric. An explicit scheme for classifying products or behaviors into categories that are steps along a continuum.

Sampling distribution. The probability distribution of a statistic calculated in all possible samples of the same size.

Sampling fluctuation. Variability in a statistic across samples.

Scaffolding. Organizing a course or curriculum to gradually build knowledge, skills, or values.

Scoring rubric. *See* **Rubric.**

Seven principles for good practice in higher education. Chickering and Gamson's (1987) summary of how to help adult students learn.

Showcase portfolio. A portfolio that documents the extent of learning by featuring the student's best work.

Specimen set. Test questions, instructions, score reports, and other materials that are provided to help professionals decide if a test is appropriate for their intended use.

Standardized test. A test that is administered to all test takers under identical conditions.

Structured group interview. A type of focus group with less interaction than traditional focus groups. Facilitation of such groups requires fewer skills than for traditional focus groups.

Summative assessment. Assessment designed to provide an evaluative summary, or assessment that occurs as students are about to complete the program being assessed.

Surface learning. Learning based on memorization of facts without deep understanding of what is learned.

Survey. A questionnaire that collects information about beliefs, experiences, or attitudes.

Test blueprint. A plan for the creation of an exam that specifies what is being assessed, at what level the assessment should be, and the relative weighting of test components.

Test-retest reliability. A reliability estimate based on assessing a group of people twice and correlating the two scores.

The fives. Gaff's (2004) exercise for stimulating discussion of general education goals and outcomes.

Think aloud. Students reflect on their thinking as they do tasks, and reviewers assess the sophistication of the thinking process.

Traditional focus group. Free-flowing discussions among participants, guided by a skilled facilitator who subtly directs the discussion in accordance with predetermined outcomes.

Triangulation. Multiple lines of evidence lead to the same conclusion.

Validity. How well a procedure assesses what it is supposed to be assessing.

Value-added assessment. Student learning is demonstrated by determining how much students have gained through participation in the program.

Warm-up question. A non-threatening question asked near the beginning of an interview or focus group.

Webfolio. A portfolio that is submitted on a web site or compact disk.

Writing-across-the-curriculum. An initiative for all faculty, regardless of discipline, to help students improve writing skills.

Bibliography

Accrediting Commission for Community and Junior Colleges/Western Association of Schools and Colleges. (2004, August). *Accreditation reference handbook.* Novato, CA: Author.

ACT. (2005). *2004 retention completion summary tables.* Iowa City, IA: Author.

Allen, M. J. (2004). *Assessing academic programs in higher education.* Bolton, MA: Anker.

Allen, M. J., & Yen, W. M. (2002). *Introduction to measurement theory.* Prospect Heights, IL: Waveland.

Alvarez-Adem, M., & Robbin, J. (2003). *Quantitative assessment project: Activity report (2002–2003).* Retrieved October 5, 2005, from the University of Wisconsin–Madison, General Education Requirements web site: http://www.ls.wisc.edu/Gened/FacStaff/QRAssessReport20022003.pdf

American Library Association. (2000). *Information literacy competency standards for higher education.* Retrieved May 21, 2005, from http://www.ala.org/ala/acrl/acrlstandards/informationliteracycompetency.htm

Anagnos, T., Dorosz, L., & Wheeler, G. (2002, June). *Course embedded assessment in large diverse general education programs.* Paper presented at the AAHE Assessment Conference, Boston, MA.

Anderson, C. (2004). Freshmen absence-based intervention at the University of Mississippi. In R. L. Swing (Ed.), *Proving and improving: Vol. II. Tools and techniques for assessing the first college year* (Monograph No. 37; pp. 19–21). Columbia, SC: University of South Carolina, National Resource Center for The First-Year Experience and Students in Transition & the Policy Center on the First Year of College.

Angelo, T. A., & Cross, K. P. (1993). *Classroom assessment techniques: A handbook for college teachers* (2nd ed.). San Francisco, CA: Jossey-Bass.

Arizona Western College. (2003). *General education and student learning outcomes assessment.* Retrieved September 27, 2005, from the Arizona Western College, General Education and Student Learning Outcome Assessment web site: http://www.azwestern.edu/assessment/general_education.php

Association of American Colleges and Universities. (2002). *Greater expectations: A new vision for learning as a nation goes to college.* Washington, DC: Author.

Association of American Colleges and Universities Board of Directors. (2004). *Our students' best work: A framework for accountability worthy of our mission.* Washington, DC: Association of American Colleges and Universities.

Association of American Colleges and Universities Greater Expectations National Panel. (2000). *Goals for liberal learning and college-level learning as stated by a selection of higher education associations, disciplinary associations, accrediting agencies, students, and colleges/universities.* Retrieved October 3, 2005, from http://www.greaterexpectations.org/briefing_papers/GoalsForLiberalLearning.html

Association of College and Research Libraries. (2000). *Information literacy competency standards for higher education.* Chicago, IL: Author.

Association of Specialized and Professional Accreditors. (2005). *Home page.* Retrieved June 7, 2005, from http://www.aspa-usa.org

Baker, R. L. (2000). 21st century learning outcomes: An integration of context and content. In C. D. Wilson, C. L. Miles, R. L. Baker, & R. L. Schoenberger (Eds.), *Learning outcomes for the 21st century: Report of a community college study* (pp. 29–39). Mission Viejo, CA: League for Innovation in the Community College.

Banta, T. W., & Associates. (2002). *Building a scholarship of assessment.* San Francisco, CA: Jossey-Bass.

Belcheir, M. J. (2003, May). *Student academic and personal growth while at Boise State: A summary of 2002 national survey of student engagement findings: Research report 2003 03.* Retrieved October 5, 2005, from the Boise State University, Institutional Assessment web site: http://www2.boisestate.edu/iassess/Reports/Reports%202003/RR%202003-03.pdf

Benjamin, R., & Chun, M. (2003, summer). A new field of dreams: The collegiate learning assessment project. *Peer Review, 5*(4), 26–29.

Bergen Community College. (n.d.). *BCC core competencies.* Retrieved September 27, 2005, from the Bergen Community College, Assessment of Student Learning web site: http://www.bergen.edu/Assessment/core.htm

Berger Institute. (n.d.). *Applying the science of learning.* Retrieved September 27, 2005, from the Claremont McKenna College, Berger Institute web site: http://berger.claremontmckenna.edu/asl//principles/lpintro.asp

Biggs, J. (2002). *Aligning the curriculum to promote good learning.* Retrieved September 26, 2005, from http://www.heacademy.ac.uk/resources.asp?process=full_record&section=generic&id=167

Bismarck State College. (2004). *General education objectives.* Retrieved September 27, 2005, from the Bismarck State College, Academic Assessment web site: http://www.bismarckstate.edu/academic/assessment/report/GenEdObjectives.pdf

Bliss, L. B. (2004). The Study Behavior Inventory. In R. L. Swing (Ed.), *Proving and improving: Vol. II. Tools and techniques for assessing the first college year* (Monograph No. 37; pp. 103–106). Columbia, SC: University of South Carolina, National Resource Center for The First-Year Experience and Students in Transition & the Policy Center on the First Year of College.

Bloom, B. S. (Ed.). (1956). *Taxonomy of educational objectives: The classification of educational goals. Handbook I: Cognitive domain.* White Plains, NY: Longman.

Born, D., & Whitfield, D. (Eds.). (2004) *Great conversations 1.* Chicago, IL: The Great Books Foundation.

Bowen, S. H. (2004, Fall). What's in a name? The persistence of "general education." *Peer Review, 7*(1), 30–31.

Bowling Green State University. (n.d.). *University learning outcomes.* Retrieved September 27, 2005, from the Bowling Green State University, Student Achievement Assessment Committee web site: http://www.bgsu.edu/offices/assessment/Outcomes.htm

Boyer, E. L. (1990). *Scholarship reconsidered: Priorities of the professoriate.* Princeton, NJ: The Carnegie Foundation for the Advancement of Teaching.

Breivik, P. S. (2005). 21st century learning and information literacy. *Change, 37*(2), 20–27.

Brigham Young University. (2004). *The university core: Rationale statements for each requirement.* Retrieved September 27, 2005, from the Brigham Young University, General Education web site: http://saugus.byu.edu/gened/forms/criteria/univcorerationales.pdf

Brigham Young University. (2005). *General education mission statement.* Retrieved September 27, 2005, from the Brigham Young University, General Education web site: http://saugus.byu.edu/gened/homepage.cfm

Brooklyn College. (1998). *Core studies 3: People, power, and politics.* Retrieved September 27, 2005, from the Brooklyn College, Core Curriculum web site: http://academic.brooklyn.cuny.edu/core3/#DESCRIPTION

Brooklyn College. (n.d.) *Core 1 course objectives.* Retrieved September 27, 2005, from the Brooklyn College, Core Curriculum web site: http://depthome.brooklyn.cuny.edu/classics/core/objctvs.htm

Business-Higher Education Forum. (2003). *Building a nation of learners: The need for changes in teaching and learning to meet global challenges.* Washington, DC: Author.

Byrne, R. (2005, May 13). In Jefferson Lecture, Yale professor defends 'value of history.' Retrieved September 27, 2005, from *The Chronicle of Higher Education* web site: http://chronicle.com/daily/2005/05/2005051303n.htm

Calder, L., & Carlson, S. (2004). Using "think alouds" to evaluate deep understanding. In R. L. Swing (Ed.), *Proving and improving: Vol. II. Tools and techniques for assessing the first college year* (Monograph No. 37; pp. 35–38). Columbia, SC: University of South Carolina, National Resource Center for The First-Year Experience and Students in Transition & the Policy Center on the First Year of College.

California State Polytechnic University–Pomona. (2003). *IGE Mission Statement.* Retrieved September 28, 2005, from the California State Polytechnic University–Pomona, Interdisciplinary General Education web site: http://www .csupomona.edu/~ige

California State University–Bakersfield. (2000a). *CSUB general education goals and objectives: Area B. Mathematics, life and physical sciences.* Retrieved September 27, 2005, from the California State University–Bakersfield, Assessment Center web site: http://www.csub.edu/assessmentcenter/MGO_web/GEweb/GEAreaB _mgos.htm

California State University–Bakersfield. (2000b). *CSUB general education goals and objectives: Area A. Communication in the English Language.* Retrieved October 3, 2005, from the California State University–Bakersfield, Assessment Center web site: http://www.csub.edu/assessmentcenter/MGO_web/GEweb/GEAreaA _mgos.htm

California State University–Los Angeles. (n.d.) *General education assessment: Goals and objectives.* Retrieved September 27, 2005, from the California State University– Los Angeles, General Education Assessment web site: http://www.calstatela.edu/ academic/aa/ugs/geassess/gegoals.htm

California State University–Monterey Bay. (2005). *University learning requirements.* Retrieved September 23, 2005, from the California State University–Monterey Bay, Catalog web site: http://csumb.edu/site/x7450.xml

California State University–Northridge. (2005). *General education: Goals and student learning outcomes.* Retrieved September 27, 2005, from the California State University–Northridge, Office of Assessment web site: http://www.csun.edu/ assessment/1_GEgoals1.html

California State University–San Bernardino. (2005). *California State University, San Bernardino outcomes assessment goals and objectives for the general education basic skills areas: Written communication, oral communication, critical thinking and mathematics.* Retrieved September 27, 2005, from the California State University–San Bernardino, Outcomes Assessment Information web site: http://gradstudies.csusb.edu/outcome/BasicSkills.html

'California Teach' first step in revising sciences. (2005, June 5). *Oakland Tribune,* p. Local 6.

Casady, M. (2005). Southwest Missouri State University. In B. F. Tobolowsky, B. E. Cox, & M. T. Wagner (Eds.), *Exploring the evidence: Vol. III. Reporting research on first-year seminars* (Monograph No. 42; pp. 139–143). Columbia, SC: University of South Carolina, National Resource Center for The First-Year Experience and Students in Transition.

Chickering, A. W., & Gamson, Z. F. (1987, March). Seven principles for good practice in undergraduate education. *AAHE Bulletin, 39*(7), 3–7.

Coastline Community College. (2004). *General education philosophy.* Retrieved September 27, 2005, from the Coastline Community College, Policies and Regulations web site: http://coastline.edu/page.asp?LinkID=365

Comeaux, P. (Ed.). (2005). *Assessing online learning.* Bolton, MA: Anker.

Community College of Denver. (2005). *Student performance objectives for transfer education (AS degree).* Retrieved September 27, 2005, from the Community College of Denver, Academic Programs web site: http://www.ccd.edu/programs/asreq.html#perf

Community College Survey of Student Engagement. (2005). *Engagement by design: 2004 findings.* Retrieved May 18, 2005, from http://www.ccsse.org/publications/CCSSE_reportfinal2004.pdf

Conference on College Composition and Communication Committee on Assessment. (1995). Writing assessment: A position statement. *College Composition and Communication, 46*(3), 430–437.

Council for Higher Education Accreditation (1998). *CHEA recognition.* Retrieved September 22, 2005, from http://www.chea.org/recognition/recognition.asp

Council of Writing Program Administrators. (2000). *WPA outcome statements for first-year composition.* Retrieved September 26, 2005, from http://www.wpacouncil.org/positions/outcomes.html

Dakota State University Assessment Office. (2000). *Executive summary: 2000 DSU assessment plan.* Retrieved September 27, 2005, from the Dakota State University, Assessment Office web site: http://www.departments.dsu.edu/assessment/executive_summary_sectionfive.htm

David, D. (2001). *Coordinator summary: General education course assessment sheet: Area S: self, society, & equality in the U.S.* Retrieved September 27, 2005, from the San José State University, Undergraduate Studies web site: http://www2.sjsu.edu/ugs/assessment/GERO107.rtf

Davidson, C. N., & Goldberg, D. T. (2004, February 13). A manifesto for the humanities in a technological age. *The Chronicle of Higher Education, 50*(23), B7.

Diamond, R. M. (1998). *Designing & assessing courses & curricula: A practical guide* (Rev. ed.). San Francisco, CA: Jossey-Bass.

Eastern New Mexico University. (2005a). *Data sources*. Retrieved September 27, 2005, from the Eastern New Mexico University, Assessment Resource Office web site: http://www.enmu.edu/academics/excellence/assessment/data -sources/index.shtml

Eastern New Mexico University. (2005b). *General education competencies*. Retrieved September 27, 2005, from the Eastern New Mexico University, Assessment Resource Office web site: http://www.enmu.edu/academics/excellence/assess ment/culture-assessment/general_education_comp.shtml

Eaton, J. S. (2003, February 28). Before you bash accreditation, consider the alternatives. *The Chronicle of Higher Education, 49*(25), B15.

Edge, H. L. (2005). Rollins College. In B. F. Tobolowsky, B. E. Cox, & M. T. Wagner (Eds.), *Exploring the evidence: Vol. III. Reporting research on first-year seminars* (Monograph No. 42; pp. 131 134). Columbia, SC: University of South Carolina, National Resource Center for The First-Year Experience and Students in Transition.

Educational Testing Service. (2005). *Major field tests*. Retrieved August 30, 2005, from http://www.ets.org/hea/mft

Emporia State University. (2001). *Status of general education assessment at ESU*. Retrieved September 27, 2005, from the Emporia State University, Assessment and Educational Measurement web site: http://www.emporia.edu/asem/GenEdAssess.htm

End, L. (2005). Mount Mary College. In B. F. Tobolowsky, B. E. Cox, & M. T. Wagner (Eds.), *Exploring the evidence: Vol. III. Reporting research on first-year seminars* (Monograph No. 42; pp. 97 100). Columbia, SC: University of South Carolina, National Resource Center for The First-Year Experience and Students in Transition.

Ewell, P. (2004). *General education and the assessment reform agenda*. Washington, DC: Association of American Colleges and Universities.

Faculty hiring in recent years has focused on part-timers at for-profit colleges, report suggests. (2005, May 20). Retrieved September 27, 2005, from *The Chronicle of Higher Education* web site: http://chronicle.com/daily/2005/05/ 2005052002n.htm

Field, K. (2004a, May 7). Poetry scholar uses Jefferson Lecture to tout the importance of arts in education. Retrieved September 27, 2005, from *The Chronicle of Higher Education* web site: http://chronicle.com/daily/2004/05/ 2004050707n.htm

Field, K. (2004b, July 9). Battling the image of 'a nerd's profession': Universities devise programs to lure more students to engineering. *The Chronicle of Higher Education, 50*(44), A15.

Foster, A. L. (2005, May 27). Student interest in computer science plummets: Technology companies struggle to fill vacant positions. *The Chronicle of Higher Education, 51*(38), A31.

Fox, P. M. (2005). State University of New York at Brockport. In B. F. Tobolowsky, B. E. Cox, & M. T. Wagner (Eds.), *Exploring the evidence: Vol. III. Reporting research on first-year seminars* (Monograph No. 42; pp. 145–149). Columbia, SC: University of South Carolina, National Resource Center for The First-Year Experience and Students in Transition.

Gaff, J. G. (2004, Fall). What is a generally educated person? *Peer Review, 7*(1), 4–7.

Gerardi, D. (2003, Spring). *Information: Core 4 online.* Retrieved September 27, 2005, from the Brooklyn College web site: http://academic.brooklyn.cuny.edu/history/dfg/core/c4dg-inf.htm

Gonyea, R. M. (2004). Assessing student expectations for college: The College Student Expectations Questionnaire. In R. L. Swing (Ed.), *Proving and improving: Vol. II. Tools and techniques for assessing the first college year* (Monograph No. 37; pp. 83–86). Columbia, SC: University of South Carolina, National Resource Center for The First-Year Experience and Students in Transition & the Policy Center on the First Year of College.

Grand Valley State University. (2005). *The general education program.* Retrieved September 27, 2005, from the Grand Valley State University, Advising Resources and Special Programs web site: http://www.gvsu.edu/gen-ed/backgrnd.htm

Gravois, J. (2005, January 17). Number of doctorates edges up slightly. *The Chronicle of Higher Education, 51*(18), A24.

Habley, W. R., & McClanahan, R. (2004). *What works in student retention? All survey colleges.* Iowa City, IA: ACT.

Halpern, D. F., & Hakel, M. D. (2003). Applying the science of learning to the university and beyond: Teaching for long-term retention and transfer. *Change, 35*(4), 36–41.

Hazard, L. L. (2005). Bryant University. In B. F. Tobolowsky, B. E. Cox, & M. T. Wagner (Eds.), *Exploring the evidence: Vol. III. Reporting research on first-year seminars* (Monograph No. 42; pp. 23–27). Columbia, SC: University of South Carolina, National Resource Center for The First-Year Experience and Students in Transition.

Hodges, E., & Yerian, J. M. (2004). The first-year Prompt Project: A qualitative research study revisited. In R. L. Swing (Ed.), *Proving and improving: Vol. II. Tools and techniques for assessing the first college year* (Monograph No. 37; pp. 47–51). Columbia, SC: University of South Carolina, National Resource Center for The First-Year Experience and Students in Transition & the Policy Center on the First Year of College.

Holst, S., & Elliott, G. (2002, May). *Finding the artificial intelligence and assessment—Best tool for the job.* Paper presented at the Pacific Planning, Assessment & Institutional Research Conference, Honolulu, HI.

House, J. D. (2004). Survey data as part of first-year assessment efforts: Using the Cooperative Institutional Research Program (CIRP) annual freshman survey. In R. L. Swing (Ed.), *Proving and improving: Vol. II. Tools and techniques for assessing the first college year* (Monograph No. 37; pp. 75–77). Columbia, SC: University of South Carolina, National Resource Center for The First-Year Experience and Students in Transition & the Policy Center on the First Year of College.

House, J. D. (2005). Northern Illinois University. In B. F. Tobolowsky, B. E. Cox, & M. T. Wagner (Eds.), *Exploring the evidence: Vol. III. Reporting research on first-year seminars* (Monograph No. 42; pp. 103–106). Columbia, SC: University of South Carolina, National Resource Center for The First-Year Experience and Students in Transition.

Huber, M. T., & Hutchings, P. (2004). *Integrative learning: Mapping the terrain.* Washington, DC: Association of American Colleges and Universities & The Carnegie Foundation for the Advancement of Teaching.

Humboldt State University. (2000). *Learning outcomes and assessment models for general education: Area B: Science.* Retrieved September 27, 2005, from the Humboldt State University, Office for Undergraduate Studies web site: http://www.humboldt.edu/~ugst/ucc/AreaB.html

Humphreys, P. A. (2004). Evaluating general education outcomes: College BASE-lining your first-year students. In R. L. Swing (Ed.), *Proving and improving: Vol. II. Tools and techniques for assessing the first college year* (Monograph No. 37; pp. 139–142). Columbia, SC: University of South Carolina, National Resource Center for The First-Year Experience and Students in Transition & the Policy Center on the First Year of College.

Huston, G. (2005). Olympic College. In B. F. Tobolowsky, B. E. Cox, & M. T. Wagner (Eds.), *Exploring the evidence: Vol. III. Reporting research on first-year seminars* (Monograph No. 42; pp. 123–126). Columbia, SC: University of South Carolina, National Resource Center for The First-Year Experience and Students in Transition.

Hutchings, P., & Shulman, L. S. (1999). The scholarship of teaching: New elaborations, new developments. *Change, 31*(5), 10–15.

IDEA Center (1998, Spring). *Kansas State University general education senior interviews: Faculty training.* Manhattan, KS: Author.

Illinois Articulation Initiative. (2005a). *Communication course descriptions.* Retrieved August 23, 2005, from http://www.itransfer.org/IAI/GenEd/comm.taf?page=courseinfo

Illinois Articulation Initiative. (2005b). *IAI course descriptions.* Retrieved May 24, 2005, from http://www.itransfer.org/IAI/FACT/Default.taf?page=CourseDescriptions

Illinois Articulation Initiative. (2005c). *Social and behavioral sciences definition.* Retrieved August 24, 2005, from http://www.itransfer.org/IAI/GenEd/SocBehSci.taf

Indiana University–Purdue University Indianapolis. (2003–2004). *IUPUI eport: Principles of undergraduate learning (PULs).* Retrieved September 28, 2005, from the Indiana University, e-Portfolio web site: http://www.eport.iu.edu/about_the_project_frameset.htm

Inver Hills Community College. (2001). *Essential skills.* Retrieved September 28, 2005, from the Inver Hills Community College, Liberal Studies/Professional Skills web site: http://depts.inverhills.edu/LSPS/essential_skills.htm

James Madison University (2005). *The goals of general education.* Retrieved September 28, 2005, from the James Madison University, General Education Program web site: http://www.jmu.edu/gened/goals.html

Johnson County Community College (2005). *Culture and ethics outcome.* Retrieved October 3, 2005, from the Johnson County Community College, General Education Learning Outcomes web site: http://www.jccc.net/home/depts/S00015/site/plan/culture

Johnson, D. W., & Johnson, F. P. (1997). *Joining together: Group theory and group skills* (6th ed.). Needham Heights, MA: Allyn and Bacon.

Katz, S. N. (2005, April 1). Liberal education on the ropes. *The Chronicle of Higher Education, 51*(30), B6.

Kellogg Community College. (2001). *General education competencies.* Retrieved September 28, 2005, from the Kellogg Community College, Academic Projects web site: http://academic.kellogg.cc.mi.us/acadproj/competencies.htm

Korn, R. (2005). Bristol Community College. In B. F. Tobolowsky, B. E. Cox, & M. T. Wagner (Eds.), *Exploring the evidence: Vol. III. Reporting research on first-year seminars* (Monograph No. 42; pp. 19–21). Columbia, SC: University of South Carolina, National Resource Center for The First-Year Experience and Students in Transition.

Krumme, G. (2002). *Major categories in the taxonomy of educational objectives.* Retrieved September 28, 2005, from the University of Washington–Seattle, Faculty web server: http://faculty.washington.edu/krumme/guides/bloom.html

Kuh, G. D., Kinzie, J., Schuh, J. H., & Whitt, E. J. (2005). Never let it rest: Lessons about student success from high-performing colleges and universities. *Change, 37*(4), 44–51.

Kuh, G. D., Kinzie, J., Schuh, J. H., Whitt, E. J., & Associates. (2005). *Student success in college: Creating conditions that matter.* San Francisco, CA: Jossey-Bass & American Association for Higher Education.

Lashley, B. (2005). Eastern Connecticut State University. In B. F. Tobolowsky, B. E. Cox, & M. T. Wagner (Eds.), *Exploring the evidence: Vol. III. Reporting research on first-year seminars* (Monograph No. 42; pp. 43–46). Columbia, SC: University of South Carolina, National Resource Center for The First-Year Experience and Students in Transition.

Laufgraben, J. L. (2005). Temple University. In B. F. Tobolowsky, B. E. Cox, & M. T. Wagner (Eds.), *Exploring the evidence: Vol. III. Reporting research on first-year seminars* (Monograph No. 42; pp. 151–154). Columbia, SC: University of South Carolina, National Resource Center for The First-Year Experience and Students in Transition.

Loacker, G. (2002). Teaching students to develop the process of self assessment. In A. Doherty, T. Riordan, & J. Roth (Eds.), *Student learning: A central focus for institutions of higher education* (pp. 29–32). Milwaukee, WI: Alverno College Institute.

Longwood University. (2004–2005). *Longwood University undergraduate catalog.* Retrieved June 9, 2005, from the Longwood University, Undergraduate Catalog 2004–2005 web site: http://www.longwood.edu/catalog/2004/General Education.htm

Lutz, D. A. (2004). CAAP general education assessment program. In R. L. Swing (Ed.), *Proving and improving: Vol. II. Tools and techniques for assessing the first college year* (Monograph No. 37; pp. 143–147). Columbia, SC: University of South Carolina, National Resource Center for The First-Year Experience and Students in Transition & the Policy Center on the First Year of College.

Macpherson, A. (2001, January 8). *Grading and assessment.* Message posted to the POD listserv, archived at http://listserv.nd.edu/archives/pod.html

Maki, P. L. (2004). *Assessing for learning: Building a sustainable commitment across the institution.* Sterling, VA: Stylus.

Mercer University. (2005). *2003–2004 general education assessment data.* Retrieved September 28, 2005, from the Mercer University, Assessment web site: http://www2.mercer.edu/Assessment/2003-2004+General+Education+Assessment+Results.htm

Mesa Community College. (2002–2003). *What are the student learning outcomes for general education?* Retrieved October 4, 2005, from http://www.mc.maricopa.edu/organizations/employee/orp/assessment/FAQ.html#Anchor-What-14210

Mesa Community College Office of Research and Planning. (2005*). Executive Summary: Student Outcomes assessment update: AY2004-05.* Retrieved October 4, 2005, from the Mesa Community College, Office of Research and Planning web site: http://www.mc.maricopa.edu/organizations/employee/orp/assessment/Executive_summary_04-05.pdf

Meuler, D. (2005). Cardinal Stritch University. In B. F. Tobolowsky, B. E. Cox, & M. T. Wagner (Eds.), *Exploring the evidence: Vol. III. Reporting research on first-year seminars* (Monograph No. 42; pp. 37–41). Columbia, SC: University of South Carolina, National Resource Center for The First-Year Experience and Students in Transition.

Middle States Commission on Higher Education. (2002). *Characteristics of excellence in higher education: Eligibility requirements and standards for accreditation.* Philadelphia, PA: Author.

Millis, B. (1999). *Using interactive focus groups for departmental course and program assessments.* Paper presented at the American Association of Higher Education Assessment Conference, Denver, CO.

Millis, B. J. (2004). Using interactive focus groups for course and program improvements. In R. L. Swing (Ed.), *Proving and improving: Vol. II. Tools and techniques for assessing the first college year* (Monograph No. 37; pp. 55–61). Columbia, SC: University of South Carolina, National Resource Center for The First-Year Experience and Students in Transition & the Policy Center on the First Year of College.

Millis. B. J. (2001). *Using interactive focus groups for departmental course and program assessments.* Retrieved September 28, 2005, from the Brevard College, Policy Center on the First Year of College web site: http://www.brevard.edu/fyc/listserv/remarks/millis.htm

Moallem, M. (2005). Designing and managing student assessment in an online learning environment. In P. Comeaux (Ed.), *Assessing online learning* (pp. 18–33). Bolton, MA: Anker.

Morgan, D. L., & Krueger, R. A. (1998). *The focus group kit* (Vols. 1–6). Thousand Oaks, CA: Sage Publications.

Mullinix, B. B. (2003). *A rubric for rubrics: A tool for assessing the quality and use of rubrics in education.* Retrieved September 28, 2005, from the Monmouth University, Faculty Resource Center web site: http://its.monmouth.edu/faculty resourcecenter/Rubrics/A%20Rubric%20for%20Rubrics.htm

Murrell, P. H. (2004). The Community College Student Experience Questionnaire. In R. L. Swing (Ed.), *Proving and improving: Vol. II. Tools and techniques for assessing the first college year* (Monograph No. 37; pp. 91–93). Columbia, SC: University of South Carolina, National Resource Center for The First-Year Experience and Students in Transition & the Policy Center on the First Year of College.

Nakamoto, J. (2005). Occidental College. In B. F. Tobolowsky, B. E. Cox, & M. T. Wagner (Eds.), *Exploring the evidence: Vol. III. Reporting research on first-year seminars* (Monograph No. 42; pp. 119–122). Columbia, SC: University of South Carolina, National Resource Center for The First-Year Experience and Students in Transition.

National Communication Association. (1996). *Speech Communication Association policy platform statement on the role of communication courses in general education.* Retrieved July 25, 2005, from http://www.natcom.org/policies/External/ GenComm.htm

National Survey of Student Engagement. (2004). *Accreditation toolkit: Western Association.* Bloomington, IN: Indiana University Bloomington Center for Postsecondary Research.

New Century College. (2002a). *Integrative studies graduation portfolio.* Retrieved September 28, 2005, from the New Century College web site: http://www .ncc.gmu.edu/intsgradport.html

New Century College. (2002b). *Integrative studies graduation portfolio guidelines (for 2002 graduates and beyond).* Retrieved September 28, 2005, from the New Century College web site: http://www.ncc.gmu.edu/intsgradport2002.html

Newman, F., Couturier, L., & Scurry, J. (2004, October 15). Higher education isn't meeting the public's needs. *The Chronicle of Higher Education, 51*(8), B6.

Noel, R. (2000, October 5). *Pilot test: GWAR assessment of critical thinking objectives.* Retrieved September 28, 2005, from the California State University–Bakersfield, Assessment Center web site: http://www.csub.edu/assessmentcenter/reports/ge/ GE_GWARCTReportF2000.doc

Noel, R. C. (2001). *Assessment of two GE arts and humanities objectives.* Retrieved September 28, 2005, from the California State University–Bakersfield, Assessment Center web site: http://www.csub.edu/assessmentcenter/reports/ge/ GE_Theme2ReportSP2001.doc

Noel-Levitz. (1998–2005). *2005 National student satisfaction and priorities report.* Retrieved September 23, 2005, from http://www.noellevitz.com/Papers+and +Research/Research/ResearchLibrary/2005+National+Satisfaction+Report.htm

Office of Assessment, Winthrop University. (2002). *Oral communication assessment May 2002: A general education report.* Retrieved September 27, 2005, from the Winthrop University, Office of Assessment web site: http://www.winthrop.edu/acad _aff/Assessment/Oral%20ASMT%20Rpt%202002editedmar31%20s2003.pdf

Office of Institutional Assessment, Boise State University. (2002, April). Academic Profile results provide baseline to measure student learning. *Assessment News, 17.* Retrieved September 28, 2005, from the Boise State University, Institutional Assessment web site: http://www2.boisestate.edu/iassess/Newsletters/Newsletter %2017.pdf

Olivet College. (n.d.). *The Olivet plan.* Retrieved September 28, 2005, from the Olivet College web site: http://www.olivetcollege.edu/about/plan.htm

Pattengale, J. (2005). Indiana Wesleyan University. In B. F. Tobolowsky, B. E. Cox, & M. T. Wagner (Eds.), *Exploring the evidence: Vol. III. Reporting research on first-year seminars* (Monograph No. 42; pp. 67–69). Columbia, SC: University of South Carolina, National Resource Center for The First-Year Experience and Students in Transition.

Peterson, M. W., & Vaughan, D. S. (2002). Promoting academic improvement: Organizational and administrative dynamics that support student assessment. In T. W. Banta & Associates (Eds.), *Building a scholarship of assessment* (pp. 26–46). San Francisco, CA: Jossey-Bass.

Portland State University. (2005). *Proposed markers of the baccalaureate.* Retrieved September 28, 2005, from the Portland State University, Portfolio web site: http://portfolio.pdx.edu/Portfolio/Learning_Markers/Markers/

Ramaley, J. A. (2004, March). *Education in the 21st century.* Paper presented at the annual meeting of the Association of American Colleges and Universities on General Education and Assessment, Long Beach, CA.

Ramaley, J. A., & Haggett, R. R. (2005). Engaged and engaging science: A component of a good liberal education. *Peer Review, 7*(2), 8–12.

Raymo, C. (2005a, May 18). *Not words, but attention.* Retrieved September 27, 2005, from http://www.sciencemusings.com/blog/blogarchive/2005_05_01 _ blogarchive.html

Raymo, C. (2005b, May 21). *The art of physics.* Retrieved September 27, 2005, from http://www.sciencemusings.com/blog/blogarchive/2005_05_01_blogarchive.html

Rose-Hulman Institute of Technology. (2002). *R-HIT student learning outcomes.* Retrieved September 28, 2005, from the Rose-Hulman Institute of Technology, RosE-Portfolio web site: http://www.rose-hulman.edu/irpa/REPS/R-HIT _Student_Learning_Outcomes_Goal.pdf

St. Cloud State University. (2005). *General education learning outcomes.* Retrieved June 5, 2005, from the St. Cloud State University, University Assessment Office web site: http://www.stcloudstate.edu/assessment/gened.asp

San Francisco State University. (1999). *General education segment I policy.* Retrieved September 28, 2005, from the San Francisco State University, Academic Senate web site: http://www.sfsu.edu/~senate/policies/S99-064.html

San José State University. (1998). *Procedures for submitting courses for GE certification.* Retrieved September 28, 2005, from the San José State University, Undergraduate Studies web site: http://www2.sjsu.edu/ugs/geguidelines.html#Procedure

San José State University. (2000). *Advanced general education: (S) Self, Society, & Equality in the U.S.* Retrieved September 28, 2005, from the San José State University, Undergraduate Studies web site: http://www2.sjsu.edu/ugs/geguidelines.html#self

Santa Clara University (2005a). *University core curriculum 2005–2006: Theme 2— Reaching out.* Retrieved September 28, 2005, from the Santa Clara University, Core Curriculum web site: http://www.scu.edu/core/theme2/index.cfm

Santa Clara University (2005b). *University core curriculum 2005–2006: Theme 3— Integrating for leadership.* Retrieved September 28, 2005, from the Santa Clara University, Core Curriculum web site: http://www.scu.edu/core/theme3/index.cfm

Santa Fe Community College. (2002). *Santa Fe's learning outcomes.* Retrieved September 28, 2005, from the Santa Fe Community College, 21st Century Learning Outcomes Project web site: http://inst.santafe.cc.fl.us/~21century/LOC.htm

Satterfield, J. (2002). *The great ideas. The University of Chicago and the ideal of liberal education.* Retrieved May 24, 2005, from the University of Chicago Library web site: http://www.lib.uchicago.edu/e/spcl/excat/ideasint.html

Sax, L. J., & Gilmartin, S. K. (2004). The CIRP Freshman Survey and YFCY: Blending old and new tools to improve assessment of first-year students. In R. L. Swing (Ed.), *Proving and improving: Vol. II. Tools and techniques for assessing the first college year* (Monograph No. 37; pp. 69–73). Columbia, SC: University of South Carolina, National Resource Center for The First-Year Experience and Students in Transition & the Policy Center on the First Year of College.

Scheffel, D. L., & Revak, M. (2004). Using archived course records for first-year program assessment. In R. L. Swing (Ed.), *Proving and improving: Vol. II. Tools and techniques for assessing the first college year* (Monograph No. 37; pp. 17–18). Columbia, SC: University of South Carolina, National Resource Center for The First-Year Experience and Students in Transition & the Policy Center on the First Year of College.

Schmidt, P. (2005, May 6). College presidents fault "weed-out" courses for driving minority students from math and science. *The Chronicle of Higher Education, 51*(35), A23.

Schneider, C. G. (2004a, Summer). Cultural pluralism and civic values. *Liberal Education, 90*(3), 2–5.

Schneider, C. G. (2004b, Summer). Setting greater expectations for quantitative learning. *Peer Review, 6*(4), 26–27.

Schoenberger, R. L.. (2000). Waukesha County Technical College. In C. D. Wilson, C. L. Miles, R. L. Baker, & R. L. Schoenberger, *Learning outcomes for the 21st century: Report of a community college study* (pp. 41–51). Mission Viejo, CA: League for Innovation in the Community College.

Schwartz, B. (2004, January 23). The tyranny of choice. *The Chronicle of Higher Education, 50*(20), B6.

Siegel, M. J. (2004). The College Student Experiences Questionnaire: Assessing quality of effort and perceived gains in student learning. In R. L. Swing (Ed.), *Proving and improving: Vol. II. Tools and techniques for assessing the first college year* (Monograph No. 37; pp. 87–90). Columbia, SC: University of South Carolina, National Resource Center for The First-Year Experience and Students in Transition & the Policy Center on the First Year of College.

Sinclair Community College. (2004). *Foundations of General Education: General Education vision statement.* Retrieved September 28, 2005, from the Sinclair Community College, General Education web site: http://www.sinclair.edu/about/gened/reports/foundations/index.cfm

Smith, P. (2004, Summer). Exploring reality: Cultural studies and critical thinking. *Liberal Education, 90*(3), 26–31.

South Dakota Board of Regents. (2004, June 24–25). *Agenda item III–B: General education.* Retrieved May 24, 2005, from http://www.sdbor.edu/administration/academics/documents/2003-04_sgr_cover_sheet_06-04BOR.pdf

Stanford University. (2005). *Requirements as opportunities.* Retrieved October 4, 2005, from http://www.stanford.edu/dept/uga/learning/3_2a_requirements.html

State Council of Higher Education for Virginia. (2002). *College of William and Mary's report of institutional effectiveness.* Retrieved September 27, 2005, from http://roie.schev.edu/four_year/CWM/body.asp?&c=1

State Council of Higher Education for Virginia. (2002). *Old Dominion University's report of institutional effectiveness.* Retrieved September 27, 2005, from http://roie.schev.edu/four_year/ODU/body.asp?&c=1

State Council of Higher Education for Virginia. (2002). *University of Virginia's report of institutional effectiveness*. Retrieved September 27, 2005, from http://roie.schev.edu/four_year/UVA/body.asp?&c=1

State Council of Higher Education for Virginia. (2002). *Virginia State University's report of institutional effectiveness*. Retrieved September 27, 2005, from http://roie.schev.edu/four_year/VSU/body.asp?&c=1

Stearns, P. N. (2004, Summer). Teaching culture. *Liberal Education, 90*(3), 6–15.

Steen, L. A. (Ed.). (2001). *Mathematics and democracy: The case for quantitative literacy*. Princeton, NJ: National Council on Education and the Disciplines.

Steen, L. A. (2004 Summer). Everything I needed to know about averages . . . I learned in college. *Peer Review, 6*(4), 4–8.

Stevens, D. D., & Levi, A. J. (2005). *Introduction to rubrics: An assessment tool to save time grading, convey effective grading and promote student learning*. Sterling, VA: Stylus.

Sticha, V. (2005). Northern Kentucky University. In B. F. Tobolowsky, B. E. Cox, & M. T. Wagner (Eds.), *Exploring the evidence: Vol. III. Reporting research on first-year seminars* (Monograph No. 42; pp. 107–112). Columbia, SC: University of South Carolina, National Resource Center for The First-Year Experience and Students in Transition.

Stony Brook University (1999). *Report of the Stony Brook task force on assessment of the diversified education curriculum: A plan for assessing general education at Stony Brook*. Retrieved September 27, 2005, from the Stony Brook University, Office of the Provost web site: http://www.sunysb.edu/provost/Reports/Assessing_Gen_Ed/AssessGenEd.pdf

Students study less than expected, survey finds: Report on 'engagement' says more seniors find college officials helpful. (2004, November 26). *The Chronicle of Higher Education, 51*(14), A1.

Subject and Area Librarians Council (2001–2005). *SOTL journals by subject*. Retrieved October 4, 2005, from the Indiana University Bloomington, Libraries web site: http://www.libraries.iub.edu/index.php?pageId=3213

Suskie, L. (2004). *Assessing student learning: A common sense guide*. Bolton, MA: Anker.

Swing, R. L. (2004a). Introduction to first-year assessment. In R. L. Swing (Ed.), *Proving and improving: Vol. II. Tools and techniques for assessing the first college year* (Monograph No. 37; pp. xiii–xxvi). Columbia, SC: University of South Carolina, National Resource Center for The First-Year Experience and Students in Transition & the Policy Center on the First Year of College.

Swing, R. L. (2004b). Overview of essays. In R. L. Swing (Ed.), *Proving and improving: Vol. II. Tools and techniques for assessing the first college year* (Monograph No. 37; pp. ix–xi). Columbia, SC: University of South Carolina, National Resource Center for The First-Year Experience and Students in Transition & the Policy Center on the First Year of College.

Tobolowsky, B. F., Cox, B. E., & Wagner, M. T. (Eds.). (2005). *Exploring the evidence: Vol. III. Reporting research on first-year seminars* (Monograph No. 42). Columbia, SC: University of South Carolina, National Resource Center for The First-Year Experience and Students in Transition.

Truman State University. (2004). *Chapter XIII: Portfolio assessment.* Retrieved September 28, 2005, from the Truman State University, Assessment web site: http://assessment.truman.edu/almanac/2004/CH13.pdf

Truman State University. (2005a). *Portfolio project.* Retrieved September 28, 2005, from the Truman State University, Assessment web site: http://assessment.truman.edu/components/portfolio/

Truman State University. (2005b). *Faculty guidelines: Guidelines for portfolio administrators.* Retrieved September 28, 2005, from the Truman State University, Assessment web site: http://assessment.truman.edu/components/portfolio/facultyguide.htm

Truman State University. (2005c). *Critical thinking and writing.* Retrieved September 28, 2005, from the Truman State University, Assessment web site: http://assessment.truman.edu/components/portfolio/Critical_Thinking_Writing.doc

Truman State University. (2005d). *Permission to use all or part of your portfolio.* Retrieved September 28, 2005, from the Truman State University, Assessment web site: http://assessment.truman.edu/components/Portfolio/Permission_Form.doc

Tucker, C. (2005, May 16). China's scientific edge. *San Francisco Chronicle*, p. B5.

U.S. Department of Education. (2005). *Financial aid for postsecondary students: Accreditation in the United States.* Retrieved June 7, 2005, from http://www.ed.gov/admins/finaid/accred/accreditation.html

University of Arizona. (2005). *General education.* Retrieved September 28, 2005, from the University of Arizona, Outcomes Assessment web site: http://outcomes.web.arizona.edu/data.php?uid=600

University of Arkansas–Fort Smith. (2003–2004). *Student learning at UA Fort Smith.* Retrieved September 28, 2005, from the University of Arkansas–Fort Smith, Student Learning web site: http://www.uafortsmith.edu/attach/Learning/StudentLearningResults/2003-2004StudentLearningReport.pdf

University of Chicago. (2000) *Liberal education at Chicago.* Retrieved September 28, 2005, from the University of Chicago, Courses and Programs of Study web site: http://collegecatalog.uchicago.edu/archives/catalog00-01/htm/liberal education.shtml

University of Iowa. (2005). *General education program.* Retrieved September 28, 2005, from the University of Iowa, College of Liberal Arts and Sciences web site: http://www.clas.uiowa.edu/faculty/gep/areas.shtml

University of Judaism. (2004). *Core curriculum brochure–freshmen 2003–2004.* Retrieved October 4, 2005, from http://www.uj.edu/Media/Images/SCM/ContentUnit/1950_2_4174.pdf

University of Missouri–Columbia. (2005). *General education assessment.* Retrieved September 28, 2005, from the University of Missouri–Columbia, Office of the Provost web site. http://provost.missouri.edu/assessment/general-education.html

University of Montana. (2002). *Criteria for general education program.* Retrieved September 28, 2005, from the University of Montana Missoula, Faculty Senate web site: http://www.umt.edu/facultysenate/ASCRCx/Adocuments/GE%20outcomes%202-14-02.htm

University of Pennsylvania (2002). *Science survey for evaluating scientific literacy at the university level.* Retrieved September 28, 2005, from the University of Pennsylvania, Center for Teaching and Learning web site: http://www.ctl.sas.upenn.edu/tools/sci_literacy_survey.html

University of South Carolina. (2003a). *Assessment criteria—Humanities/cultural.* Retrieved September 28, 2005, from the University of South Carolina, Institutional Planning and Assessment web site: http://ipr.sc.edu/effectiveness/assessment/criteria/humcultl.htm

University of South Carolina. (2003b). *Assessment criteria—math.* Retrieved September 28, 2005, from the University of South Carolina, Institutional Planning and Assessment web site: http://ipr.sc.edu/effectiveness/assessment/criteria/math.htm

University of South Carolina. (2003c). *Assessment criteria—oral communication.* Retrieved September 28, 2005, from the University of South Carolina, Institutional Planning and Assessment web site: http://ipr.sc.edu/effectiveness/assessment/criteria/oral.htm

University of Wisconsin–Green Bay. (2004a). *General education assessment program.* Retrieved September 28, 2005, from the University of Wisconsin–Green Bay, Assessment and Testing Services web site: http://www.uwgb.edu/assessment/GEA.htm

University of Wisconsin–Green Bay. (2004b). *Student perspectives on the UW–Green Bay learning experience.* Retrieved September 28, 2005, from the University of Wisconsin–Green Bay, Assessment and Testing Services web site: http://www.uwgb.edu/assessment/CompReport_2004.pdf

University of Wisconsin–Superior. (2002). *Welcome to your electronic portfolio.* Retrieved September 28, 2005, from the University of Wisconsin–Superior, Electronic Portfolio web site: http://www2.uwsuper.edu/assessment/

Walvoord, B. E., & Anderson, V. J. (1998). *Effective grading: A tool for learning and assessment.* San Francisco, CA: Jossey-Bass.

Ward, D. (2005). University of Texas–El Paso. In B. F. Tobolowsky, B. E. Cox, & M. T. Wagner (Eds.), *Exploring the evidence: Vol. III. Reporting research on first-year seminars* (Monograph No. 42; pp. 179–182). Columbia, SC: University of South Carolina, National Resource Center for The First-Year Experience and Students in Transition.

Ward, J. P. (2004). Using EnrollmentSearch to track first-year success. In R. L. Swing (Ed.), *Proving and improving: Vol. II. Tools and techniques for assessing the first college year* (Monograph No. 37; pp. 11–15). Columbia, SC: University of South Carolina, National Resource Center for The First-Year Experience and Students in Transition & the Policy Center on the First Year of College.

Washington State University. (2002). *Definition and purposes of general education.* Retrieved September 28, 2005, from the Washington State University, General Education Programs web site: http://www.wsu.edu/gened/curric-outcomes/goalsoutcomes-index.html

Weimer, M. (2002). *Learner-centered teaching: Five key changes to practice.* San Francisco, CA: Jossey-Bass.

Weinstein, C. E., Julie, A. L., Corliss, S. B., Cho, Y., & Palmer, D. R. (2004). Knowing *how* to learn is as important as knowing *what* to learn: The Learning and Study Strategies Inventory. In R. L. Swing (Ed.), *Proving and improving: Vol. II. Tools and techniques for assessing the first college year* (Monograph No. 37; pp. 95–98). Columbia, SC: University of South Carolina, National Resource Center for The First-Year Experience and Students in Transition & the Policy Center on the First Year of College.

Weinstein, C. E., King, C. A., Hsieh, P. P., Acee, T. W., & Palmer, D. R. (2004). What students expect may not be what they get: The PEEK (Perceptions, Expectations, Emotions and Knowledge about College). In R. L. Swing (Ed.), *Proving and improving: Vol. II. Tools and techniques for assessing the first college year* (Monograph No. 37; pp. 79–81). Columbia, SC: University of South Carolina, National Resource Center for The First-Year Experience and Students in Transition & the Policy Center on the First Year of College.

Western Association of Schools and Colleges Accrediting Commission for Senior Colleges and Universities (2001). *Handbook of accreditation.* Alameda, CA: Western Association of Schools and Colleges.

Wiggins, G. (1998). *Educative assessment: Designing assessments to inform and improve student performance.* San Francisco, CA: Jossey-Bass.

Wilson, C. D., Miles, C. L., Baker, R. L., & Schoenberger, R. L. (2000). *Learning outcomes for the 21st century: Report of a community college study.* Mission Viejo, CA: League for Innovation in the Community College.

Wood, F. B. (2005). Southeastern Louisiana University. In B. F. Tobolowsky, B. E. Cox, & M. T. Wagner (Eds.), *Exploring the evidence: Vol. III. Reporting research on first-year seminars* (Monograph No. 42; pp. 135–138). Columbia, SC: University of South Carolina, National Resource Center for The First-Year Experience and Students in Transition.

Index